THE SIKHS

THE SIKHS

Khushwant Singh

HarperCollins *Publishers* India

First published in India by
HarperCollins *Publishers* in 2006
A-75, Sector 57, Noida, Uttar Pradesh 201301, India
www.harpercollins.co.in

This edition published in India by
HarperCollins *Publishers* in 2019

2 4 6 8 10 9 7 5 3 1

P-ISBN: 978-93-5302-689-9
E-ISBN: 978-93-5357-466-6

Typeset in 11.5/15 Bembo Std at
Manipal Digital Systems, Manipal

Printed and bound at
Thomson Press (India) Ltd

CONTENTS

Preface   ix

PART I

Chapter 1   Founding of the Faith   3

Chapter 2   The Sikh Religion   23

Chapter 3   Rise of the Sikh Confederacy   40

Chapter 4   The Kingdom of the Sikhs   50

Chapter 5   The End of the Sikh Kingdom   64

PART II

Introduction   85

Chapter 6   Movements of Religious Reformation   87

Chapter 7   The Singh Sabha and Social Reform   98

Chapter 8   Akali Agitation for Sikh Shrines   103

Chapter 9   The Ghadr Rebellion and Marxism   121

Chapter 10 Political Groups   141

Chapter 11 Partition Holocaust and the Exodus   156

PART III

Chapter 12 The Cultural Heritage   169

PART IV

Chapter 13 The Future   191

         Afterword   201
         Index   237

PREFACE

The chief reason for my writing an account of my people is the melancholic thought that contemporary with my labours are being written the last chapters of the story of the Sikhs. It would be proper that some estimate of Sikh religion, history, tradition, and political and cultural achievements be made by someone who identified with them by faith and association. It may be somewhat premature and lacking in historical perspective; it may be somewhat biased and lacking in the objective approach of the outsider. But it has the advantage of being the point of view of the believer mentally and emotionally involved in the vicissitudes of the community.

Not many books have been written on the Sikhs in the English language. Apart from passing references in travellers' diaries and articles in journals, little was known of these people to the Western world till Sir John Malcolm's *Sketch of the Sikhs* appeared in 1812. It was followed twenty-two years later by Prinsep's *Origin of the Sikh Power in the Punjab*. In 1842 a more detailed account of the Sikhs was published by MacGregor in two volumes. These and other smaller works published in between served to create an interest which was increased by the many inaccuracies apparent in their texts.

The first real work of scholarship was undertaken by Captain J.D. Cunningham, who spent eight years of his service (1838–46) in close contact with the Sikhs. In 1849 (the year of annexation of the Sikh kingdom) his *History of the Sikhs* was published. The first edition was proscribed. Cunningham lost his post in the Political Service and was sent back to the army. He died two years later. In 1853 a second edition appeared with an introduction by his brother stating that the author 'fell victim to the truth related in the book. He wrote history in advance of his time and suffered for it.' The author had himself corrected the proofs of his second edition before his death. In the preface to this edition he wrote: 'It has been remarked by some public critics and private friends that the author leans unduly towards the Sikhs, and that an officer in the Indian Army should appear to say he sees aught unwise or objectionable in the acts of the East India Company and its delegates is at least strange.' Bearing in mind the fact that Captain Cunningham's association with the Sikhs extended over the period of the Anglo-Sikh wars and the subsequent annexation of the Sikh kingdom by the British, another passage in his preface to the second edition is equally significant. 'The wisdom of England', he wrote, 'is not to be measured by the views and acts of any one of her sons, but is rather to be deduced from the characters of many. In India it is to be gathered in part from the high, but not always scrupulous, qualities which distinguished Clive, Hastings and Wellesley, who acquired and secured the Empire.'

The second edition was also proscribed. Both editions contained, according to the editor of the subsequent editions, 'statements of an injudicious nature'.

It is a pity that political considerations should have required the deliberate distortion of historical facts and rendered suspect an otherwise excellent work of objective scholarship.

The first attempt to interpret the religion of the Sikhs to the West was also a failure. In 1869 Dr Ernest Trumpp, Regius Professor of Oriental Languages at the University of Munich, was commissioned by the secretary of state for India to translate the Sikh Scripture, the Granth Sahib. He was not very successful in this mission. After two years of work, he came to the conclusion that 'the language of the Granth had become already obsolete to a great extent'. He got very little assistance from Sikh scholars – in fact, he was sure that none existed. 'The Sikhs', he wrote, 'in consequence of their former warlike manner of life and troublous times, had lost all their learning.' When Dr Trumpp's translation finally appeared in 1877, it proved offensive to Sikh susceptibilities. In order to repair the damage caused to 'the loyal Sikhs', M.A. Macauliffe was commissioned to undertake the work. Macauliffe described Trumpp's work as 'highly inaccurate and unidiomatic ... whenever he saw an opportunity of defaming the Gurus, the sacred book and the religion of the Sikhs, he eagerly availed himself of it'. Macauliffe admitted that the object of his work was 'to make reparations to the Sikhs ... without criticism or expression of opinion of his own'.

Macauliffe's *The Sikh Religion* was published in six volumes in 1909. With justifiable pride he wrote: 'I bring from the East what is practically an unknown religion.' His translation of the Granth was done in co-operation with Sikh theologians and is literal. But unfortunately, its accuracy is marred by its unattractiveness. It fails to do justice to the poetic excellence of the original. Besides that, Macauliffe incorporated in his work many of the legends which grew around the Gurus and were believed only by the gullible. These shortcomings detract a great deal from his otherwise extremely valuable work.

Although I have neither the desire nor the competence to undertake an exhaustive work on the Sikh religion, I consider it necessary to draw the reader's attention to the absence of a concise and readable account of Sikhism. I am more concerned with history than with religion.

Since Cunningham and Macauliffe, several periods of Sikh history have been dealt with by Indian and English authors. Lives of individual Gurus, the rise of the Sikhs to political power, and the biographies of Banda Singh and Ranjit Singh have been published. It is a sorry admission that hitherto no complete history of the Sikhs has been written by a Sikh – and no history dealing with the affairs of the community after 1849 has been published at all. It is true that after the dissolution of the Sikh kingdom the history of the Sikhs becomes, as it were, merged with the history of the rest of India. Nevertheless, several movements took place in the last hundred years which were wholly or mostly concerned with the Sikhs. The revolt of the Kookas in 1872 and the Singh Sabha movement of the early part of the twentieth century were wholly Sikh in character. The struggle for the acquisition of Sikh shrines was also in the beginning a purely Sikh movement. The terrorist activities of the Ghadr revolutionaries were largely Sikh in inception and personnel, although their impact was national. No account of any of these movements has ever been written.

I have had the privilege of meeting people who were the leading characters in many of these movements, and of being entrusted with original documents in their possession. I was also fortunate in having spent a part of my diplomatic service in Canada, where I was able to see back numbers of newspapers and files dealing with the origin and activities of the Ghadr party. In London, I have had access to the manuscripts, records, old newspapers and books at the India Office Library, which (apart perhaps from the British Museum Library) is the most exhaustive source of information on Indo-British history that exists. All this I have endeavoured to put together in this book.

I have to acknowledge assistance given to me in my work by many people and organizations, and would specially like to express my gratitude to Sir Edward MacLagan, one-time governor of the Punjab, for the use of personal documents dealing with the Akali agitation; to the Nirankari and Namdhari organizations for material concerning their sects; to Lord Hailey, former governor of the Punjab, and to Mrs Sidney Ralli of the *Onlooker* for the loan of old books from their private collections; to Dr Edmund Leach and Miss Elizabeth Batt of the London School of Economics for advice and assistance in locating sources of information; to Dr Balbir Singh for correcting the chapter dealing with the Singh Sabha movements; to N. Iqbal Singh and Jagmohan Mahajan for reading the manuscript and advising on it; above all, to my secretary, Eardley Wildman, without whose co-operation this book would not have been written.

Khushwant Singh

PART I

Chapter 1

FOUNDING OF THE FAITH

The Land and the People

A glance at the map of northern India yields an important clue to the history and temperament of the people who inhabit it. The northern and western bastions consist of a range of mountains which, but for some breaches in them, cut off the western world from India. Sheltered behind these mountainous walls are the plains of the Punjab, stretching from the river Indus in the north and west to the Yamuna in the south-east. Between the Indus and the Yamuna are the rivers Jhelum, Chenab, Beas, Ravi and Sutlej, which give to the area the name Punjab, the land of the five waters. On the banks of these rivers, but at safe distances from their wayward courses, have sprung up a dozen or so commercial towns. Between them are rich wheat lands, on which more than nine-tenths of the population lives.

While the north and west are demarcated by mountains, the southern and south-eastern limits are separated from Sindh and Rajputana by miles of arid waste, which divides not only

3

the desert from the town but also peoples of different speech, culture and outlook on life. The eastern end is not so marked either in the nature of its terrain or in the type of its people. The only real division is of speech and of a consciousness on the one side of belonging to the Punjab and on the other of not being a Punjabi.

This geographical location has fostered in the people of the Punjab feelings of both fear and pride. Since the earliest known period of the history of India, gaps in the mountain walls in the north-west have let in invaders who have spent themselves in plundering the cities and plains. The Punjabis developed a frontier consciousness, looking with apprehension towards the mountain passes through which every few years came death and destruction. Despite the richness of the soil and the abundance of harvests, there was never any prolonged prosperity nor ever any promise of long life. Chronic turbulence produced a restive temperament. At the same time, the Punjabi became conscious of being the most important defender of India. He developed a patriotism which was at once bitter towards the invader but benign, and often contemptuous, towards his own countrymen, whose fate and fortune depended so much on his courage and fortitude.

Little, if anything, is known of the original inhabitants of the Punjab. The earliest traces of civilization that have been unearthed at Mohenjodaro in the Indus Valley and at Harappa in the Punjab have been put down to a period around 3000 B.C. The people who are said to have lived in these cities were Dravidians, who came in from the north and drove the aboriginals towards the east and south of India. A thousand years or so later the Dravidians were in their own turn driven east and south by the Aryans. After the Aryans came the Greeks (under Alexander), Scythians, Parthians, Ionians, Bactrians, Huns and possibly many others in minor invasions. Each wave of invasion left its deposits of race, religion, language and customs. All of them were absorbed and became part of the substrata of the Punjab soil.

The advent of Islam brought to India yet another stream of invaders. These were Arabs, Persians, Turks, Mongols and Afghans. They were as different from each other in race, language, and culture as their predecessors and the people they conquered. But they were bound by a common allegiance to Islam. This important factor marked them out as invaders with a difference. The non-Muslim invasions had been more triumphs of arms than of ways of life. Their language and culture were absorbed in the Indian, their religion became one of the many apartments in the palatial mansion of Hinduism. Islam, on the other hand, would brook no compromise. The Muslims would not even make terms that would let the Indian alone in his faith. From A.D. 780 onwards, almost year after year, came waves of Islamic conquest vying with each other in the massacre of Hindus, destruction of their temples, and forcible conversions. One important consequence of this Muslim attitude was that for the first time in India's history there came to live within her borders a people, alien in their faith and values, who were not content merely to preserve their own identity but who insisted on imposing their beliefs on others. The reaction was the emergence of an Indian consciousness which embraced all non-Muslims. It expressed itself politically in militarism and philosophically in the emergence of Hindu schools of thought, which borrowed the best of Islamic beliefs to combat it. The Sikhs were the most outstanding example of Hindu renaissance produced by Islam — an edifice built as it were with Hindu bricks and Muslim mortar.

The Background

Sikhism, as has already been indicated, is the outcome of a conflict between Hinduism and Islam. In order to understand the particular pattern of compromise which it adopted, it is necessary to know something of the development of the Islamic and Hindu schools of thought which paved the way for its emergence. It is also important to be acquainted with the political situation which gave its inherent pacifism a militant exterior.

Islamic Sufism

Soon after the death of Prophet Mohammed (A.D. 623) Arab armies began to invade the neighbouring countries and impose their faith on non-Arab people. In its early expansionist phase, when Islam spread to Iraq, Turkistan, Persia and Afghanistan, it came into contact with Christianity, Judaism, Buddhism, Zoroastrianism and, above all, Neo-Platonic Greek philosophy. The different races and religious creeds, which joined the Islamic brotherhood, brought with them doctrines and practices that were not strictly in accordance with the gospel of the Prophet. Out of these contacts and influences emerged a school of theological intellectuals, who lived in monasteries and spent their time in prayer and philosophic speculation. They subsequently took upon themselves the task of interpreting Islam to non-Muslims. To make Islam emotionally satisfying, they made several concessions to the practices of other creeds. From the very start, they accepted the toleration of non-Muslims as a cardinal principle of faith. This was the school of the Sufis.

Before the Muslim invaders came to India, Sufism had become firmly rooted in Persia. Some aspects of its belief and practice were akin to those in vogue with some Hindu orders in India. These we should note briefly.

Although Sufism adhered to the strict monotheism of Islam, nevertheless, it allowed the seeds of pantheism to germinate. The text of the Koran itself said: 'Wherever ye turn, there is the face of Allah' (ii, 209). This implied a radical change of emphasis from the 'There is no God but God' of the iconoclast. It was willing to understand the Hindu pantheon instead of smashing it.

Sufism did not accept the strict Muslim interpretation of life hereafter. It took from the Buddhists the theory of nirvana or salvation, in which the personality of the worshipper merged (*fana*) with God. In fact, the worshipper became God himself – 'I went from God to God, until they cried from me in me: "O thou I"' (Bayazid). The Hindus too knew of the state of divine merger 'Aham Brahma Asmi' – 'I am God'. Sufis laid down rules of conduct which led by stages (*maqamat*) towards salvation. They stressed the importance of a religious mentor (*pir*) to guide the initiate (*murshid*) in prayer, vigil and fasting. The Hindus also believed that a Guru's guidance was necessary for the salvation of the disciple (*chela*). The Sufi recited the praises of God in the Koran in a loud sing-song (*dhikr*) till he shut himself off from the world and sank into a meditative trance. He used song and music to help him in fixing his mind. The Hindus too set great store on meditation. Religious music (*kirtan*) and dancing in temples were similarly popular with them. The Sufis went on pilgrimage to the tombs of other Sufis, lit oil lamps on them and venerated them as a Hindu did his idols in the temple.

Sufism came to India along with the Muslim invasions. It made its home in the deserts of Sindh. For some time the Sufis patiently watched the Muslim rulers losing their impatient battle of conversion by the sword. Having got the measure of Hindu religion and its way of life, they went out to proselytize. They did not cut off the heads of those who were unwilling nor, like the Hindus, relegate the convert to be an outcaste. The new Muslims were given titles of honour, such as Shaikh, Malik, Khalifa and Mu'min. The convert could still meditate, become an ascetic, go to shrines, and give offerings of food, as he had done when a Hindu.

If he wanted to worship a human being, or an object, there was the Sufi saint or his tomb. The success of Sufism in winning Hindu converts was phenomenal. By the fifteenth century, there were more than fourteen orders of Sufis flourishing in various parts of northern India. More than three-quarters of the Muslims of India owed allegiance to one or other of these orders, and large numbers of Hindus were known to worship at their centres.

Hindu Bhaktas

In India itself, movements to break the shackles of caste imposed by the Brahmins on Hindusim had started before the impact of Islam. Islam only quickened their pace. Where the contact was close, it also influenced their philosophy. In the first century A.D., the Alwars in southern India set up a school advocating fervent worship through devotional hymn-singing and meditation. It paved the way for Ramanuja (1017–37), the leader of what came subsequently to be known as the Bhakti movement. The movement, which within the Hindu framework emphasized the worship of Vishu, the Preserver, and his reincarnations in preference to the other two gods of the trinity, viz., Brahma, the Creator, and Siva, the Destroyer, had a different import in practice. Vishnu, in fact, became the one god almost in a monotheistic sense. His worshippers called themselves Vaishnavites.

The reincarnations which became the subject of devotion were Rama and/or Krishna. The form of devotion was song and meditation. The devotional path was indicated by the mentor to his disciple. The barriers of caste, even of religion, were ignored or overlooked.

A significant aspect of Vaishnavite monotheism was also the acceptance of the idea that God was more an abstract conception than a concrete something, either personified or idolized. Although most of Vaishnavite ritual centred around worship of idols, they were not looked upon as gods in the sense of having power, but as media for communion with the power that was God. The fact that God was all pervading, formless and beyond description was not a Vaishnavite discovery. It only emphasized one of the many Hindu concepts of God. As early as A.D. 600, Sankara had said:

> O Lord, pardon my three sins.
> I have in contemplation clothed in form Thee who art formless.
> I have in praise described Thee who art ineffable. And in visiting temples I have ignored Thine omnipresence.

The Bhakta school spread its influence all over India. Chaitanya led it in the east, Tukaram, Namdev and Trilochan in central India, Sadhana, Ramanand, Pipa, Mirabai, Tulsidas, and, above all, Kabir, were its leaders in the north.

Kabir (d. 1398) was a Muslim disciple of the Hindu Ramanand. He combined in his teaching his own faith and that of his teacher. Being a Muslim he was a monotheist and against the worship of idols. 'If God is a stone', he said, 'I will worship a mountain.' He did not invest God with a particular personality, and used Hindu and Muslim nomenclature indiscriminately in describing Him. He did not believe in the unique mission of Prophet Mohammed but, like the other Bhaktas, believed in the necessity of every person attaching himself to a spiritual mentor who would guide him on the right path. He believed in prayer and devotion with the use of song and music. He accepted the Hindu theory of retributive justice – karma, and life hereafter. Being a Muslim, he rejected outright the system which made him an outcaste.

Sikh religion is a product of the Sufi and Bhakta schools of thought. The two people who probably influenced the founder, Guru Nanak, were the Bhakta Kabir on one side and the Sufi

Shaikh Ibrahim Farid (1450–1535). Unfortunately, not much is known of the life of Farid, apart from the fact that he was a descendant of the Sufi Faridudin Shakargunj of Pak Pattan (in the Punjab) for whom Guru Nanak had great admiration and whose works are incorporated in the Granth. Faridudin himself was a disciple of the famous mystic Qutubuddin (*d.* 1172) of the Chisti order.

The Times

The state of affairs in northern India preceding the birth of Nanak can be described in one word as chaotic. The reigning dynasty of the Lodhis had begun to break up. In 1398, Timur had invaded India and devastated the plains up to Delhi. Even twenty years later, the country had not recovered from the blow, and a contemporary writer described the principal city of the province, Lahore, as a town 'in which no living thing except the owl of ill omen had its abode'. In Delhi itself, the authority of the Lodhis did not extend beyond the city walls. There was lawlessness born out of uncertainty. From 1519 the Mughal Babar started his incursions. After invading India thrice, he finally came to establish his dynasty in 1526. But for the first few years his own authority and that of his son was repeatedly challenged, and insecurity continued. The common people suffered at the hands of marauders all claiming sovereignty for themselves. There is a legend that Nanak was himself imprisoned by Babar. Even if that be doubtful, he had something to say of the tyranny and repression. 'The age', he said, 'is a knife. Kings are butchers. They dispense justice when their palms are filled … Wealth and beauty which afforded men pleasure have now become their bane … Decency and laws have vanished; falsehood stalks abroad … The vocation of priests is gone and the devil reads the marriage vows. Paeans of murder are sung. Blood is shed in place of saffron … Then came Babar to Hindustan. Death disguised as a Mughal made war on us. There was slaughter and lamentation. Did not Thou, O Lord, feel the pain?' It was veritably Kalyug, the dark age of the Hindus, when, in the words of Nanak, 'true men speak the truth and suffer for it; when penitents cannot perform penance; when he who repeats God's name meets obloquy.' It was a time when a person with a sensitive mind would begin to doubt the ultimate triumph of right over wrong. He might seek escape in asceticism and solitary meditation; he might find the answer in either renouncing the world altogether as damned beyond redemption or coming back to it determined to redeem it.

Founding of the Faith

Nanak

Guru Nanak (1469–1539) was the son of a petty official living in a village some thirty miles from Lahore. He took to studying the Hindu and Muslim religions almost from his boyhood, and found himself constantly involved in argument and discussion with itinerant holy men. Although he married and reared a family, the urge to find spiritual truth for himself proved too great. He temporarily abandoned his family and became a wanderer. He fasted, prayed and meditated. After many years of ascetic life, thought and contemplation, he felt qualified to convey his experiences to the people. He started with the simple statement: 'There is no Hindu, there is no Mussulman.' He took as his companions a low-caste Hindu and a Muslim musician, and the three went preaching from hamlet to hamlet. The Guru composed his sermons in verse, which his Muslim colleague set to music and sang with the lute. His teachings fired the imagination of the Punjab peasantry and a large number of followers gathered around him. At first they were merely known as his disciples, in Sanskrit *shish*. Some time later these disciples became a homogeneous group whose faith was exclusively the teachings of Nanak. The '*shish*' became the Sikh (corruption of the Sanskrit word).

Nanak was content to be a teacher. He made no claims to divinity or to kinship with God. 'I came in the course of nature', he said, 'and according to God's order shall I depart.' He did not invest his writings with the garb of prophecy, nor his word with the sanctity of a 'message'. His teaching was essentially a crusade against cant and humbug in religion, and he had the courage to pattern his life according to his teachings. Two incidents in his life illustrate his method of approach. He went to bathe in the Ganga as all devout Hindus did. The Brahmins bathed and threw water towards the rising sun as an offering to their dead ancestors. Nanak faced the other way and threw water in the opposite direction. When questioned, he answered: 'I am watering my fields in the Punjab. If you can throw water to the dead in heaven, it should be easier to send it to another place on earth.' On another occasion, he happened to fall asleep with his feet towards Mecca. An outraged priest woke him up and rudely drew his attention to the fact. Nanak simply said: 'If you think I show disrespect by having my feet towards the house of God, turn them in some other direction where God does not dwell.'

As he himself had combined his mission with the domestic obligations of a husband and father, he advocated a way of life which allowed for the discharge of civic obligations with the spiritual. He was strongly opposed to asceticism involving renunciation of the world:

> Religion lieth not in the patched coat the yogi wears,
> Not in the staff he bears
> Nor in the ashes on his body.

Religion lieth not in rings in the ears, Not in a shaven head
Nor in the blowing of the conch shell.
If thou must the path of true religion see
Amongst the world's impurities, be of impurities free.

There are no totally reliable accounts of Nanak's travels. By
the time his biography came to be written, sixty or eighty years
after his death, a mass of legend had been built around incidents
of his life. He apparently travelled all over India and even as far
as Persia or Arabia. His life was mostly spent in bringing Hindus
and Muslims together. His personal success in this direction was
remarkable. He was acclaimed by both communities. When he
died, his body became a subject of dispute. The Muslims wanted
to bury him, the Hindus to cremate him. Even to this day, he is
regarded in the Punjab as a symbol of harmony between the two
major communities. A popular couplet describes him:

Guru Nanak Shah Fakir.
Hindu ka Guru, Mussulman ka Pir.

(Guru nanak, the King of fakirs.
To the Hindu a Guru, to the Mussulman a Pir.)

The success of Nanak's mission in the short space of twenty
to thirty years of teaching calls for comment. It was partly due
to the fact that the ground had already been prepared for him
by the Sufis and the Bhaktas. It was chiefly due to his own
personality, in which he combined a gentle disposition with a
stern and uncompromising attachment to principle; humility
with a conviction of the greatness of his mission; and, above all, a
kindly sense of humour, with which he got the people to see the
ridiculous without being ridiculed. He made them come to him,

not through a sense of remorse or repentance, but as to one who
was at once warm-hearted and understanding – a friend and a
father. He did not spare himself from his humour:

> When I am quiet, they say I have no knowledge;
> When I speak, I talk too much they say;
> When I sit, they say an unwelcome guest has come to stay;
> When I depart, I have deserted my family and run away.
> When I bow, they say it is of fear that I pray.
> Nothing can I do that in peace I may spend my time.
> Preserve Thy servant's honour now and hereafter,
> O Lord sublime.

The following that Nanak had created in his lifetime could
at best be described as a group dissenting from both Hinduism
and Islam. It was left to his successors to mould this group into a
community with its own language and literature, religious beliefs
and institutions, traditions and conventions.

Nanak's Successors

Nanak was followed by nine other Gurus. Succession was not
determined by the prevailing laws of inheritance, but with the
object of finding a teacher most fitted to safeguard and develop
the spiritual legacy left by Nanak. It provided for two centuries
a remarkable continuity in the functions of leadership, when one
Guru succeeded the other 'as one lamp lights another'. These
200 years witnessed the consummation of the religious aspect of
Sikhism. They also saw nascent Hindu nationalism grow to political
power and pave the way for the setting up of a Sikh state. Of the
ten Gurus, the second, fourth, fifth, sixth and tenth were chiefly
responsible for measures which fostered communal consciousness
and welded the Sikhs into an independent community.

The second Guru, Angad (1504–1552), was a disciple of Nanak and was chosen by him as his successor in preference to his own sons. (The third Guru, Amar Das, was in similar fashion chosen from amongst the disciples.) Angad invented the Gurmukhi script by combining the scripts present in a northern India. He then proceeded to collect the writings of Nanak and added some of his own to the compilation. Angad established centres (*manjis*) for the propagation of Nanak's teachings. These *manjis* became meeting places for Sikhs, and later on temples (gurdwaras) sprang up in their place.

The fourth Guru, Ram Das (1534–1581), laid the foundation of the temple at Amritsar. This temple was elevated into the Holy of Holies by his successor, Arjun. During the Sikh rule of the Punjab, it was reconstructed in marble and covered with gold leaf and became the most important Sikh shrine.

The fifth Guru, Arjun (1563–1606), was the one to take definite steps towards organizing the Sikh community. What Angad had started, he completed. He, along with his chief disciple Gurdas (1559–1637), continued the compilation started by the second Guru, and incorporated in it the writings of Hindu and Muslim saints. This became the Adi Granth, the holy scripture of the Sikhs. He was also responsible for the construction of temples at Turun Tarun, Amritsar and Kartarpur, which became places of pilgrimage. Guru Arjun's organizing activities attracted the notice of the Muslim rulers. He was arrested and, after considerable torture, executed at Lahore. He became the first and the most important martyr in Sikh history.

A passage in Arjun's writing illustrates how much the Sikhs had in less than a hundred years of Nanak's death freed themselves of their Hindu and Muslim affinities:

I do not keep the Hindu fast, nor the Muslim Ramadan.
I serve Him alone who is my refuge.

I serve the one Master, who is also Allah.
I have broken with the Hindu and the Muslim,
I will not worship with the Hindu, nor like the
   Muslim go to Mecca.
I shall serve him and no other.
I will not pray to idols nor say the Muslim prayer.
I shall put my heart at the feet of the one Supreme
   Being,
For we are neither Hindus nor Mussulmans.

After the death of Arjun, Sikhism went through a transformation. It is said that the last message Arjun sent to his son was: 'Let him sit fully armed on his throne and maintain any army to the best of his ability.' Hargobind (1606–1645) accepted his father's advice and decided to train his followers in the art of defence. He girded himself with two swords, one signifying the spiritual and the other temporal leadership. He realized that building an army at a time when all non-Muslims were being persecuted would not be easy. In fact, the Emperor Jehangir had once jailed him for non-payment of land revenue owed by his father. Hargobind collaborated with the Mughal authorities for some years and, at the same time, built up a private army. The Sikhs grumbled that he was 'too much occupied with Mohammedans and military exercises'. But Hargobind's 'occupation' with Mohammedans was mainly to legalize irregularities. By the time of his death, the Sikhs had already become a fighting force of considerable importance in the hill tracts and won several engagements against Hindu chieftains and local Muslim militia.

The final transformation of the Sikhs into a militant sect came with the last of the ten Gurus, Gobind Singh. In the autumn of 1675 Gobind's father, Tegh Bahadur, was summoned to Delhi by the Mughal Emperor Aurangzeb and ordered to accept conversion to

Islam. The legend goes that he refused and volunteered to perform a miracle whereby the executioner's sword would fail to sever his head from his body. He wrote some words on a piece of paper and tied it round his neck with a thread like a charm. When he was decapitated the message on the paper was seen to read: '*Sirr diya, pur sirrar na diya*' (I gave my head but not my faith). It is also said that Tegh Bahadur repeated Arjun's advice to his son about arming the Sikhs.

The Khalsa of Gobind Singh

Guru Gobind Singh (1675–1708) assumed the leadership of the Sikh community when he was only ten years of age. He spent the first few years in studying Persian, Sanskrit and the Hindu scriptures, and preparing himself for his mission. Although the fate of his father had made a profound impression on his sensitive mind, he never lost sight of the fact that the issues involved were of greater magnitude than the mere wreaking of vengeance. Of his father's death he said: 'Tegh Bahadur died to protect the frontal marks and the sacred threads of the Hindus.' Of his own mission he wrote: 'To uphold right in every place, to destroy sin and evil have I come. That righteousness may flourish, that the good may live and tyranny be uprooted from the land.' (*Vichitra Natak* – 'The Divine Drama'.)

He realized that a change in ideology was necessary for the fulfilment of his temporal work. If his followers were to be saved from extinction, they had not only to be taught the use of arms but also convinced of the morality of the use of force. 'When all other means have failed, it is righteous to draw the sword', he said.

'Light thine understanding as a lamp. Take the broom of divine knowledge and sweep away the filth of timidity.' Even the conception of God became a militant one. He was timeless as death. His symbol was steel. Armed with these mental concepts,

Gobind Singh set about 'training the sparrow to hunt the hawk and one man to fight a legion'.

On the Hindu new year's day in 1699, Gobind Singh assembled his followers and initiated five of them, known as Punj Piyaras, the Five Beloved, into a new fraternity which he named the Khalsa or 'the pure'. Of these five, one was a Brahmin, one a Kshatriya, and three belonged to the lower castes. They were made to drink out of the same bowl and given new names with the suffix 'Singh' (lion) attached to them. They swore to observe the 'Five Ks', namely, to wear their hair and beard unshorn (*kesh*); to carry a comb in the hair (*kungha*); to wear a pair of shorts (*kuchha*); to wear a steel bangle on the right wrist (*kara*); and to carry a sword (*kirpan*). The Khalsa was also enjoined to observe four rules of conduct (*rahat*): not to cut the hair; abstain from smoking tobacco and consuming alcoholic drinks; not to eat kosher meat; and refrain from carnal intercourse with Muslims. Gobind Singh further bade the initiates rid themselves of their family ties, their professions, their creed and ritual, and have no loyalties except to the new fraternity. After baptizing the five, he had himself baptized by them.

At the end of the ceremony, he hailed the five with the new greeting – '*Wah guru ji da Khalsa – Wah guru ji di Fateh*' (The Khalsa are the chosen of God – Victory be to our God). With the belief in the sanctity of their mission he gave his followers a promise of temporal success. '*Raj kareyga khalsa*', he said:

The Khalsa shall rule ...
Their enemies will be scattered,
Only they that seek refuge shall be saved.

The reason which prompted Gobind Singh to introduce forms and symbols has never been adequately explained. Neither he nor any of his contemporaries throw any light on the subject. Some of the symbolism is, however, intelligible in its historical background.

The ceremony of baptism at which these vows were taken consisted of drinking sweetened water out of a common bowl. This was obviously intended to break through the orthodox Hindu practice of regarding anything touched by a person of lower caste as polluted. Sikhs were recruited from all castes and drank the baptismal water as nectar (*amrit*). The use of 'Singh' as a name was a step in the same direction. Since an individual's caste could be ascertained by his family name, with its abolition the 'Singhs' became one family. Besides being casteless, the name Singh had psychological value for a militant community.

Rules regarding abstinence from alcohol and tobacco are matters of personal ethics known to other religious codes. Sikhs have become more particular about tobacco, as abstinence from smoking together with the wearing of long hair and beards have in fact become the only things which distinguish them from Hindus. The provision against eating kosher meat (halal), where the animal is killed by being slowly bled to death, was both a protest against the cruelty to animals and refusal to eat meat slaughtered by Muslim butchers over which a passage of the Koran had been read.

The carrying of the *kirpan* and wearing of *kachha* were rules of discipline for soldiers. The *kachha* was in all probability the Punjabi fighters' uniform, unlike the loose and cumbersome *dhoti* of the peasant. Prohibition of carnal intercourse with Muslims was introduced to safeguard the person of women from molestation when Sikh bands raided Muslim towns and villages.

Several theories have been advanced to explain the innovation of growing the hair and the beard. It has been suggested that this was not an innovation at all and that Guru Gobind Singh's predecessors had all conformed to the tradition of Indian ascetics, who never cut their hair or beards. By making it obligatory for his followers, the Guru intended to emphasize the ideal of ascetic saintliness which he enjoined upon his followers. He wanted them to be soldier–saints. Another version is that, prior to launching on this venture, Gobind had spent a long time invoking the blessings of Durga, the Hindu goddess of destruction. Since she was always portrayed with long unshorn tresses, the Guru believed that in deference to his patron goddess he and his followers should also leave their hair unshorn.

A simpler and more plausible explanation is that in preparing his men for action against the Muslims, Guru Gobind Singh had to take account of the somewhat awesome aspect of the hirsute tribesmen from the North-west Frontier, who kept their long hair loose on their shoulders and let their beards grow. He made it a rule for his followers to do likewise so that appearance would no longer terrify. It is also likely that by having his followers wear emblems which made them easily recognizable, the Guru wanted to raise a body of men who would not be able to deny their faith when questioned, but whose external appearance would invite persecution and breed courage to resist it.

The carrying of the comb (*kungha*) in the hair is complementary to growing the hair long. It usually consists of a small two-square-inch comb under the turban. The steel bangle (*kara*) is said to be symbolic of restraint and is worn on the right hand like a 'moral handcuff'. Historically the *kara* can be traced to the practice of tying charms on the wrists of soldiers before they went to battle.

Gobind Singh completed the religious facet of Sikhism. He turned the innocuous band of pacifists into armed crusaders. Those who did not accept his innovations of forms and symbols remained just Sikhs, usually described as Sahajdharis or 'those who take time'; those who did, became the Khalsa.

A significant step Gobind took was to declare the line of Gurus at an end. He did this while all his four sons were alive. He divided the concept of Guruship into three, viz., personal, religious and temporal. The first he said would end with him. The second would subsist for ever in the Scriptures, and the Granth was henceforth to be considered as the symbolic representation of the ten Gurus. Temporal leadership he vested in the community. In actual practice it meant that all decisions taken by the majority of a representative assembly became binding on the rest as if it were the order of the Guru himself (*gurumatta*).

Gobind Singh's career as a military leader is significant as the first serious attempt to overthrow the Mughal Empire in the north. Even prior to 1699 he had built himself a fort at Paonta on the banks of the Yamuna. He followed it up by building four more at Anandpur, Lohgarh, Keshgarh and Fatchgarh. He employed Pathan mercenaries, and they along with his own followers fought successful skirmishes with neighbouring hill chieftains. After the formation of the Khalsa militia in 1699, as expected, the Mughal armies came upon him. In 1701 the governors of Sirhind and Lahore assaulted the fort of Anandpur. After three years the fort fell to the besiegers, but the Guru escaped. In his flight, he was separated from his family and his mother and two of his younger sons were captured. By order of the governor of Sirhind the boys, aged 9 and 10, were executed by being buried alive. Their grandmother died of grief. At Chamkaur the Guru was once again besieged and lost his remaining two sons and many of his most devoted followers. He himself escaped in disguise with the Muslim army in hot pursuit. At Muktsar in Ferozepur District he turned on his pursuers and defeated their vanguard, only to flee again till he was out of reach. From there in easy stages he went south towards the Deccan.

Although Guru Gobind did not win any spectacular victories, and in fact, apart from minor successes against hill chiefs, fought a losing battle from fortress to fortress, he never gave up his resolve to continue the crusade. Some time before his death, Emperor Aurangzeb summoned the Guru to his court at Delhi in the belief that adversity would have humbled his pride and he would be willing to make terms. Gobind answered the summons by a long letter written in Persian verse which he entitled the *Zafarnama* or the 'Epistle of Victory'. In this he recounted all the misdeeds of the Mughal rule with the defiant note: 'What use is it when you put out a few sparks and raise a mighty flame?'

His last days were spent in the Deccan with the Emperor Bahadur Shah, who had succeeded Aurangzeb and was more friendly to him. It appears that the Guru had asked Bahadur Shah for action against the governor of Sirhind for the murder of his infant sons. Before obtaining redress, Gobind fell victim to a murderous assault by one of his own Muslim retainers. It is likely that his assailant was a hireling of Wazir Khan, the Sirhind governor.

At the time of his death neither Guru Gobind nor any of his followers owned any territory or had any personal possessions. The foundations of the future Sikh state had, however, been firmly laid in the minds of his disciples, who came to believe in it as an article of faith, and like their Guru asked for no nobler end than to die for it:

> With clasped hands this boon I crave,
> When time it is to end my life
> Let me fall in mighty strife.
>
> – Gobind

Chapter 2

THE SIKH RELIGION

A Sikh has been defined as 'one who believes in the ten Gurus and the Granth Sahib'. This definition is not exhaustive. There are people who call themselves Sikhs but do not believe in all the ten Gurus, e.g., followers of unsuccessful claimants to the title like Adasis, Minas and Ram Raiy as noted in the family tree of the ten Gurus. There are others who believe that the line of Gurus continued after the tenth and follow the precepts of a living Guru, e.g., Nirankaris and Namdharis. Similarly, some Sikhs challenge the authenticity of certain passages of the Granth Sahib, while others insist on including extraneous writings in it. Besides these, there are numerous subsects distinguished by allegiance to one or other Guru or claiming that the real Guru had been overlooked in deciding the succession. But despite these discrepant factors, it can be safely asserted that the belief in the ten Gurus and the authorized version of the Granth Sahib is the common basic factor of the Sikh community, and it covers the vast majority of them. The only practical sectional division of the Sikh community is into the orthodox Khalsa and the clean-shaven Sahajdhari.

Conception of God

The Sikhs believe in the unity of God and equate God with truth.
Although Sikh monotheism has an abstract quality, there is nothing
vague about it. The preamble to the morning prayer Jupji, which is
recited as an introduction to all religious ceremonial and is known
as the Mool Mantra, the basic belief, states:

> There is one God.
> He is the supreme truth.
> He, the creator.
> Is without fear and without hate.
> He, the omnipresent,
> Pervades the universe.
> He is not born,
> Nor does he die to be born again.
> Before Time itself
> There was truth.
> When time began to run its course
> He was the truth.
> Even now, He is the truth.
> Evermore shall truth prevail.
>
> – Nanak

There was a change of emphasis in the conception of God in
the writing of the tenth Guru, Gobind Singh. To him, although
God was still one, the aspect of timelessness and of the power to
destroy was more important than the creative. 'I performed great
austerities and worshipped great death', he wrote.

Gobind Singh elevated death and time to the status of God. He
enjoined respect, if not worship, for steel (*sarb loh*) as the symbol of
destruction. He described God as Akal Purukh (timeless):

Time is the only God,
The primal and the final,
The creator and the destroyer.
How can words describe him?

An excellent example of his notion of God is in one of his compositions translated by Macauliffe:

Eternal God, Thou art our shield,
The dagger, knife, the sword we wield.
To us protector there is given
The timeless, deathless, Lord of Heaven,
To us all-steel's unvanquished might,
To us all-time's resistless flight,
But chiefly Thou, protector brave,
All-steel, wilt Thine own servant save.

The attitude of the two Gurus, which seems at first sight to be divergent, is not really so. The basic factors in the conception of God were oneness and truth. Other attributes, such as omnipresence, omniscience, formlessness, timelessness and the power to destroy (evil), were complementary and also referred to frequently by Nanak. Guru Gobind gave them prominence by constant emphasis.

Although God has no form (*nirankar*) or substance and is beyond human comprehension, by righteous living one can invoke His grace.

In the first verse of the morning prayer, Nanak said:

Not by thought alone
Can He be known,
Tho' one think a hundred thousand times.

Not in solemn silence,
Nor in deep meditation.
Though fasting yields an abundance of virtue,
It cannot appease the hunger for truth.
No! by none of these
Nor by a hundred thousand other devices
Can God be reached.
How then shall truth be known?
How the veil of false illusion torn?
O Nanak: thus runneth the writ divine.
The righteous path let it be thine.

Sikh emphasis on action as a means to salvation is a departure
from the predestination, and consequent passiveness, of the Hindu
belief. Nanak, who was fond of using rural similes, wrote:

As a team of oxen are we driven
By the ploughman, our teacher.
By the furrows made are thus writ
Our actions – on the earth, our paper.
The sweat of labour is as beads
Falling by the ploughman as seeds sown,
We reap according to our measure
Some for ourselves to keep, some to others give.
O Nanak, this is the way to truly live.

And again:

If thou wouldst the fruits of salvation cultivate
And let the love of the Lord in thy heart germinate,
Thy body be as the fallow land
Where in thy heart the Farmer sows his seeds

Of righteous action and good deeds,
Then with the name of God irrigate.

Although Sikhism accepts the Hindu theory of karma and life
hereafter, it escapes the maze in which life, death and rebirth go
on as it were independent of human volition. The Sikh religion
states categorically that the first form given to life is the human
('Thou has the body of man, now is thy turn to meet God'
[Arjun]). Human actions determine the subsequent forms of life
to be assumed after death. It also believes that by righteous living
and grace it is possible to escape the vicious circle of life and death
and attain salvation:

He who made the night and day,
The days of the week and the seasons,
He who made the breezes blow, the waters run,
The fires and the lower regions,
Made the earth – the temple of law.

He who made creatures of diverse kinds
With a multitude of names,
Made this law –
By thought and deed be judged forsooth
For God is true and dispenses truth.
There the elect His court adorn,
And God Himself their actions honours.
There are sorted deeds that were done and bore fruit
From those that to action could never ripen.
This, O Nanak, shall hereafter happen.

– Nanak

The Sikh religion, believing as it does in the unity and
formlessness of God, expressly forbids, in no uncertain terms, the
worship of idols and emblems:

They who worship strange gods
Cursed shall be their lives, cursed their habitations.
Poison shall be their food — each morsel,
Poisoned too shall be their garments.
In life for them is misery,
In life hereafter, hell.

> — Amar Das, third Guru

Some worship stones and on their heads they bear them,
Some the phallus — strung in necklaces wear its emblem.
Some behold their god in the south, some to the west bow
    their head.
Some worship images, others busy praying to the dead.
The world is thus bound in false ritual
And God's secret is still unread.

> — Guru Gobind

Guru Nanak, while attending the evening service at a Hindu temple where a salver full of small oil lamps and incense was being waved in front of the idol before it was laid to rest for the night, composed this verse:

The firmament is Thy salver,
The sun and moon Thy lamps,
The galaxy of stars
Are as pearls scattered.
The woods of sandal are Thine incense,
The forests Thy flowers,
But what worship is this
O Destroyer of Fear?

The Guru or the Teacher

God being an abstraction, godliness is conceived more as an attribute than a concrete something which can be acquired by a person or a thing The way of acquiring godliness or salvation is to obey the will of God. The means of ascertaining God's will are, as in other theological systems, unspecified and subject to human speculation. They are largely rules of moral conduct, which are the basis of human society. Sikh religion advocates association with men of religion for guidance. Hence the importance of the guru or the teacher and institution of discipleship.

The Sikhs do not worship human beings as incarnations of God. The Sikh Gurus themselves insisted that they were human like other human beings and were on no account to be worshipped. Guru Nanak constantly referred to himself as the slave and servant of God. Guru Gobind Singh, who was the author of most of the Sikh practice and ritual, was conscious of the danger of having divinity imposed on him by his followers. He explained his mission in life:

> For though my thoughts were lost in prayer
> At the feet of Almighty God,
> I was ordained to establish a sect and lay down its rules.
> But whosoever regards me as Lord
> Shall be damned and destroyed.
> I am – and of this let there be no doubt –
> I am but the slave of God, as other men are,
> A beholder of the wonders of creation.

In another passage he refuted the claims to divinity and reincarnation made by others:

God has no friends nor enemies.
He needs no hallelujahs nor cares about curses.
Being the first and timeless
How could he manifest himself through those
Who are born and die?

Godliness being the aim of human endeavour, the lives
and teachings of the Gurus are looked upon as aids towards its
attainment. 'On meeting a true Guru doubt is dispelled and
wanderings of the mind restrained' (Nanak).

The Scripture – Granth Sahib

The compilation of the Granth Sahib was largely the work of
the fifth Guru, Arjun, and his disciple, Gurdas. This compilation
is known as the Adi Granth, the first scripture. It is different from
the Dasam Granth, the tenth scripture of the tenth Guru, Gobind
Singh, which was compiled by his disciple Mani Singh.

By the ordinance of Guru Gobind himself, the Adi Granth
alone was given the status of the Holy Scripture, as symbolic
representation of all the ten Gurus. His own Dasam Granth is read
with reverence but does not form part of the ritual, except at the
ceremony of baptism.

The Adi Granth or the Granth Sahib contains the writings
of the first five Gurus, the ninth Guru, Tegh Bahadur, and a
couplet by Guru Gobind Singh. A large part of the book consists
of the writings of Hindu and Muslim saints of the time, chiefly
those of the Muslim Kabir. The compositions of the bards who
accompanied the different Gurus are also incorporated in it.

The language used by the Sikh Gurus was Punjabi of the
fifteenth and sixteenth centuries. Other writings are in old
Hindi, Persian, Sanskrit, Gujarati, Maharathi and other dialects

of northern India. The entire work is set to measures of classical Indian music.

All the words appearing in each line are joined together, causing considerable confusion in the interpretation of the text. It is frequently impossible to tell whether there is one word or two words put together. Despite this the Granth is a unique historical document. It is perhaps the only kind of writing of a scriptural nature which has preserved without embellishment or misconstruction in the original writings of the religious leaders. It has saved the literary works of other poets of the time from the vagaries of human memory.

The Granth Sahib is the central object of Sikh worship and ritual. In all temples, copies of the Granth are placed under a canopy. The book itself is draped in cloth, usually richly embroidered. It is opened with a prayer and a ceremony each morning and similarly closed in the evening. Worshippers appear before it barefoot and with their heads covered. They make obeisance by rubbing their foreheads to the ground before it. Offerings of money or food are placed on the cloth draping the book.

A ceremony of non-stop reading of the Granth Sahib by relays of worshippers, known as the Akhand Path, takes two days and nights and is performed on important religious festivals and private functions. A simpler ceremony is the Saptah Path, a cover-to-cover reading in seven days. This is frequently undertaken in homes with private chapels, where assistance from outside is not easily available.

Sikh children are named by being given a name beginning with the first letter appearing on the page at which the Granth may open. Sikh youths are baptized with recitation of prayers in front of the Granth. Sikh couples are married to the singing of hymns from the Granth, while they walk round it four times. On death, hymns are read aloud in the dying person's ears. On cremation, they are chanted as the flames consume the body.

Despite all this, the Granth is not like an idol in a Hindu temple or a crucifix in a Catholic church. It is the source and not the object of prayer or worship. The Sikhs revere it because it contains the teachings of their Gurus. It is more a book of divine wisdom than the word of God.

Pilgrimage

Sikhs do not believe in 'sacred' rivers and mountains, nor do they pray to stone images. 'To worship an image, to make a pilgrimage to a shrine, to remain in a desert, and yet have the mind impure, is all in vain. To be saved, worship only the Truth' (Nanak).

Although there are no places or occasions marked out for pilgrimage, Sikhs assemble on the birthdays of the Gurus at their birthplaces. Prior to the partition of the Punjab, the martyrdom of the fifth Guru, Arjun, used to be celebrated by mammoth gatherings of Sikhs in Lahore. The martyrdom of Guru Tegh Bahadur is still celebrated annually in Delhi. The more important shrines – the birthplace of Nanak, the site of Arjun's execution in Lahore, the temples in Amritsar and Turun Tarun, the birthplace of Gobind Singh in Patna and the site of his death in Hyderabad, Deccan – are visited by Sikhs at all times.

Society and Caste

Sikh tradition elevates society to the status of the law-giver and judge. The last Guru devised means by which the will of society could be ascertained and enforced. A resolution (*mata*) passed by elected representatives of the congregation became a *gurumata* (the order of the Guru). A *gurumata* could even dispense with forms and conventions initiated by the Gurus themselves. Gurdas put it somewhat tersely:

Where there is one Sikh, there is one Sikh.
Where there are two Sikhs, there is an assembly of saints.
Where there are five Sikhs, there is God.

Consistent with giving society the democratic right to lay down the law, the Gurus categorically rejected the Hindu caste system, which put certain sections of the people outside its pale. Nanak chose a Muslim musician, who would normally have been an outcaste, as a companion. His writings abound with passages describing as ungodly the conduct of those who condemn God's creatures to untouchability:

There are ignoble amongst the noblest
And pure amongst the despised.
The former shalt thou avoid,
And be the dust under the foot of the other.

The second Guru, Angad, said:

The Hindus say there are four castes
But they are all of one seed.
'Tis like clay of which pots are made
In diverse shapes and forms – yet the clay is the same.
So is the body of men made of five elements.
How can one amongst them be high and another low?

Gobind's first five disciples included three who were of lower castes. With determined deliberation he said he would mix the four castes into one – like the four constituents of pan (betel leaf) which when chewed produce just one colour.

Besides condemning the actual segregation of people on the basis of birth, Sikhism refused to compromise with practices

that were the outcome of caste distinctions but were masked as
hygienic. The sanctity of the kitchen and of food were amongst
the most conspicuous of these. About them Nanak said:

Once we say: 'This is pure, this unclean',
See that in all things there is life unseen.
There are worms in wood and cowdung cakes.
There is life in the corn ground into bread.
There is life in the water which makes it green.
How then be clean when impurity is over the kitchen spread?
Impurity of the heart is greed,
Of tongue, untruth.
Impurity of the eyes is coveting
Another's wealth, his wife, her comeliness.
Impurity of the ears is listening to calumny.

Prayer

A feature of the Sikh religion which is particularly striking is its
emphasis on prayer. The form of prayer is usually the repetition
of the name of God and chanting hymns of praise. This was
popularized by the Bhakti cult and Sikhism is its chief exponent
today. The Sikh Scriptures abound with exhortations to repeat 'the
true name' as a purification from sin and impious thoughts:

As hands or feet besmirched with slime,
Water washes white;
As garments dark with grime,
Rinsed with soap are made light;
So when sin soils the soul
Prayer alone shall make it whole.

Words do not the saint or sinner make.

Action alone is written in the book of fate,
What we sow that alone we take;
O Nanak, be saved or for ever transmigrate.

                                                  – Nanak

At the same time there are positive injunctions against austere asceticism involving renunciation of society, celibacy and penance. All the Gurus led normal family lives, discharging their obligations as householders as well as being the spiritual mentors of their people. The concept of righteous living was to them meaningless except in the context of the community. There is constant reference by them to being in the world but not being worldly. The ideal is to achieve saintliness as a member of society, to have a spiritual existence with the necessary material requisites – '*raj men jog kamayo*':

The lotus in the water is not wet
Nor the water-fowl in the stream.
If man would live, but by the world untouched,
Meditate and repeat the name of the Lord Supreme.

                                                  – Nanak

Gobind was more forthright in his denunciation of asceticism. He compared a yogi's penance with the crane which stood impassive in the water with its eyes shut as if in prayer but all the time mindful of the frogs about it. He also disapproved of making vegetarianism and austerity in food into a fetish and a part of religion. 'Practise asceticism in this way', he said:

Let thine own house be the forest,
Thy heart the anchorite.

Eat little, sleep little.

Learn to love, be merciful and forbear.
Be mild, be patient.
Have no lust, nor wrath,
Greed nor obstinacy.

Priesthood

The Sikhs do not have priests. All adults, irrespective of status or sex, are competent to perform religious ceremonial. A class of professional scripture readers (*granthis*) and musicians (*ragis*) has come into existence, but they function mainly in big cities where the size of the congregation renders some sort of institutionalization necessary.

Pacifism and the Use of Force

Sikh pacifism in religion and the Sikh militarism present a contradiction which can only be explained by a reference to history. A strictly pacifist faith is difficult to reconcile with a spartan military tradition, except through the formula that, when the faith itself is threatened with extinction, force may be used to preserve it. This indeed was Guru Gobind Singh's explanation of the steps he took. In a Persian couplet, he said:

Chu kar uz hama har heel te dar guzusht
Halal ust burdan ba shamsheer dust.

When all other means have failed
It is righteous to draw the sword.

It is possible that if the state of affairs in the Punjab had returned to a peaceful normality, the Sikh sword might have been sheathed and the gospel of Nanak, which preached peace and humility, become symbolic of the Sikh faith. As it was, the period following Gobind Singh was the most turbulent one known to Indian history. The decaying Mughal Empire took to making scapegoats of minorities to explain away its failures. There were pogroms of unprecedented savagery in which the small community of the Sikhs was almost exterminated. Coincident with persecution within the country came new Muslim invasions from the north, which destroyed any people or institution which they deemed un-Islamic. In such circumstances, martial traditions were forged, which became an integral part of Sikh life and gave the Sikhs the reputation of being a fighting people.

Sikhism and Its Relation to Hinduism and Islam

Sikh religion, which in its inception was a synthesis of Hinduism and Islam, began to manifest a tendency to revert to the Hindu fold at an early stage in its development. Although in its general system of belief it was closer to Islam than Hinduism, in practice, in ritual, and above all in social affinities, it never quite succeeded in freeing itself of Hindu influence. The trend towards a merger back into Hinduism was evident immediately after the Gurus.

Sikhism did not succeed in breaking the caste system. If intermarriage is considered the test of equality, at no time was there much intercaste marriage between Sikhs converted from different Hindu castes.

The untouchable converted to Sikhism remained an outcaste for purposes of matrimonial alliances. Although he was no longer untouchable in the sense of not being touched and sat in temples along with other Sikhs, in time caste taboos regarding food came back, and Sikhs of higher castes refused to eat with untouchable Sikhs and in villages separate wells were provided for them. Amongst the other four castes, Sikhs did not continue the observance of the rigid rules of the Hindus and intermarriage was commoner with them than with the Hindus. The chief reason for this was the emergence of a new order of caste hierarchy within the Sikh social set-up which cut across the Hindu pattern. The majority of the early converts were Jats who belonged to the lowest of the four castes, the Sudras. When the Sikhs came to power, the Jats became the ruling class and the aristocracy. Sikh converts from higher castes became the middle and lower middle classes, ever willing to raise their social status by alliance with lower caste Jats.

The Sikh attitude to cow slaughter was another move in the same direction. Veneration of the cow was not part of the teaching of the Sikh Gurus and, apart from a passing reference in the writings of Guru Gobind regretting the existence of cow slaughter, it had no scriptural backing. Nevertheless, the Sikhs became more zealous protectors of the cow than even the Hindus and during Sikh rule, cow slaughter was rigorously suppressed.

Within a hundred years of Guru Gobind Singh's death, rituals in Sikh gurdwaras were almost like that in Hindu temples, and more often than not were presided over by priests who were usually Hindu rather than Sikh. Sikhs began to wear caste marks; Sikh weddings and funerals followed Hindu patterns; ashes of the dead were carried to the Ganga and offerings were made to ancestors. Amongst the ruling class and the aristocracy the trend towards Hinduism was even more marked. On birth, horoscopes were cast by pandits. Brahmin priests invested Sikh rulers on their thrones with the burning of sacrificial fires and chanting of Vedic hymns. Marriages took place with Hindu women and were performed by Hindu priests. At death, wives were burnt along with their husbands. The cremation of Ranjit Singh, the Sikh ruler, was accompanied by the burning of his widows and even his favourite pigeons.

This affinity with Hinduism explains both the Sikh drift-away from Islamic associations and the pattern of Sikh reformation movements, which sought to maintain Sikh identity distinct from the Hindu. It also explains the Sikh attachment to external forms and symbols, which came progressively to have more of a sociological than a religious significance. They became symbolic of belonging to a group and not necessarily of observing its religious ordinances.

Chapter 3

RISE OF THE SIKH CONFEDERACY

Gobind Singh spent most of his life in desultory fighting. His area of operations was confined to the vicinity of the Himalayan foothills in the Punjab. Here, for many years, he fought the Mughal governors and their Hindu satellites. But neither he nor his associates were able to hold any territory. The Guru actually lost his family and personal possessions in the struggle. All he bequeathed to his followers was a tradition of reckless valour and faith in the ultimate and inevitable victory of the Sikhs.

Although Gobind Singh had declared the institution of guruship at an end, he realized the necessity of giving his followers a leader who could keep them together. Shortly before his death, he had met and befriended a Hindu hermit, Lachman Das, to whom he entrusted the secular affairs of his people.

Banda

Lachman Das, renamed Banda Singh Bahadur (1708–1726), was in his late thirties when he met the Guru in the Deccan. His association with Gobind Singh was by all accounts a very brief one, possibly of a couple of months. It is likely that he, being a Hindu from the north, was well acquainted with the Guru's mission and had, prior to the meeting and conversion, been involved in some capacity in the rebellion against Muslim tyranny. That is the only explanation of his selection in preference to several old and faithful comrades who were still in the Guru's camp.

Banda left the Deccan bearing Gobind Singh's banner, a battle drum and five arrows. He issued a manifesto in the name of the Guru calling the Sikhs to arms, to avenge the murder of the Guru's children. All over the country the peasantry rose and Banda laid waste large tracts in south-eastern Punjab. In the summer of 1710, he captured Sirhind along with its governor, Wazir Khan, who had tormented the Guru in his lifetime and killed his family. Banda wreaked terrible vengeance on his master's oppressors. The town was razed to the ground and the entire Muslim population put to the sword. From there he moved north to Ludhiana, Jullundur, Hoshiarpur and Pathankot, and then south-east to Karnal and across the Yamuna to Saharanpur. He struck coins in the names of Nanak and Gobind Singh and appointed Sikh governors to the captured towns.

The Muslims were thoroughly alarmed at Banda's success. The governor of Lahore called for a holy war against the Sikhs. Emperor Bahadur Shah abandoned his expeditions against the Mahrattas and Rajputs and hurried north. He outlawed the Sikh community and ordered 'all Hindus employed in the Imperial offices to get their beards shaved'. Banda was driven from the plains and took shelter in the hills.

As soon as Bahadur Shah turned his back to return to Delhi, Banda descended on the plains calling on 'the Khalsa of the great immortal God' to fight the Mughal. Once again the Sikhs flocked to his colours and marched across the plains of southern Punjab.

This time their ventures were assisted by the death of Bahadur Shah and the quarrels between his successors.

In 1713, Farukhsiyar ascended the throne of Delhi.

He appointed two energetic men, Abdus Samad Khan and his son Zakarya Khan, as governors of Lahore and Jammu, respectively, with explicit orders to destroy the power of the Sikhs. These two mustered all their strength and moved against Banda. Fortunately for them, dissensions had arisen in Banda's camp, which had materially reduced his strength.

Banda had attempted to introduce certain religious innovations amongst the Sikhs, which were resented by the orthodox elements led by Guru Gobind Singh's widow, Sundri. Sundri was revered by the whole community as the mother of the Sikhs. Banda had himself somewhat changed in his personal habits. From the hermit of a Deccan monastery, he had become a petty king, living in regal pomp with courtiers and a couple of wives. Amongst a people who had exaggerated respect for asceticism and had come to believe in Banda's miraculous powers, this caused serious misgiving. On the actual field of battle, some of his most trusted lieutenants disagreed with his strategy and deserted him.

In the December of 1715, Banda was surrounded by the Mughal forces near Gurdaspur and starved into surrendering. From the Punjab, he, his family and several hundred of his soldiers were led in chains to Delhi. There his wife was forced into the royal harem, and the prisoners were publicly beheaded. On 9 June 1716, Banda himself was led to the scaffold. His infant son was placed in his lap for him to kill. The sadistic orgy came to an end with the torture and execution of Banda himself.

For some years after Banda's death the Sikhs disappeared from the Punjab as a political force. Old dissensions gained a new lease of life. Disapproval of Banda's innovations were looked upon by his followers, the Bandei Khalsa, as a disavowal of his enterprise.

In these dissensions, the influence of Sundri decided the issue against the Bandei. The religious affairs of the community were entrusted to Mani Singh, a contemporary of the last Guru, who was appointed head priest of the temple at Amritsar.

Anarchy and Persecution

While the Sikhs were busy putting their house in order, the affairs of the Mughal Government at Delhi began to deteriorate rapidly. In all parts of India, governors threw off allegiance to the Central Government and proclaimed themselves independent sovereigns. In the south the Mahrattas had consolidated their power and had moved north within gunshot of Delhi. All around the capital itself the Jats were in open revolt. The Mughal monarch Farukhsiyar was engaged in a desperate but losing battle against the elements of disintegration.

Unfortunately for the Sikhs, the only part of India where the dissolution of the Mughal Empire was not accompanied by the total collapse of local administration was the Punjab. Here the provincial governors, although of dubious loyalty to their sovereign, were men of unusual ability. From Abdus Samad Khan the governorship went to his son Zakarya Khan and then in succession to the latter's two sons, Yahya and Shah Nawaz. After them came the ablest of the lot, Mir Mannu. Despite their own troubles with the government at Delhi and with the Afghans from the north, they never hesitated in their determination to put down the Sikhs. In fact, the measures they took were in terms of savage repression out of all proportion to the problem. But the series of invasions from Afghanistan, starting with that of Nadir Shah in 1738 and followed by nine others by Ahmed Shah Abdali from 1748 to 1767, seriously dislocated administration each time, and the Sikhs were able to consolidate their strength in the hills and occasionally to wreak vengeance on their erstwhile oppressors.

The first governor to launch a campaign to exterminate the Sikh religion was Abdus Samad Khan, aptly called 'the sword of the state'. A contemporary Persian chronicler records that 'he filled the extensive plain with blood as if it had been a dish'. A price was put on the head of all Sikhs and the local bureaucracy went about hunting them as if they were wild animals. Large numbers abjured their faith to save their lives. Others retreated into the mountainous regions in the north. But once every year they ran the gauntlet of the Muslim armies by going to Amritsar to bathe in the pool surrounding the shrine.

Sikh Reorganization

By the time Abdus Samad Khan died in 1737, the Sikhs had succeeded to some extent in reorganizing their scattered forces under the leadership of Kapur Singh, later entitled the nawab. He divided the army into the old army (Budha Dal) and the young army (Taruna Dal). The latter were again subdivided into several minor units and allocated specific areas of operation. Associated with Nawab Kapur Singh at the time were several other men of considerable political and military capabilities. Outstanding amongst them were Jassa Singh Ahluwalia (founder of the present state of Kapurthala), Charat Singh Sukerchakia (grandfather of Ranjit Singh, the first Sikh ruler of the Punjab), Ala Singh (founder of Patiala state), and Jassa Singh Ramgarhia. When the Persian ruler Nadir Shah invaded India in 1738–39, he had occasion to see something of the Sikh armies. He had marched across the Punjab, plundered Delhi, and was on his way back with his booty and a large train of enslaved Hindu women. The Sikhs emerged from their mountain haunts, relieved Nadir Shah of his loot, and released most of his Hindu captives. It is said that Nadir Shah questioned Zakarya Khan of the whereabouts of the people who had the audacity to prey on his troops. Zakarya Khan replied: 'Their homes are their saddles. They are fakirs who visit their Guru's tank twice a year, bathe in it, and disappear.' Nadir Shah warned the governor saying: 'Take care, the day is not distant when these rebels will take possession of your country.'

In 1748, Ahmed Shah Abdali began the first of his series of nine invasions, ending in 1767. Each time he crossed the Punjab on his way to Delhi, he disrupted provincial administration and destroyed its links with the Central Government. The Sikhs were tactful and retired into the mountains and wooded tracts, content to prey on the stragglers of the invader's forces. Their strength consequently remained unimpaired. On the other hand, the enemies of the Sikhs fought Abdali and were laid low. Thus were the Mughals and their governors destroyed. So also were the Mahrattas in 1761, at Panipat, just when their power was at its zenith and their expanding empire had begun to cast its shadow over the nebulous kingdom of the Sikhs.

Several attempts were made between these invasions to exterminate the Sikhs. The temple at Amritsar was blown up many times, and the countryside was combed to apprehend Sikhs. They were beheaded in batches in the marketplace at Lahore for their refusal to abjure their faith. Amongst the people who suffered death were revered leaders like Mani Singh. The site of their executions became a place of pilgrimage. It was renamed Shahidgunj – the place of martyrdom.

Sikh strength continued to grow in the face of suppression. In 1757, Sikh raiders occupied Lahore for a brief period but withdrew with the advance of Abdali. Two years later, in alliance with the Mahrattas and the local governor, Adeena Beg Khan, they re-entered the city and evacuated it again in the face of Abdali. While Abdali was occupied in fighting the Mahrattas, the Sikhs convened a general assembly at Amritsar and resolved to take Lahore permanently. As soon as the Afghans returned home after defeating the Mahrattas, they ousted his nominee and reoccupied the city for the third time (October 1761). Abdali came down once more on them, and on 5 February 1762 he surprised and surrounded their armies near Malerkotla and killed over 30,000. This defeat is still remembered bitterly as the Ghallu-ghara or the 'great massacre'. But even this reverse did not smash Sikh power. A few months after the massacre they defeated Afghan forces at Amritsar and recaptured most of southern Punjab. Two years later Abdali had to undertake yet another expedition against them. The Sikh armies met him in open combat near Amritsar and forced him to retire. On Abdali's last invasion in 1767, Sikh horsemen harassed the Afghan armies right up to Peshawar and occupied the northern district of Rawalpindi. Fighting the Sikhs was like slashing a sword through a pond.

All the time the contest with the Afghans was going on, the Sikhs continued to consolidate their hold on the outlying districts by building a chain of forts and organizing a regular revenue system. They took towns, villages and small states under their rule on payment of protection money. When Jassa Singh Ahluwalia finally entered Lahore, Sikh power had spread well beyond the frontiers of the Punjab, from across the Indus in the west to the Ganga in the east, the Himalayas in the north to the Thar desert in the south. With justified pride he struck coins in the name of the new confederation with the inscription:

By the grace of God and the sword – to victory.
Thus was ordained by Nanak and Guru Gobind.

Confederate Organization

The political and military organization evolved by the Sikhs during the period between the death of Banda and the rise of Ranjit Singh deserves attention. There was no systematic planning behind the organization, but because of the necessity of having to break up every few months to scatter in all parts of the country, they evolved a system admirably suited to the state of affairs and unique in its democratic concepts. It has already been stated that immediately after Banda's execution the Sikh fighting forces were divided into the Budha and the Taruna Dals (old and young armies). These two divisions subsequently broke up into twelve *misls* or militias operating in different parts of the province. The twelve *misls* were:

Bhangi
Ahluwalia
Ramgarhia
Sukerchakia
Kanheya
Nakkai
Phoolkia
Singhpuria
Nishania
Krora Singhia
Dulewalia
Shahid.

Some *misls* took their names from their leader, e.g., the Ahluwalias after Jassa Singh Ahluwalia; some from the personal habits of the leader, e.g., the Bhangis from the founder's addiction to bhang (hashish); some from symbols, e.g., the Nishania – the standard-bearers; others from the area of activity, e.g., Nakkaisi. Their fighting strength varied from 10,000 to 20,000 horsemen of the most powerful, the Bhangis, to a few hundred of the smaller ones. In the beginning when the *misls* were engaged purely in marauding, all the members had an equal voice in its deliberations and activities. All shared the booty alike. The leader held his post

purely because of his capacity for leadership. Twice a year, on the
Hindu new year's day in spring (Baisakhi) and the festival of the
lamps (Diwali) in autumn, the *misl*s gathered at Amritsar. Here
past successes and failures were discussed, future plans made, duties
apportioned, defaulters penalized, and contributions levied. Every
individual had the right to speak, and indeed at times so much
misused it as to paralyse proceedings. No chief dared to browbeat
the commonest soldier. But leaders were acknowledged and
respected. The first was Nawab Kapur Singh, who was followed
by the greatest leader of the time, Jassa Singh Ahluwalia. The
biennial deliberations were described as the meetings of the Sarbat
Khalsa and their resolutions were considered binding on the entire
community.

The *misl* organization did not maintain its democratic character
for very long. As soon as the Sikhs settled down as landowners,
property rights became hereditary and the disparity in wealth
introduced an extraneous element in the choice of leadership.

The actual history of the *misl*s and their area of operation is
also significant. Any map of the time will show that of the twelve
*misl*s the three most powerful, the Bhangi, Kanheya and the
Sukerchakia, operated in the area north of the Sutlej where the
population was predominantly Muslim. These three flourished in
the order mentioned.

The Bhangis at one time covered an area from Kashmir in the
north to Multan in the south, and Attock in the west to Lahore in
the east. They held these tracts with interruptions throughout the
period of Abdali's invasions. In 1765, the *misl* had occupied Lahore
for a short period. The Bhangis were at the zenith of their power
under the founder, Hari Singh, and his first two successors, Jhanda
Singh and Ganda Singh. This *misl*, as well as the Kanheyas, was
absorbed by the Sukerchakias.

The Kanheyas were in possession of the area north of
Amritsar. Their chief, Jai Singh, was, at an early stage, involved

in intrigues against the Bhangis, whom he defeated with the aid of the Sukerchakias. The Sukerchakias and the Ramgarhias then combined to defeat Jai Singh, and slew his son Gurbaksh Singh. With the defeat of the Kanheya chieftain, power passed to the Sukerchakias, whose leader Maha Singh became the most powerful Sikh chief. He made peace with the Kanheyas by marrying his son Ranjit Singh to the daughter of Jai Singh's dead son. Not only did he thereby acquire the territories won by the Kanheyas from the Bhangis, but also, on the death of Jai Singh, the Kanheya's own lands. Maha Singh died before he could consolidate his hold on northern Punjab. This was left to his son, Ranjit Singh.

There were other smaller *misls* north of the Sutlej that played important roles in the struggle for power. Ranjit Singh was able to absorb them in his domains. He might easily have extended his territories to the *misls* south of the river but for the interference of the English, who were at the time already in power at Delhi. They took under their protection the most powerful of the southern *misls*, the Phoolkias, who covered the territory from the Sutlej to the Yamuna. In so doing they followed the Afghan policy of dividing the trans-Sutlej areas from the cis-Sutlej. The division separated the Majha Sikhs of the north from the Malwa Sikhs of the east − a division based almost entirely on difference of dialect but capable of political exploitation. The immediate effect was, however, to confine Sikh domains to an area where the population was largely non-Sikh. The majority of the community was thereby prevented from taking part in a venture the fulfilment of which had been an article of faith with preceding generations.

Chapter 4

THE KINGDOM OF THE SIKHS

Ranjit Singh was a boy of twelve when his father, Maha Singh, died. At the time his *misl*, the Sukerchakias, were the most powerful in the Punjab and occupied the territory between the Ravi and the Chenab, with their headquarters at Gujranwala. By his marriage to the daughter of the Kanheya chief, Ranjit acquired a future interest in the tracts possessed by them between the Ravi and the Beas. He also came under the care and guidance of an astute and able woman, his mother in-law, Sada Kaur, who helped him to gain ascendancy over the other *misls*.

By the time Ranjit was seventeen and able to manage his own affairs, the other *misls* were in a state of disintegration. His father-in-law, the Kanheya chief, was dead. So were the heads of the once powerful Bhangis and the Ahluwalias. The Ramgarhia Jassa Singh was too old to matter. The Phoolkias in the south-east had been weakened by family disputes and invasions of the Mahrattas and the English adventurer, George Thomas. It became quite obvious to Ranjit Singh that the days of the Sikh confederacy were over, and the only chance of resisting the encroachments on the Sikh possessions by the encircling powers, Mahrattas, British, Gurkhas,

Dogras and Afghans, was to consolidate the loose confederacy into a kingdom. This was the task Ranjit Singh set himself: first, to unite the Sikh factions; then to convince his covetous neighbours that the Punjab was to be the homeland of the Sikhs, not a province of an alien empire. In both these aims he acted not in his own name or that of the Sukerchakias, but in the name of the entire body of Sikhs, the Khalsaji.

Ranjit Singh's first move was towards the capital city of Lahore. It was nominally under the dominion of the ruler of Afghanistan, but actually held by the Bhangi Sardars since its occupation by the Sikhs. In 1798, Shah Zaman, in keeping with the tradition of his ancestors, invaded India for the third time and occupied Lahore. On his way back he lost several guns in the Jhelum which Ranjit Singh recovered for him. In return, the city of Lahore was granted to Ranjit Singh. Ranjit ousted the Bhangi Sardars without difficulty and transferred his seat of government from Gujranwala to the capital. He then proceeded to drive the Bhangis out of Amritsar and set the seal of sanctity on his secular power. He took the city of Kasur from the Pathans. Within eight years he was in effective occupation of the lands between the Jhelum and the Sutlej and ready to meet the challenge from his neighbours.

Dogras and Gurkhas

The first to threaten Ranjit Singh were the hill men from the north and north-east, the Dogras and the Gurkhas. The Dogra ruler, Sansar Chand of Katoch, descended from the hills, took Hoshiarpur, and occupied the adjacent territory. About the same time, the Gurkhas under Amar Singh Thapa started to move westward from Garhwal and came into clash with the Dogras. Both appealed for assistance to Ranjit Singh. Ranjit took Kangra from the Dogras, and Sansar Chand came virtually under the Sikh ruler's protection. The enraged Gurkhas invited the British to join them in invading the Sikh kingdom and the British invited Ranjit Singh to go across their territory to fight the Gurkhas. The end of these intrigues and counterintrigues was a triumph for Ranjit, who kept aloof and let the British fight the Gurkhas and defeat them. Thus, although the north and north-eastern borders were rendered safe from invasion, in the east British power had become greater and more menacing. The only people to challenge British supremacy in the region were the Mahrattas.

The Mahrattas

The two Mahratta chiefs who had extended their dominions up to the borders of the Punjab were Madhaji Scindia and Jaswant Rao Holkar. Both were, in turn, involved in troubles with the British and appealed to the Sikhs for assistance. At first Madhaji Scindia, who had extended his power north of Delhi, asked his French generals, Perron and Bourquin, to contact Ranjit Singh for a joint invasion of English-held territories. When his plan failed, Perron invaded southern Punjab and proceeded to make alliances with local Sikh chiefs. He defeated George Thomas, who had carved out a petty kingdom for himself near Jind, and drove him out of the Punjab. But before his ambition of extending Mahratta power to the Indus could materialize, his master got involved in fighting the English. Perron was recalled. Scindia himself was defeated in a series of battles with the English and ceased to menace the Sikh kingdom.

In 1805, Jaswant Rao Holkar was also defeated by the English and arrived at Amritsar with a part of his army. He asked the Sikhs to join him in fighting the English. General Lake in pursuit of Holkar asked Ranjit to eject him from Amritsar and marched northward with his forces. Ranjit realized the gravity of the situation and called a meeting of the Sarbat Khalsa at Amritsar. Holkar's motives were ascertained. The wily Mahratta was only interested in utilizing the Sikhs to recover his domains and share the loot that might fall to their joint forces. Ranjit described him as a *pukka huramzada* (absolute bastard), and ordered him to quit the Sikh territories. The English armies afterwards withdrew to Delhi.

The English

With the defeat of the Gurkhas and the Mahrattas, an Anglo-Sikh frontier extending from the Himalayas down to the deserts of Rajputana came into existence. Hitherto the two powers were only vaguely conscious of each other without any specific policy. Ranjit Singh had little occasion to think of the English prior to their contact as neighbours. His ambition was limited to consolidating the Sikh chiefs into one Punjab power. The British were somewhat quicker in their appraisal of the Sikhs and formulated their plan of action. As early as 1784, Governor-General Warren Hastings wrote that the Sikh power extended 'from the most western branch of Attock to the walls of Delhi'. He was conscious of the danger to England of a union between the Sikhs and the Mahrattas and was determined to prevent it, and indeed to prevent either Indian power from growing too strong. Regarding the Sikhs, he advised his government to take 'seasonable means of opposition ... not to permit the people to grow into maturity without interruption'. The one 'seasonable means' which Warren Hastings suggested was, as the Afghans had done before him, to divide the Sikhs by separating those living south of the Sutlej from their co-religionists in the north. The division was roughly that of the Malwa from the Majha Sikhs. 'The Sikhs in Lahore and Multan form altogether a very respectable power', he wrote. 'But', he added, 'Sikh chiefs immediately to the northward of Delhi are totally unconnected with these and are in fact nothing more than a number of petty plunderers.'

Ranjit was at first not quite aware of this plan nor of the designs of the English to extend their dominions. In 1805 he crossed the Sutlej and levied tribute on the Sikh chiefs of Patiala, Nabha, Jind and Kythal. He also took the town of Ludhiana. Two years later, he again came down to Patiala to adjudicate in the domestic affairs of the ruling family and visited the neighbouring Sikh states. But by this time British policy had changed. In Europe, the treaty of Tilsit between Czar Alexander and Napoleon Bonaparte caused serious misgivings in English political circles. It was believed that both France and Russia coveted British possessions in India and were planning to use Turkey, Persia, Afghanistan and the Sikhs in furtherance of their designs. To countenance these moves from the Indian end, envoys were sent to Afghanistan and Lahore.

Charles Metcalfe, who was assistant to the resident at Delhi and was sent to Ranjit Singh, had a difficult task. Without offending the Sikh ruler he had to persuade him to acknowledge British hegemony over the lands south of the Sutlej. The Sikh chiefs and Ranjit Singh had been led to believe that Britain had no interests beyond Delhi and recognized Ranjit's suzerainty over all Sikh territories. During Ranjit's second visit to the south, a deputation representing Patiala, Jind and Kythal had asked the British for protection against Ranjit Singh and had been refused. On the other hand, when Ranjit Singh himself asked the deputations to come to him, they had done so and accepted his assurances. The new position taken by Metcalfe was rightly viewed by Ranjit to be a flagrant violation of precedent and he emphasized this by crossing the Sutlej a third time and visiting Faridkot, Ambala and Thanesar. At Patiala, he was welcomed by the ruler and the two exchanged turbans to symbolize everlasting friendship. Metcalfe protested against this act of 'hostility' but his government was not yet in a position to go to war with the Sikhs.

Meanwhile, the situation in Europe changed. The Spaniards had risen in revolt against France and there was no likelihood of French invasion. Relations with Turkey had improved and led ultimately to the signing of the Treaty of the Dardanelles. Britain could now dictate its terms to the Sikhs. Ranjit was told categorically that the cis-Sutlej states were under its protection and any interference by him would be countered by force. The protected chiefs themselves were informed that they had no choice in the matter of being protected (and one, Kalsia, had to be actually coerced into it). In January 1809, British troops moved through the cis-Sutlej Sikh states of Boorea and Patiala on to Ludhiana. The commander, Sir David Ochterlory, made a proclamation that he was there to defend British possessions and proceeded to fortify Ludhiana. Metcalfe himself made contacts with disgruntled elements in Ranjit Singh's court to 'put his own government's hands on the cords that could, if necessity arose, pull tight a wide net of conspiracy' (Thomas).

For some time, Ranjit Singh thought of going to war. His troops moved to the Sutlej frontiers and the garrisons at Govindgarh and Phillaur were strengthened. But he soon realized that his armies were as yet no match for the British and to be incited by acts of provocation would provide them with the excuse they wanted to absorb his dominions. On 25 April 1809 he signed a treaty of 'friendship' conceding all the British demands. His views on the nature of this treaty were well summed up in the conversation he had with Metcalfe prior to the signing. He said: 'Do not let the same injury arise in friendship, which would be the result of enmity.'

There are two aspects of this treaty which need special notice. In the first place, although the British Government agreed to have no concern 'with the territories and subjects of the Raja to the northward of the river Sutlej', in actual interpretation, this was limited to Ranjit's affairs with the Afghans. When he tried to proceed towards Sindh, he received another check from the British, who took the local Amirs under their protection. The other clause which subsequently caused confusion was the one which, although restricting Ranjit Singh's kingdom to the north of the Sutlej, allowed him to retain his possessions south of the river which he had acquired before the arrival of Metcalfe. In these possessions he was allowed to maintain troops necessary for internal duties. In other words, his sovereignty over some areas south of the Sutlej was acknowledged. One of these was the town of Ferozepur, which, up to 1805, was admitted by the British to rest solely within the care of the maharaja. Subsequently, the maharaja's claim to it was denied since it was a 'post of consequence' only forty miles from Lahore. In 1824, when it was proposed by a woman estate holder of Ferozepur that the British openly take the city in return for an equivalent area in the south, the governor-general did not altogether reject the proposal but was unable to accept it as 'it would doubtless excite alarm and suspicion in the mind of Ranjit Singh and perhaps not unnaturally be objected to by him as an encroachment'. Ferozepur was, however, occupied by the British in 1835 and strongly garrisoned three years later. The significance of these moves lies in the fact that, after the death of Ranjit Singh, the first clash of arms between the Sikhs and the English was in this region.

Reorganization

Ranjit's dealings with the English made it abundantly clear that if the Sikh state was to subsist at all, it would have to be strengthened, both militarily and politically. All citizens of the Punjab, irrespective of their race or religion, had to be associated with the state and taught the use of the latest instruments of warfare. Ranjit Singh's new army recruited Gurkhas, Biharis, Oriyas, Punjabi Mussulmans, and Pathans along with Sikhs. Sikh cavalrymen were induced to take service in the infantry and equipped with matchlocks. Foundries were set up in Lahore to manufacture cannon and Mussulman gunners trained to man them. European officers were employed to drill the troops. At one time nearly three dozen of them were in Ranjit's service. Outstanding amongst them were French Generals Ventura, Allard and Court. Ventura was in charge of the household cavalry and was for some time governor of Derajat. Allard was governor of Peshawar and Court in command of the Gurkhas. An Italian, Avitabile, commanded a battalion of infantry and rose to be governor of Wazirabad and Peshawar successively. An Irishman, Colonel Gardner, commanded a section of the artillery. Other nationals in his employ were English, American, German, Spanish, Austrian and Greek. Although Ranjit Singh was friendly to all of them, and some – like Allard – he held in great esteem, he did not trust them when it came to dealings with foreign powers. 'German, French or English', he said, 'all these European rascals are alike.' (Not one of these European officers fought on the Sikh side in the Anglo–Sikh wars. Many volunteered for service with the English.) Generals who actually led his armies in the field of battle were all Punjabis: Mohkam Chand, Diwan Chand, Fateh Singh Ahluwalia, Hari Singh Nalwa and Akali Phoola Singh. Along with the strengthening of the army came the association with the Sikh Government of several able counsellors. The most important of these was Fakir Azizuddin, who became Ranjit Singh's chief adviser on diplomatic matters. The Sikh maharaja had enough confidence in his Muslim counsellor to trust him in dealing with his co-religionists from Afghanistan. Raja Dina Nath was put in charge of fiscal affairs.

The Afghans

After the diplomatic defeat at the hands of the English, Ranjit Singh turned his attention to the north. With the disintegration of the Mughal empire, most of northern India had passed from the Indian administrative orbit to the Afghan. Although Abdali was himself unable to govern India, he had nominated governors for all conquered provinces. These men owed allegiance to him and his successors on the throne of Kabul. It was to Abdali's descendant Shah Zaman that Ranjit had looked for confirmation of his seizure of Lahore rather than the Mughal court at Delhi. Hence, in pursuit of his plans to take Kashmir, the North-west Frontier and Multan, Ranjit had to find Afghan pawns to play his game.

In April 1809, when Ranjit signed the treaty with the English, the Afghan throne was occupied by Shah Shuja. The Shah's hold on his kingdom was precarious. On his western frontiers he was threatened by the Persians. In Kabul itself, his brother Shah Mahmud disputed his authority and eventually ousted him. In Kashmir and Peshawar the powerful family of Barakzais paid scant respect to the Kabul throne and actually became king-makers. In Multan and Sindh the local governors had long ceased paying any tribute to the Afghans.

Opportunity to intervene in Afghan affairs presented itself soon after the checkmate from the English. Shah Shuja was ejected from Kabul by his brother and came to Ranjit for assistance. His help was also sought by the two other claimants, Shah Zaman and Shah Mahmud. Meanwhile, the Barakzai family had come on the scene as rival arbiters of the destiny of the Kabul throne. The eldest Barakzai brother, Fateh Khan, backed Shah Mahmud and took Peshawar and Kashmir for him. His other brothers were already in possession of Ghazni and Kabul. Ranjit Singh backed Shah Shuja, recovered Peshawar and defeated the Afghans at Attock.

He brought Shah Shuja to Lahore and took the famous diamond Koh-i-noor from him. Shuja fled from Sikh 'protection' and sought asylum with the English. Fateh Khan Barakzai was assassinated by Shah Mahmud's son Kamram. His brother, Azim Khan Barakzai, left Kashmir to avenge his murder. In Azim's absence Ranjit Singh took Kashmir. Azim Khan returned at the head of a vast horde of Afghan tribesmen in a holy war against the Sikhs. Ranjit defeated them. Peshawar and the North-west Frontier up to the Khyber pass finally passed into Sikh hands.

Ranjit Singh's troops then moved southwards along the Indus, subduing Muslim tribes, the Gakkhars, Awans and Tiwanas. Multan, which had previously fought off or bribed the invaders, fell in 1818.

Although Afghan possessions in India had all been recovered by Ranjit Singh, Afghan troubles were not quite over. Two more attempts to oust the Sikh hold on the frontier were made in the name of religion. One was led by a Wahabi fanatic, Syed Ahmed. He roused the frontier tribesmen against the Sikhs, took the district of Hazara and captured Peshawar. For three years the Wahabis kept Sikh armies at bay until they were scattered and their leader slain by Hari Singh Nalwa in 1831. In 1835 the Barakzais, this time under Dost Mohammed, made one more attempt to recover Peshawar. He assembled an army of 40,000 tribesmen, consisting of Turks, Uzbeks, Qazilbashes, Afridis and the Yusufzais. The Muslims of Sindh and Behawalpur also promised their support. But Dost Mohammed's venture went off like a damp squib. After facing the Sikh armies for seven days, he lost heart and retreated without a fight. Two years later, he partly redeemed his lost reputation at Jamrud, where he defeated a small Sikh force and killed their most famous general, Hari Singh Nalwa. But the battle was of little consequence in Sikh-Afghan affairs.

For some time Ranjit Singh toyed with the idea of crossing the Khyber pass and invading Afghanistan. Shah Shuja had again come to Ranjit Singh for assistance in recovering his throne. The relationship between the two had changed so much that Ranjit had the audacity to suggest that Shuja's son should pay tribute at his court and the slaughter of kine be forbidden in all Shah's territories. The Afghan was unable to accede to these demands but acknowledged Ranjit's right to hold the territories he had wrested from the Afghans. Before Ranjit could launch on further ventures, the English once more forestalled him.

Ranjit Singh had not seriously thought of invading Afghanistan. He had used Shah Shuja strictly for his own ends, particularly in his squabbles with the Barakzais. The English were more ambitious. A subservient Afghan monarch would solve two of their major problems. He would create a friendly buffer state between them and the Russians and Persians. He would also define the final limits to the Sikh kingdom. A tripartite treaty was negotiated amongst the English, Shah Shuja and Ranjit Singh. Its ostensible object was to put Shah Shuja on the Afghan throne. One of the clauses provided for the surrender of the Shah's claims on Sindh in lieu of compensation to be fixed by the British. Ranjit Singh was unwilling to sign the treaty but, as in the past, his relations with the British were not really on equal terms. On 25 July 1838, he put his signature to it. Once having done so, he faithfully carried out his word and the British troops were on the march across his dominions into Afghanistan. A year later Ranjit Singh was dead.

Ranjit Singh's Character

In order to estimate the achievements of Ranjit Singh, one has to take into account the state of affairs in the country when he, a lad of seventeen, set out to create a kingdom. Although the Sikhs as a people had extended their power from the Indus to the Ganga, within themselves their quarrels had rendered their confederation extremely vulnerable. On all frontiers, hostile powers sought to add portions of the Punjab to their domains. The Afghans considered the whole province as a part of their territory and continued their periodical invasions to emphasize that fact. The Dogras and Gurkhas in the north, the English and the Mahrattas in the east, had all at different times succeeded in inciting one Sikh faction against another and making serious inroads into their territory. Out of this state of internal chaos, and under a chronic threat of external aggression, Ranjit produced a state, stable within and so powerful without that on all frontiers save one, it sent the tides of invasion rolling back beyond the frontiers of Hindustan. For the first time in the history of India, Indians marched up to the north-western passes of Khyber and dictated the law to people who had for centuries been accustomed to rule over them. They went north beyond the hills and valleys of Kashmir to Ladakh, Baltistan and Tibet. They went south into Sindh, from where the Muslim invaders had first conquered India. This in itself gives Ranjit Singh a unique place in the history of India and as a feat of arms rivals that of his European contemporary Napoleon Bonaparte. But like Bonaparte, Ranjit suffered his reverses at the hands of the English. The former was beaten in battle. The latter avoided it by discreetly accepting a diplomatic demarche. There is little doubt that if Ranjit Singh had accepted the challenge so wilfully flung at him in 1809, when the cis-Sutlej Sikhs were weaned away from his protection, he would have lost and his ambition to create a united Sikh state remained a dream. But later on, when he had built up his armed strength, there was less justification for accepting treaties which threw a cordon around his kingdom and allowed alien armies passage across his domains. On several occasions he thought of going to war against the English – and had indeed

been egged on to do so in turn by the Gurkhas, Mahrattas and the
Jats, but either through temerity ('he is not famous for desperate
enterprises' [Metcalfe]) or through distrust of promises of assistance,
he never did so. He undoubtedly knew that war against English
expansionism was inevitable. It is said that once while studying the
map of India he asked the significance of the red with which the
rest of the country was coloured. When told that it represented
British possessions, he said, '*Ek roz sub lal ho jaiga*' (one day it will
all be red). While he lived, he could have led a united country in
a venture where the chances of success were reasonable. He must
also have known that after him the forces of disintegration would
dissipate the strength of Sikh resistance and make it an easy victim
to aggression. This chance he did not take.

As a person Ranjit Singh had several characteristics which
made him particularly beloved to his people. Although he became
a monarch, he never lost the human touch nor sympathy for the
peasant folk from whom he came. Being illiterate, he learnt from
life rather than from books, and life taught him humility and
kindness in dealings with his fellow men. He dressed in plain white
amid the gaudy pomp of his court. He addressed his subordinates
with courtesy and tolerated rude familiarity from others. He was
humble, even obsequious, in his dealings with men of religion,
irrespective of their faith. The Sikhs he honoured as co-religionists
and colleagues. Others also he respected, and was known to step
down from his throne to wipe the dust off the feet of Muslim
mendicants with his long grey beard. Although stern as a ruler,
he was never known to have indulged in cruelty or revenge.
Throughout his life he never passed a sentence of death.

Although Ranjit Singh was 'not famous for desperate
enterprises', he was never found wanting in personal bravery. On
all battlefields where he led his armies, he was known to have
fought in the forefront, risking his life like a common soldier. He

took liberties with his own life but did not want to jeopardize the existence of the state. He was doggedly single-minded in gaining his objective and used craft, cunning, diplomacy, bullying, haughtiness, humility and compromise, as was necessary for the occasion. A popular anecdote indicates some of the secrets of his success. It is said that one of his courtesans frivolously alluded to his ugliness – he was blind in one eye and pock-marked. ('Without exaggeration the most ugly and unprepossessing man I saw throughout the Punjab' [Baron Hügel].) She asked: 'When God was doling out good looks where were you?' The monarch replied: 'When you were occupied with your looks, I was busy seeking power.'

Chapter 5

THE END OF THE SIKH KINGDOM

The Army

Most of Ranjit Singh's time as a ruler was devoted to fighting, the earlier part in consolidating the Sikh homeland and the latter in extending his frontiers northwards. All this time he was uneasily aware of English intentions and had to build up an army capable of resisting aggression from that quarter. He did so with great thoroughness and efficiency. A powerful mercenary army of nearly 40,000 men was raised, drilled and equipped with the latest weapons of war. The scales of pay in his army were the same as those of the East India Company's forces. But unfortunately an army of that size involved a high cost of maintenance – which, in turn, required an efficient administrative and fiscal system to bring in a regular revenue. Ranjit Singh had neither the time nor apparently the temperament to look into these matters.

In the early years of expansion, he was able to maintain his army from the booty that came with conquest. But after that source was exhausted, the pay of his soldiers fell sadly in arrears. Signs of disaffection were in evidence before his death. In May 1836, the troops in Kashmir mutinied because they had not been paid for over a year. The mutiny was suppressed after the shooting of twenty-two men. Other incidents involving bloodshed took place in regiments led by Jamadar Khushal Singh and General Ventura. In the case of Ventura's troops, an entire battalion of Gurkhas abandoned their posts in Peshawar and marched back to Lahore to demand their wages.

After the death of Ranjit Singh matters deteriorated very rapidly. Civil administration, which had never been a strong point of the Sikh Government, went to pieces. Ranjit Singh had not bothered to train a body of civil servants or even initiated any of his men in the affairs of state. He had ruled personally with the assistance of a few trusted friends. While he had both the personality and the weight of established authority behind him, his successors, whose rights to the throne were always being questioned, had neither. They had to win support of the army to enable them to oust their rivals. They could only do this by promises of extra remuneration. In the absence of revenue, these promises were seldom fulfilled – and the army went out of hand altogether.

As the army assumed the role of king-maker, its constitution also underwent a change. Matters of salary became one of direct and periodical negotiation between the soldiers and the incumbent of the throne. The role of the officer became merely that of drilling and leading the troops in action. He had no power to punish or reward, or consequently to demand discipline. The soldiers themselves elected representatives (*panch*s), who negotiated with parties for their pay and decided whether or not to undertake a particular expedition.

This government by the *panch*s grew because the soldiers who were villagers were accustomed to having rural affairs handled by elected panchayats. The system was not suited to army administration. It cut at the roots of the two most important factors in the efficiency of an army, viz., unquestioned loyalty to the throne and obedience to the officer.

Rival Factions

Ranjit Singh had a paralytic stroke some days before he died. This laid him prostrate and speechless. He was, therefore, unable to leave instructions regarding his succession and the constitution of the court. There were doubts regarding the legitimacy of some of his sons. The eldest, Kharak Singh, was, in addition, an opium addict. The uncertainty of succession produced several factions, of which two, the Dogras and the Sandhawalias, played important roles in the years that followed. They were the brains behind the intrigues, the army was the power, and the claimants to the throne were the pawns.

The Dogra family had risen from the status of domestic servants of Ranjit Singh to be rulers of the province of Jammu. There were three brothers, Dhian Singh, Gulab Singh and Suchet Singh, and a son of Dhian Singh, Hira Singh. Frequently the family itself was divided in its loyalties to the claimants to the throne. Of the four members mentioned, three, i.e., Dhian Singh, his son Hira Singh, and Suchet Singh, came to a violent end in pursuit of their designs. Gulab Singh was able to steer clear and ultimately became the ruler of Jammu and Kashmir.

The Sandhawalias were relatives of Ranjit Singh. Kharak Singh's wife, Chand Kaur, was a member of that family. Their interest in the affairs of the royal household was also proprietary. After the death of Kharak Singh and his son Naonihal Singh, they claimed the succession for Chand Kaur – and thereafter for themselves. The chief members of the Sandhawalia family at the time were

Attar Singh and Lehna Singh and their nephew Ajit Singh. All three came to a violent end.

Ranjit's Successors

Kharak Singh, Naonihal Singh

After the death of Ranjit Singh, Prince Kharak Singh ascended the throne with a favourite, Cheyt Singh, as adviser. Two months later, he was imprisoned by his own son, Naonihal Singh, and Cheyt Singh was murdered. Naonihal was acknowledged king with Dhian Singh Dogra as his chief minister. The young prince showed promise of making a good and strong ruler. He restored law and order in the kingdom and diverted his turbulent army to further fields of conquest. General Ventura led his troops to Mandi and Suket. Gulab Singh went further north and took Ladakh and parts of Baltistan. But Naonihal was not destined to live long. Two years after he became king, he was murdered on his way back from the funeral of his father.

Sher Singh

After the death of Naonihal, the Dogras and the Sandhawalias openly espoused the cause of rival claimants. Dhian Singh Dogra supported Prince Sher Singh. The Sandhawalias supported Naonihal Singh's widowed mother, Chand Kaur, whom they proclaimed to be the Queen Mother. Within two months Chand Kaur was ousted by Sher Singh, and later murdered. A year and a half later, Sher Singh, his son Pratap Singh, and the chief minister, Dhian Singh Dogra, were murdered by the Sandhawalias. Dhian

Singh Dogra's murder was avenged by his son Hira Singh, who succeeded in killing Lehna Singh and Ajit Singh Sandhawalia.

Dalip Singh

In September 1842, the last Sikh ruler ascended the Lahore throne. This was the nine-year-old prince Dalip Singh. His chief minister was Hira Singh Dogra. The rival factions now were Hira Singh on one side, Dalip's mother, Jindan, and her brother, with the remaining Sandhawalia, Sardar Attar Singh, on the other. For some time Hira Singh was able to hold his own. Attar Singh was killed in an attempt to remove him. But Hira Singh lasted only two years and was himself murdered and replaced by Jindan's brother Jawahar Singh. A few months later Jawahar Singh was murdered by his own soldiers, leaving Dalip Singh as king with his mother Jindan as regent.

All this time that the assassin's dagger determined the destinies of the Sikh throne, the Khalsa army continued to grow. Five years after Ranjit Singh's death it had more than trebled itself in numbers. It had no unified command and even within the units, it was the elected *panch*s who were usually ordinary soldiers, who mattered and not the officers. Most of the European officers had fled the Sikh kingdom. Some had gone over to the English.

British Preparations

The state of affairs at Lahore was watched with great interest by the British Government. Plans to annex the Punjab would have probably been put into action had the venture in Afghanistan gone well. But the intervention in Afghanistan ended in a fiasco. The English had succeeded in putting on the throne their nominee

Shah Shuja – but within two years Shuja was ousted and the British troops massacred. Their reputation suffered grievously. The temptation to re-establish it at the expense of the Sikhs was great. In 1841, Mr Clerk, the agent at Ludhiana, had ordered the troops at Sirhind and Ambala to proceed to the Sikh frontier and asked the protected states for assistance. His plan of intervening in Sikh affairs was considered premature by his government and cancelled. This was not the only evidence of British intentions. In 1841, Sir William Macnaughton, who was the envoy of the British Government to Shah Shuja, wrote to Lord Auckland, the governor-general, urging him 'to crush the Singhs, macadamize the Punjab and annex Peshawar'. He advocated the handing over of Peshawar to Shah Shuja. Captain Barnes, an envoy who was sent to enquire into conditions in the Punjab, disagreed with him and wanted the city given to Dost Mohammed. But both agreed that the Sikhs were to be dispossessed of their country, if necessary by force, in any case without justification. Lord Ellenborough, who succeeded Lord Auckland, wrote in somewhat the same tone to the Duke of Wellington. In a letter dated 20 October 1843, he said: 'The time cannot be far distant when the Punjab will fall into our management ... I do not look to this state of things as likely to occur next year, but as being ultimately inevitable, if we do not bring on union against ourselves and indisposition to our rule by some precipitate interference. I should tell you, however, that there is, as there long has been, a great disposition, even in quarters not military, to disturb the game.' In another letter also addressed to the duke, written in February 1844, Lord Ellenborough wrote: 'I earnestly hope that we may not be obliged to cross the Sutlej in December next. We shall not be ready so soon ... I am quietly doing what I can to strengthen and equip the army.'

In 1843 Major Broadfoot was appointed agent at the Lahore court. The Sikhs had unpleasant memories of Broadfoot's behaviour in the initial stages of the Afghan campaign. He had, on more than one occasion, without provocation turned his troops against the escort provided by the Lahore authorities for his journey across the Punjab. No actual fighting had taken place, but that was due to General Ventura's tact in handling the situation. This appointment caused uneasiness in the court circles. Coupled with this was the British Government's announcement that Sikh possessions to the south of the Sutlej would be taken by escheat after the death of Dalip Singh. Some estates in Ferozepur, which should on the death of the holders have become the property of the Lahore ruler, were actually taken over.

The chief cause of precipitating hostilities was the military measures taken by the British on their side. It should be borne in mind that at no time did the English have any fears of aggression on the part of the Sikhs, and they held the Sikh army in great contempt. In official despatches they were described as 'rabble' and rated lower than the Afghan and even the hill men from Jammu. In view of this opinion, it is hardly likely that these measures could in any sense have been for the security of their possessions.

Up to 1838, the British army in the Punjab consisted of one regiment in the hills as security against Gurkha inroads and two at Ludhiana. The total armed force consisted of 2,500 men with six guns. Immediately after the death of Ranjit Singh this was increased to 8,000. Ferozepur, which being the subject of dispute had hitherto remained unfortified, was made into a cantonment. In Lord Ellenborough's time the strength of the army was further raised to 14,000 men, and three more towns – Ambala, Kasauli and Simla – were garrisoned. Finally, Lord Hardinge increased the army in the Punjab to 32,000 with sixty-eight guns and stationed a reserve force of 10,000 at Meerut. Early in 1845, seventy 30-ton boats built in Bombay were transported to the Punjab. They arrived in Ferozepur in the autumn. The commander then proceeded to train his men in bridge building on the Sutlej under the eyes of the Sikh forces on the other side.

With all these preparations came the inevitable border incidents. Up to then, military police of either side had crossed the border in pursuit of criminals without any complications arising. In the autumn of 1845, Sikh cavalry in pursuit of marauders were fired on near Ferozepur and later near Multan. In both cases, they retreated somewhat bewildered at the treatment, but did not dare to retaliate.

In July 1845, Lord Ellenborough was replaced by Lord Hardinge, a soldier of repute. A few months later he was on his way to the Punjab to consult with the commander-in-chief, Lord Gough. They met in December at Ambala to plan their campaign. The location of the pontoon bridge at Ferozepur left no doubt as to where the first blow would be struck. On 11 December, Sikh troops began to ford the Sutlej a few miles above Ferozepur. They decided that if the English wanted war they should have it on their own territory.

The time chosen for the commencement of hostilities was auspicious for the English. The Sikh court was in a state of panic. A boy of nine sat on the throne, and his mother, the Queen Regent, herself more concerned with her own and her son's personal welfare than the future of the state, was surrounded by traitors. The army clamoured for war against insult and imminent aggression and had no commander to lead it. Both the chief minister, Lal Singh, and the commander-in-chief, Tej Singh, were in correspondence with the English before the war started. Soon after the Sikh forces had crossed the Sutlej, Lal Singh wrote to Captain Nicholson 'to say that he would show his good wishes by keeping back his force for two days from joining the infantry or regulars ... if I would consider him and Rani Jindan our friends'. So the Anglo-Sikh wars started with traitors in command of the Khalsa army.

The First Anglo-Sikh War

Sikh troops forded the Sutlej at two points. The first crossing was made near Ferozepur. Here two engagements were fought. The first was at Mukdi (18 December 1845), where the British forces were badly mauled and left in a state of utter confusion. But Lal Singh was true to his word and kept his army back from delivering the coup de grace. The British were able to reorganize and with further reinforcements defeated the Sikhs at Ferozepur (21 December 1845). The next crossing was made up the river by Tej Singh's army and an engagement fought at Aliwal on 28 January 1846. On 10 February, the Sutlej campaign ended with a complete defeat of the Sikh army at Sabraon. The British forces marched on to the Sikh capital and on 8 March was signed the Treaty of Lahore. The signatories on behalf of the Sikh Durbar were Lal Singh and Tej Singh.

The Treaty of Lahore

The English were not yet ready to annex the whole of the Punjab. There were still about 30,000 Sikh soldiers under arms scattered in the north-western parts of the province, and a precipitate annexation might have brought about a united front amongst the rival Sikh factions, or at least a protracted guerilla warfare. The portion conquered, i.e., the Jullundur Doab, was annexed. The Treaty of Lahore constituted what was deemed a necessary prelude to the annexation of the remaining part of the Sikh kingdom. Henry Lawrence was appointed agent at Lahore with a force of English infantry 'for the purpose of protecting the person of the Maharaja'. The powers of the agent, although undefined, were later referred to by Lord Hardinge as 'on the same footing as the Lieutenant Governor' (letter to Currie dated 10 December 1846).

Besides being agent, Lawrence was made president of a council of eight Sardars to look after Prince Dalip Singh and his court. He also brought with him a large number of officers who were scattered over various parts of the province. Notable amongst them were Nicholson, Edwards, Lumsden, McGregor, Abbot and Taylor. A war indemnity of Rs 1.5 crore was imposed, and since only one-third of that sum could be recovered, Kashmir and Hazara were taken in lieu. Kashmir was then handed over to Gulab Singh Dogra ('the worst native I came in contact with' [H. Edwards], 'the mildest mannered man that ever scuttled a ship or cut a throat' [Byrons Lambro]), with orders to the Sikh durbar to put him in possession. Thus were the Hindu and Muslim areas segregated from their Sikh alliance. This was Hardinge's plan, as he wrote in a despatch early in February 1846:'I shall demand 1½ crore in money as compensation; and if I can make Gulab Singh and the hill tribes independent, including Kashmir, I shall have weakened this warlike republic.' Besides these clauses, others restricted the strength of the Sikh army and forbade the employment of foreigners without the consent of the British Government. An amusing postscript to the treaty was the undertaking on the part of the British Government not to interfere in the internal affairs of the Lahore state.

Lord Hardinge was quite clear in his mind that the treaty was just to give him breathing space. In a letter to Henry Lawrence dated 23 October 1847, he wrote: 'In all our measures taken during the minority, we must bear in mind that by the treaty of Lahore, March 1846, the Punjab never was intended to be an independent state ... In fact the native prince is in fetters, and under our protection, and must do our bidding.'

British interpretation of the clause about noninterference in internal affairs was made within one month of the treaty over an affair referred to as the 'cow row'. One day in April 1846, an English sentry was obstructed in his way by a herd of cows. He removed the obstruction by slashing some of the animals with his sword. Hindus and Sikhs, who venerated the cow, were perturbed and the shops in the city were closed in protest. The British agent with a party of horsemen went into the town to explain the incident, but were pelted with stones from roofs of adjoining houses. The agent was offended and ordered the durbar to make amends by handing over the instigators of the outrage. Next day, the young maharaja was taken by Lal Singh to make his apologies. But that was not enough. The houses from which the offensive missiles had been hurled were razed to the ground. One man was executed and two jailed. The European sentry was 'warned to be more careful how he used his sword in future'.

This and other incidents brought home to Rani Jindan and the traitor Lal Singh that the English meant to annex the Punjab – not to look after their interests or those of the young maharaja. Their attitude began to change. When the British ordered the Sikhs to hand over Kashmir to Gulab Singh, Lal Singh sent secret letters to the durbar's Muslim governor to resist. These letters were handed over to the agent. Lal Singh was tried, found guilty and exiled. He went unwept and unhonoured.

Tej Singh continued his anti-durbar activities and was honoured by the British. In August 1847, the young maharaja was ordered to invest him and some other Sardars with titles. When it came to Tej Singh's turn, the maharaja refused. The agent rightly suspected Rani Jindan to be behind this incident and decided to banish her from the Punjab. Attempts to foist on her a false accusation of conspiracy to murder the agent did not succeed. But she was removed to Sheikhupura and her allowance arbitrarily reduced. Henry Lawrence then read a proclamation announcing this decision: 'The Governor-General of India feels the interest of a father in the education and guardianship of the young prince.' It had 'become absolutely necessary to separate the Maharaja from the Maharani his mother'. And finally: 'Let us therefore rejoice throughout the kingdom that the Right Honourable the Governor-General of India had so much at heart the peace and security of this country, the firm establishment of the state, and the honour of the Maharaja.'

In September 1847, the exiled maharani wrote in exasperation to the officiating resident: 'Do you make out my allowance to be Rs 4,000 p.m.? I will take what was fixed by treaty ... Either do away with the treaty or observe it.' In an earlier letter she complained: 'Surely royalty was never treated before in the way you are treating us! Instead of being secretly king of the country, why don't you declare yourself so? You talk about friendship and then put us in prison! ... You establish traitors at Lahore, and then at their bidding you are going to kill the whole of the Punjab.'

The Second Anglo-Sikh War

Having had more than two years in which to consolidate their gains, the British were now ready for the final act. Lord Dalhousie replaced Lord Hardinge. He was, in his own words, 'of strong and deliberate opinion that the British Government is bound not to put aside or neglect such rightful opportunities of acquiring territory as may from time to time present themselves' and again, in August 1848, 'the right to annex the Punjab is beyond cavil'. In October of the same year, he wrote: 'The task before me is the utter destruction and prostration of the Sikh power, the subversion of its dynasty, and the subjection of its people. This must be done promptly, fully and finally.'

This plan was put in action soon after Dalhousie's arrival. The excuse was provided by a minor insurrection in Multan, where two English officers had been murdered by Sikh soldiers attached to the Hindu Governor Mulraj. Mulraj was in no way connected with the murder (one of the dying men himself wrote a note to that effect). But Mulraj was compelled by his soldiers to become the leader of the revolt. The rebellion would have fizzled out and the terrified Mulraj easily made to surrender, as indeed he was within a few days of the insurrection, but that was not the plan. It was decided to invest the affair with the status of a Sikh rising and so take the Punjab 'fully and finally'. And a national rising in due course it did become. Sher Singh, who was ordered by the British to quell Mulraj's rebellion in the name of the Sikh Durbar, found that his soldiers were not willing to fight their fellow countrymen. Their minds had been inflamed by the exile of Rani Jindan, the Queen Mother, to Benares. Sher Singh went over to Mulraj. He issued a proclamation which read: 'It is well known to all the inhabitants of the Punjab ... with what oppression, tyranny and undue violence the English have treated the widow of the great Maharaja Ranjit Singh, and what cruelty they have shown towards the people of the country.' It asked the Sikhs to rise against the foreign intruders.

In the north, Sher Singh's father, Chattar Singh, was placed in a similar predicament by Captain James Abbot, who was to aid and advise the Sardar. Being suspicious of the Sardar's motives (Chattar Singh's daughter was engaged to marry the young maharaja), he raised and armed the Mohammedan peasantry and 'called upon them, by the memory of their murdered parents, friends and relatives, to rise and aid me in destroying the Sikh forces in detail'. Up till then Chattar Singh had made no move which could justify Abbot's action. The resident himself censured the English captain and exonerated the Sardar. In a note he said: 'No overt act of rebellion was committed by them till the initiative was taken by you.' Nevertheless, the step had been taken and the government decided to utilize it to their best advantage. In a tone of jubilation, Dalhousie wrote: 'The rebellion of Raja Sher Singh followed by his army, the rebellion of Sardar Chattar Singh with the Durbar army under his command, the state of the troops and of the Sikh population everywhere, have brought matters to that crisis I have for months been looking for; and we are now, not on the eve of, but in the midst of, war with the Sikh nation and the kingdom of the Punjab.'

Most of this complicated conspiracy hatched in the minds of the English rulers and their agents was lost on the simple English soldiers who were commanded to carry out their bidding. General Gough, who led the English armies, did not know till after leaving Lahore for the front that 'war was to be against and not in support of the Durbar. I do not know', he said, 'whether we are at peace or war, or who it is we are fighting for.'

So the second Sikh war came to be fought. In October and November 1848 there were several engagements in which the Sikh armies were beaten, ending with the seizure and destruction of Multan in January 1849 and a total defeat at Chillianwala a few weeks later. On 10 March 1849, the Sikh Generals Chattar Singh and Sher Singh presented their swords in token of submission. Four days later, 18,000 Sikh soldiers laid down arms at a ceremonial parade. On the morning of 29 March the sun finally set on Ranjit Singh's short-lived empire. His ministers collected at a durbar at Lahore and read a proclamation from Dalhousie which said: 'The kingdom of the Punjab is at an end. All the territories of Maharaja Dalip Singh are now and henceforth a portion of the British Empire.'

Dina Nath, the Hindu minister, argued while the proclamation was being read: 'If France after the defeat and imprisonment of Bonaparte had been restored to its legitimate ruler, then it would be no extraordinary act of British clemency if the Punjab should be restored to the Maharaja.'

Sickle to the Harvest

The first few months after the annexation were spent in 'macadamizing the Singhs'. Dalip Singh was taken away to Fatehgarh in the United Provinces and put under the care of Sir John Login of the Bengal Army. After two years of Login's tutelage the young maharaja announced his intention of renouncing his faith and turning Christian. He was duly baptized, granted a pension, sent to England, and given an estate in Suffolk. The *Lahore Chronicle* of 8 June 1850 produced a sketch of the estate with the gleeful caption: 'The extent of His Highness's dominions is now measured by square yards.' In another issue dated 26 February, the paper quoted the *Delhi Gazette* for an 'announcement of a momentous event'. It said: 'Dalip Singh, ex-sovereign of the Punjab, has eaten beef steak! The King of the Sikhs has ceased to be a Sikh ... he has sold his claim to the allegiance of his people by a juicy mouthful.'

In England Dalip Singh married an Egyptian woman who bore him several children. None of them had any issue. He himself came to India twice, once to fetch his mother, once again to take her body back for cremation. In 1886 he made an attempt to return home to settle, but was not allowed to proceed beyond Aden. He had been reconverted to his own religion. In 1893 he died in Paris. Ranjit Singh's male line became extinct in 1926 with the death of Dalip Singh's second son.

The properties of the Lahore Durbar were put up for auction at Lahore in February 1851 by a firm of English auctioneers and sold. The Koh-i-Noor diamond was taken to England and became a part of the British Crown.

The leaders of the Sikh revolt were brought to trial. Mulraj was at first sentenced to death. But later he, along with Chattar Singh and Sher Singh and some other Sardars, was exiled. The properties of all who were connected with the Sikh resistance were confiscated. The entire province was disarmed. Then Lord Dalhousie himself came on a victorious tour of the new domains. On 22 November 1849 he visited the Golden Temple at Amritsar and in full view of thousands of Sikhs walked through the sacred precincts with his shoes on. The temple had been specially lit in his honour.

This process of humiliating vanquished foes went on for some time. On 4 September 1850 the *Lahore Chronicle* published a letter signed by 'an impartial observer' protesting that 'some officers residing near the Residency are in the habit of shooting pellets at natives, respectable or low, and setting dogs at them'.

The Punjab Board

When the second Sikh war ended affairs of the Punjab were under the control of the three Lawrence brothers. George was stationed at Peshawar, Henry was resident at Lahore and John was in charge of the eastern districts. Military affairs were in the hands of Sir Charles Napier, who together with his predecessor, Lord Gough, had won the second Sikh war. Above these officials was the young governor-general, Lord Dalhousie, and his trusted adviser, Sir John Currie. From the very outset there was trouble amongst them.

Henry Lawrence had been the longest in India and had established a mild form of personal monarchy in the Punjab. He was against annexing the Punjab and confiscating the *jagirs* and estates of the Sikh Sardars, most of whom were known to him. His brother John disagreed with him on both points. Dalhousie would not turn from his duty 'by a feeling of misplaced and mis-timed compassion for the fate of a child', and John echoed his sentiment by repeating: Annex it now.' Dalhousie had further cause to dislike Henry's assumed lordship over the Punjab and had constantly to keep him reminded of who was the governor-general, and finally to dismiss him. Sir Charles Napier disagreed with all of them.

He described Henry as 'a good fellow' though he 'doubted his capacity'. John he thought was clever, 'but a man may have good sense and yet not be fit to rule a large country'. He also disliked Dalhousie's overbearing attitude. The controversy went beyond notes on files. Napier wrote a treatise on 'Indian misgovernment'. Henry replied through an article in the *Calcutta Review.*

Dalhousie first constituted a board to govern the Punjab. It consisted of Henry Lawrence as president and in charge of matters of defence and settlement with the Sikh Sardars; his brother, John Lawrence, in charge of revenue matters; and C.G. Mansel to organize the judicial system. It was constituted on the principle of divided labour and common responsibility. Individually, the members did notable work. Law and order were restored; a police force was raised; civil and criminal courts were established; land revenue was put on a regular basis; and roads and canals begun. But disputes between the brothers, between Henry and Lord Dalhousie, and between Sir Charles Napier and all the others, prevented its functioning as a team. After three years of trial Lord Dalhousie abolished it and put John Lawrence solely in charge as chief commissioner of the Punjab. Henry was sent to a post elsewhere. Then Dalhousie and John Lawrence got working on moulding the province to their heart's desire.

Dalhousie's Achievements

The success of Dalhousie's Punjab policy can be gauged from the fact that within eight years of his unwarranted aggression against the Sikh state, he was so able to convert the masses that not only did they refuse to grasp the opportunity of regaining their independence presented by the Mutiny in 1857, but also they actually went to the assistance of the British in quelling it. There were many reasons for this.

In the first place, after the death of Ranjit Singh, no Sikh had been able to control the government and particularly the Khalsa army. The state of misrule that existed from 1839 to 1849 made the idea of an independent Sikh state somewhat of a dream, if not a nightmare.

Secondly, Dalhousie was astute enough to direct his punishment only to the landed aristocracy (which was practically abolished), and thus indirectly rewarded the peasant proprietors, who formed the backbone of the Sikh nation. He confiscated the *jagirs*. 'The people', he wrote, 'would gain by the extinction of *jagirs*, which were given on condition of military or religious service.' Only the large holdings that were on the southern side of the Sutlej were recognized and perpetuated. These belonged to Sikhs who were under British protection even during the reign of Ranjit Singh and at no time identified themselves with the Sikh state.

Thirdly, English commanders had been much impressed by the discipline and bravery of the Sikh troops and Dalhousie accepted their suggestion of incorporating them into the British Army. After the first Sikh war, orders were given for the formation of two Sikh battalions, one at Ferozepur and the other at Ludhiana. After the annexation and disbandment of the Sikh army, three armed services were formed in the Punjab and in each the Sikhs were recruited. These were the Punjab Irregular Frontier Force, the Corps of Guides and the Military Police. At their inception, a few Sikhs were taken in these units, which consisted mainly of Pathans, Punjabi Mussulmans and Gurkhas. After the Mutiny, the Sikh percentage in the British Indian Army was raised beyond all proportion to their numbers. This had another effect of far-reaching consequence to the Sikh community. The army insisted on the Sikh recruits being Kesadhari (the Khalsa with unshorn locks). The first announcement of this decision was published in the *Lahore Chronicle* as early as 19 March 1851. The 'Enlistment of

Sikhs' notice stated that 'no Sikh is to be required to cut either his hair or his beard, and all who enter the service with *kes* are to be required to continue to wear the hair after that fashion'. This was confirmed by an order of the commander-in-chief which read: 'Every countenance and encouragement is to be given to their comparative freedom from the bigoted prejudices of caste, every means adopted to preserve intact the distinctive characteristics of their race, their peculiar conventions and social customs.' It not only made the British Army popular with orthodox elements, it preserved the Sikh identity as distinct from the Hindu – a differentiation which was fast beginning to disappear.

Finally, Dalhousie's work in the opening of old and building of new canals (Bari-Doab), of roads (chiefly the Grand Trunk Road running from Delhi to Peshawar), in introducing railways and postal and telegraphic communication, brought to the whole of India, particularly to the Punjab, an era of economic prosperity which stood out in marked contrast to the turmoil that had preceded it. In the first three years of British rule, the Punjab produced a surplus budget of over Rs 400,000 a year.

It is then a matter of little surprise that the Punjab, including the Sikhs, was not willing to join the mutineers in 1857. When victory seemed assured to the English, all Punjabis, Muslims, Hindus and Sikhs alike, protested their loyalty to the British Crown. For the Sikhs there was yet another reason for backing the English. They did not look upon the Mutiny as a war of independence. It was, as a matter of fact, largely an affair of the Bihari Hindu and the Mussulman with a sprinkling of Mahrattas. There was little identity of purpose between the 'revolutionaries'. The Mahrattas wanted to restore Mahratta rule. The Muslims had already put a descendant of the Mughals on the throne in Delhi. The Sikhs rightly suspected it to be an attempt to re-establish Mughal rule in India, of which they had bitter memories.

PART II

INTRODUCTION

With the annexation of the Punjab, the history of the Sikhs was merged with that of the other communities. There were, however, religious, reformist, political and revolutionary movements that were largely or wholly Sikh in character and personnel. I have taken these out of the context of historical sequence of events in the country for the purposes of this section. In doing so, I have taken the liberty of assuming knowledge of contemporary affairs, both national and international. Thus, although I may make no specific reference to the rise of nationalism, the introduction of democratic institutions, the growth of separatist tendencies in certain communities, the world wars and the rise of international communism, all that is said in these chapters is to be read with these developments in the background.

Chapter 6 deals with two movements of religious revival. Chapter 7 is concerned with the Singh Sabha, a movement of social reform with stress on education and literature. Chapter 8 deals with the Akali agitation, which in the beginning was a movement started with the sole object of taking over Sikh shrines and bringing them under communal control, but which got involved in political disputes with the government and became one – the most successful one – of the nation-wide movements of passive resistance organized by the Indian National Congress and the Muslim Khilafatists. Chapter 9 deals with the history of the Sikh émigré revolutionary groups in the United States and Canada, their return home, and the formation of Marxist parties in the Punjab. Subsequent chapters give accounts of Sikh politics between the two world wars, leading up to the partition of the province and the independence of India.

Chapter 6

MOVEMENTS OF RELIGIOUS REFORMATION

Nirankaris

The Nirankari was a Sikh puritan movement started with the object of stemming the tide into Hinduism. Tendencies to revert to the Hindu fold had become stronger as the Sikhs attained temporal power. By the time of Ranjit Singh, Hinduism had practically come back into its own. Spartan Sikh traditions had given way to tawdry Brahminical ritual. Distinctions of caste were observed. Idols were worshipped alongside the Sikh scripture. Widows were incarcerated if not burnt with their dead husbands. When Ranjit Singh died several of his wives were cremated with him as was customary amongst aristocratic Hindu families – but expressly forbidden by the Sikh Gurus. Sikhs had simply become Hindus who grew their hair long and did not cut their beards.

The originator of the Nirankari movement was Dyal Das (1783–1855), the son of a bullion exchange merchant of Peshawar. His interest in the Sikh faith came from his mother, whose father had seen service with the last Guru, Gobind Singh. It is interesting to note that, although Dyal Das spent his entire life in preaching against Hindu encroachments on the Sikh way of life, he himself was never baptized in the traditional way and did not grow his hair long. Apparently, what he intended to revive was the Sikhism of the earlier Gurus and not that of Guru Gobind Singh.

The main item in Dyal Das's preaching was a protest against the worship of idols by Sikhs – even when it took the form of setting up images of their own Gurus. Nanak, he said, was known as Nanak Nirankari – Nanak the formless. All idol worship or worship of any thing or person, which was corporeal, was sacreligious. The watchwords he coined were:

Dhun dhun nirunkar,
Jo deh dhari sub khwar.

Glory to the Formless One.
Gods corporeal thou must shun.

Along with the enjoinder against idol worship, he urged his followers to give up Hindu ritual at wedding ceremonies, to stop going on pilgrimages and offering food to dead ancestors. He asked the Sikhs to restrict the amount of dowries given to daughters and to provide for widowed women's remarriage.

There was nothing very startling in the preaching of Dyal Das, and, at the initial stages of his career, he received a large appreciative audience. At Rawalpindi, where he set himself up as a greengrocer, he built a temple of his own to propagate his creed. It is said that Ranjit Singh himself came to pay him homage and gave a grant for the upkeep of another temple which was built by one of Dyal Das's disciples.

Opposition to Dyal Das's movement came from both the Hindus and the Sikhs. The Hindus naturally resented his preaching against their form of worship. The Sikhs opposed him mainly because, despite his own humble way of living and pursuit of ideals, his followers had elevated him into another guru – precisely what Dyal Das himself had been declaiming against. He was ostracized by the orthodox Sikhs of Rawalpindi and had to move outside the town. On the banks of the Layee, a small stream running beside the town, he built his own place of worship. When he died in 1855, the local Sikhs refused to allow his cremation in the communal grounds and his body was consigned to the waters of the stream.

Dyal Das was followed by two sons. The first, Bhai Ohara or Darbara Singh (1855–1870) was successful in persuading the Sikhs in northern India to adopt ceremonial conforming to the Scriptural injunctions. He set up forty centres for the propagation of his father's teachings which he had published in 1857 in the *Hukum Nania*, the 'Book of Ordinances'. The Nirankaris claim with some justification that Darbara Singh was responsible for popularizing most of the prevailing ceremonies connected with birth, marriage and death. Prior to 1855 almost all ceremonies in Sikh houses were conducted according to Hindu rites.

Darbara Singh, along with his brother and successor Rattan Chand (1870–1908), built a temple where their father had died. The place was named Dyal Sar in memory of the founder. Dyal Das's sandals were placed on a pedestal and became an object of reverence, and the temple became a place of pilgrimage for Nirankaris. Rattan Chand also organized Nirankari communities in other towns.

Rattan Chand was followed by his son Gurdit Singh, who died in 1947 and was succeeded by his son, Hara Singh.

It is difficult to estimate the number of the Nirankari subsect. According to Major Bingley, the author of the *Handbook for*

Sikhs, in 1891 there were 46,610. Since there was no clear line demarcating a Nirankari Sikh from another and intermarriage was common, Bingley's figures must have been purely conjectural.

Before 1947 Nirankari missionary activity had been largely confined to the Sikh communities living in the North-west Frontier Province, Rawalpindi District and Kashmir. After the partition of the Punjab, the Nirankaris had to abandon their headquarters at Dyal Sar in Rawalpindi and their scene of activities moved to East Punjab.

The orthodox Sikhs disowned the Nirankari sect. Nirankaris recognized their own gurus as successors to the ten accepted by the Sikhs. Two of these, Dyal Das and Rattan Chand, were not even baptized into the Khalsa fraternity. Besides that, the Nirankaris disapproved of militant Sikhism, whose worship involved an invocation to arms in every prayer and whose words of greeting to each other were 'Victory to the Guru'. The Nirankaris greeted each other with the simple 'Dhun Nirankar' – 'Glory to the Formless One'.

Namdharis or Kookas

The Kooka or Namdhari movement was, like the Nirankari, a movement of religious revival. It started in the last few years of Sikh rule. The initiator, Bhagat Jawahar Mal, also known as Sain Sahib (*d.* 1862), and his disciple Baba Balak Singh, had a considerable reputation as men of learning and piety and attracted many followers to their centre at Hazro (North-west Frontier Province) known as the Jagiasi Abhiasi Ashram.

Bhagat Jawahar Mal and Balak Singh had for their mission two objects: firstly, that of purging the Sikhs of some obnoxious Hindu practices which had gained currency despite the injunction of the Gurus against them, e.g., caste distinctions and taboos, incarceration of widows, and the worship of idols, tombs and ascetics; and secondly, that of reforming the Sikh nobility. The Sikh aristocracy, which had risen from the ranks of common peasants, had acquired enormous wealth and power. Many of these newly rich had taken to a dissolute life of drink and debauchery. Bhagat Jawahar Mal aimed at bringing them back to the path of righteousness. The objects of the Namdhari movement were very similar to those of the Nirankari, but whereas the Nirankaris restricted their activities to religious affairs, the Namdharis got involved in political matters.

After the annexation of the Punjab the movement underwent a change. To the zeal for religious and social reformation was added a feeling of resentment against the new rulers and an ambition to restore Sikh sovereignty. The leadership of the Namdharis fell into the hands of a remarkable man who shared these feelings and was willing to risk giving them a trial. This was Ram Singh of village Bhayani in District Ludhiana.

Ram Singh (1815–1885) was the son of a carpenter. In his early youth he joined Prince Naonihal Singh's army as a soldier and served in it for eight years. Army manoeuvres took him north and he came into contact with Balak Singh. After the first Sikh war he resigned his commission and retired to his village in Bhayani, where he set himself up as a manufacturer of coats of mail. To this he added preaching and propagating the teachings of Bhagat Jawahar Mal and Balak Singh.

Within a few years Ram Singh acquired a large following. On the Hindu new year's day in 1857 he, following the precedent of Guru Gobind Singh, baptized five of his disciples as members of the new community, which he named the Namdharis. (They also came to be known as Kookas because of the cries (kooks) they emitted in a state of religious frenzy.) In addition to the vows prescribed by Guru Gobind, Ram Singh enjoined his Sikhs to observe other rules, which he divided into personal, social, religious and political. They were:

(a) Personal:	Not to eat meat or drink alcohol.
	Not to covet another's property or women.
	Not to lie.
	Not to accept interest on loans.
(b) Social:	Not to kill female children or sell them.
	Not to allow marriages of infants under the age of 16 or arrange marriages by exchange.
	Not to give expensive gifts on weddings. Not to castrate domestic animals.
(c) Religious:	To rise at dawn, bathe and pray with rosaries made with wool.
	To wear their turbans straight (unlike those of other Sikhs, the two sides of whose turbans meet at an angle on the forehead).
	To protect cows and other animals from slaughter.
(d) Political:	Not to accept service with the government.
	Not to send children to government schools.
	Not to use courts of law but settle disputes in panchayats.
	Not to use foreign goods.
	Not to use the government postal service.

[All these vows were incorporated in an epistle (*Rahatnama*) which Ram Singh issued to his followers in 1863.]

Within a couple of years the number of Ram Singh's followers increased to over 50,000, spread all over the Punjab. He set up *suba*s (governors) and *naib suba*s (deputy governors) to organize the Kookas and arranged military training for them. He started his own postal service. He sent a delegation to Nepal and his gesture of friendship was reciprocated by the Nepalese court by a return of presents. Ram Singh abandoned the earlier quietist way of life. He came to be surrounded by a following of horsemen and himself rode a favourite mare and was addressed as 'Chiniwala Padshah' – 'Lord of the Chini horse' (from the name of the animal).

When the English established themselves as rulers of the Punjab, the only organized body of men that constantly drew their attention were the Namdharis. For some years they just watched them without undue interference. This attitude came to an end with the Mutiny. Then all native organizations became suspect. At first the government examined the Namdhari headquarters at Hazro. In 1863 a police post was set up at Bhayani and Ram Singh and his *subas* interned within the village limits. These restrictions were relaxed three years later, but the police continued to keep a close watch on Kooka activities.

Cow Slaughter Agitation

In 1871 some Kookas got into trouble with the government over the slaughter of cows, and soon the whole organization was drawn in. After the first Sikh war and partial annexation of the Punjab, John Lawrence, acting on behalf of the British Government, had given an undertaking that, in the territories that had passed from the Sikh to the British rule, no acts offensive to Sikh susceptibilities would be allowed. The slaughter of kine was, as under Sikh rule, forbidden. A wooden tablet with an inscription mentioning Lawrence's undertaking was hung outside the Golden Temple at Amritsar (and was removed only in 1922). This undertaking was not honoured and, within a few years of the new rule, beef began to be sold in all large cities. In Amritsar a large abattoir was constructed near the entrance to one of the streets leading to the Golden Temple. It caused much heart-burning to the Sikhs.

Several abortive attempts were made to burn this establishment and terrorize the butchers. Finally, on 14 June 1871 a small band of Kookas raided it, killed four butchers and severely wounded another three. A month later another raid took place at Raikot in Ludhiana District and three butchers were killed and thirteen wounded. The Kookas who took part in these murderous assaults were tried and hanged. Amongst the five men who went to the gallows for the Rakoit murders were two believed by the Kookas to be innocent.

Ram Singh publicly condemned the assaults on the butchers and suffered some unpopularity amongst his followers for doing so. There is reason to believe that the Kookas who had committed these murders and evaded arrest were compelled by Ram Singh to surrender to the police and save the lives of innocent men in custody. Even the authorities had to concede that they could find no connection between Ram Singh and the crimes committed by some of his followers.

All through the summer of 1871 the trouble simmered. The Kookas, who were already in a state of agitation, were stung by the executions of their fellows, particularly of the two men they believed to be innocent. Some of them decided to ignore Ram Singh and avenge themselves on the butchers. Early in 1872 information about cow-killing in the Muslim state of Malerkotla was received by the Kookas. A band of some one hundred of them proceeded to the state. They raided the house of the Sikh jagirdar of Malaudh to furnish themselves with arms and money. All that they actually succeeded in getting was sixteen horses at the expense of two Kookas killed and four others wounded. The next day (15 January 1872) Hira Singh's band reached Malerkotla to settle matters with the authorities. They got involved in a fracas with the nawab's soldiers and fighting broke out. They killed eight of the Malerkotla soldiers and wounded another fifteen. They themselves lost seven men with ten wounded.

Disheartened by their adversities, the Kookas retired into the woods, pursued by the Nawab's militia. There, the units of the British army and those of the rulers of Patiala and Nabha surrounded them. Sixty eight Kookas were captured and brought to Malerkotla. On 16 January 1872, Mr L. Cowan, deputy commissioner of Jullundur, arrived on the scene. In his diary of that date he recorded: 'I propose blowing away from guns or hanging the prisoners tomorrow morning at daybreak.'

On the morning of 17 January, the prisoners were lined up on the parade ground at Malerkotla. At noon Cowan received a note from Forsyth, commissioner of Ambala Division (and his superior officer), asking him to wait. This note, wrote Cowan in his diary, he put in his pocket 'and thought no more about it'. Since the offence had not been committed in British territory but in an Indian state, Cowan decided that a trial was unnecessary. He passed sentence of death on fifty Kookas and, at 4 p.m., ordered their execution. In batches the Kookas were led to the mouths of cannon and blasted off. At 7 p.m., when the last batch of six men had been lashed to the guns, Cowan received an official order from Forsyth to send him the prisoners for trial. 'After reading Mr Forsyth's letter', reported Cowan in a subsequent note to the government, 'I handed it to Colonel Perkins with the remark that it would be impossible to stay the execution of the men already tied to the guns; that such a proceeding would have the worst effect on the people around us; and so the last six rebels were blown away as had been the forty-three before them.' The fiftieth Kooka broke away from the guard, rushed at Cowan and caught him by the beard. He was cut down with the sabres of the native officers in attendance.

On 18 January, Forsyth after hearing of Cowan's action wrote to him: 'My dear Cowan, I fully approve and confirm all you have done. You have acted admirably. I am coming out.' It may not be out of place to mention that during the Mutiny Forsyth held the post of commissioner for the punishment of rebels.

The next day Forsyth 'came out'. Sixteen Kookas who were concerned with the raid on the house of the jagirdar of Malaudh in British territory were tried summarily and hanged. Namdhari headquarters at Bhayani was searched for arms, but the only incriminating articles discovered were a pair of *kukris* presented by the ruler of Nepal. Ram Singh and twelve of his chief supporters were arrested and deported. Ram Singh lived in exile in Rangoon for thirteen years and died there in 1885.

An enquiry was held into the actions of Cowan and his commissioner, Forsyth. The secretary to the Governor-General of India reported that 'His Excellency is under the painful necessity of affirming that the course followed by Mr Cowan was illegal, that it was not palliated by any public necessity, and that it was characterised by incidents which give it a complexion of barbarity.'

Sir Henry Cotton in his *Indian and Home Memoirs* wrote: 'For my part I can recall nothing during my service in India more revolting and more shocking than these executions, and there are many who thought as I did and still think that the final orders of the Government of India were lamentably inadequate.'

Inadequate was an unhappy euphemism. The execution without trial of sixty-six men, the arbitrary sentences of transportation and imprisonment passed on scores of others, and the condemnation of Ram Singh and his deportation, were countenanced by action that was characteristic of the conception of justice at the time. Cowan was pensioned off. Forsyth was simply transferred to another division. On appeal to the viceroy, Forsyth was compensated by being appointed envoy on a mission to Kashgar. He was subsequently knighted. Forsyth recorded in his autobiography that, having taken the responsibility of Cowan's acts upon himself, he wrote a letter approving of the measures taken by Cowan. But since the government had dismissed Cowan 'I did my utmost to help him when he was turned out of the service by procuring a very good appointment for him in India'. The Anglo-Indian press applauded the Malerkotla executions as an example of 'stern justice'.

With the deportation of Ram Singh, Kooka political activity came to an abrupt end. Ram Singh was succeeded by his younger brother, Budh Singh, who became head of the organization with a new name, Guru Hari Singh. He was succeeded by his son, Pratap Singh. Both of Ram Singh's successors restricted their activity to purely religious and social affairs. Pratap Singh was likely to be succeeded by his elder son Jagjit Singh.

It is impossible to estimate the numbers of this subsect. For many years after 1872, the Kookas got the popularity enjoyed by persecuted groups in any country under alien rule. Their religious beliefs were, however, accepted by only some sections of the Ramgarhia (carpenter) caste to which Ram Singh himself belonged, with a sprinkling of Jats. Most of the other Sikhs disapprove of their belief in gurus other than the ten historical ones. The importance of the Kookas arises not from their numbers but from the fact that they are a compact body of men always united in action. Their missionaries work energetically in the villages and hundreds of Kooka gurdwaras have been erected in recent times all over the province. These factors contribute towards making the Namdhari Guru one of the leading figures in the Sikh community.

Chapter 7

THE SINGH SABHA AND
SOCIAL REFORM

The name Singh Sabha is loosely used for a movement of reform in matters religious, social, literary and political. In some ways this movement picked up the thread from where the Namdharis had been forced to drop it. Its achievements, however, were more substantial. One reason for this was that more emphasis was put on religious, social and literary activities than on political matters. Even the politics of the individuals associated with the movement found favour with the authorities, and, consequently, considerable co-operation was forthcoming from the government.

The spur to activity was provided by anti-Sikh elements within and without the community. Efforts of Christian and Hindu missionaries to win over the Sikh masses to their respective folds had alarmed the orthodox elements. Some attempts to check anti-Sikh propaganda had, in turn, brought forth hostile comment on the Sikh Gurus and their religious institutions. Within the community itself disruptive forces had disintegrated the small sect into those who stood for Sikhism as a new faith with an independent entity, and those who considered it as a branch of Hindu protestants still owing allegiance to Hindu deities and conventions. A vast majority were with the former group, but a small and important minority were with the latter. Amongst them were the priests (mahants) of the Sikh gurdwaras who were members of the Udasi subsect, which had never accepted Guru Gobind Singh's forms and symbols of the Khalsa.

The immediate reason for the starting of the movement was provided by an incident which took place in Amritsar. A Hindu missionary erected a pulpit in the vicinity of the Golden Temple and openly vilified the teachings and achievements of the Sikh Gurus. The Sikhs of Amritsar were stung into activity. In 1873 an association styled the Sri Guru Singh Sabha was formed. A plan to organize educational facilities for Sikhs, with particular emphasis on the teaching of Gurmukhi and the Scriptures, was put into action. A Khalsa school was opened in Amritsar and the university authorities were persuaded to introduce Gurmukhi as a subject for higher studies in the Oriental College at Lahore. Manuscripts dealing with Sikh history were translated into Gurmukhi. Commentaries on the Sikh Scriptures were written and widely distributed. To assist all these manifold activities, journals dealing with communal matters were started in various languages.

The movement became popular with the Sikh middle class. In 1879 a Singh Sabha was established at Lahore through the efforts of Gurmukh Singh. After a year a joint board under the name of General Sabha was brought into existence at Amritsar, the Lahore Singh Sabha having become a branch of it. The moving spirit of the association was, again, Gurmukh Singh of the Oriental College of Lahore, who was the most important figure in the Singh Sabha movement. Collaborating with him was Jawahir Singh, a clerk in the railway offices.

The work of the Khalsa Diwan went on smoothly till 1886. Several new *sabha*s were opened at various centres. A charitable

hospital and many Khalsa schools were started. A resolution for the
establishment of a Khalsa College was also adopted. In the same year
some difference arose between the Amritsar and Lahore centres,
and Gurmukh Singh was compelled to set up an independent
association at Lahore under the patronage of Atar Singh of Bhadaur,
who later became its president (1889). The government associated
itself with the Lahore association's efforts. The viceroy, Lord
Lansdowne, in a speech delivered at Patiala on 23 October 1890,
said: 'With this movement the Government of India is in hearty
sympathy. We appreciate the many admirable qualities of the Sikh
nation, and it is a pleasure to us to know that, while in days gone
by we recognized in them a gallant and formidable foe, we are today able to give them a foremost place amongst the true and loyal
subjects of Her Majesty the Queen Empress.' In 1894 the governor
of the Punjab and the commander-in-chief agreed to become its
patrons. The Sikhs themselves were proud of the government's co-
operation. The secretary of the Khalsa College council referred to
his Eurpoean colleagues in the council as people 'activated by no
other motives than those of philanthropy, of friendliness towards
the Sikhs, and we are very grateful to them'.

The rivalry between the Amritsar and the Lahore associations
continued for some years. But this did not impede the progress
of the movement. For the first time Sikh missionaries went out
to proselytize. Sahib Singh Dedi, Attar Singh, and later on Sangat
Singh of Kamalia, carried out a campaign of conversion in northern
Punjab and in Sindh, and large masses of urban Hindus joined the
Sikh fold. Sikh religious writing was given a new lease of life by
the enthusiastic labours of a band of writers. Vir Singh founded the
Khalsa Tract Society and a weekly theological journal, the *Khalsa
Samachar*. Kahan Singh of Nabha produced an encyclopaedia of
Sikh religion and culture. Dit Singh was another prose writer of
note. Above all, the Sikhs were fortunate in getting the services

of Mr Macauliffe, who produced his volumes on the history of
the Sikh religion, which to this day remain the chief work on the
Sikh faith in the English language. The greatest achievement of the
diwans was the foundation of the Khalsa College at Amritsar in
1892, which is the most important landmark in the history of the
movement. Associated with the institution were several prominent
Englishmen.

In 1902 the Amritsar and Lahore associations fused together
under the title 'Chief Khalsa Diwan' and all the Sikh Sabhas were
brought under its guidance and superintendence. Sundar Singh
Majithia made his debut into Sikh affairs as the secretary of the
new diwan and the college. From this time till his death in 1940,
he was the central figure in Sikh social and political life. In 1904, a
conference was held on the college premises under the presidency
of Maharaja Hira Singh of Nabha and the institution was put on
a sound financial basis by endowments. Sir Charles Rivaz, the
lieutenant governor, himself organized the raising of funds from
Sikh landowners for the purpose.

In 1908 an educational committee was formed and from then
onwards annual educational conferences were held in different
parts of the Punjab. New schools, colleges, orphanages, and other
educational institutions followed in the wake of these conferences.
Notable amongst them were the Khalsa College at Gujranwala
and a girls' school at Ferozepur, the Kanya Maha Vidyala.

By the beginning of the 1914–18 war the Singh Sabha had
begun to give way to another movement, later known as Akali.
The methods of the Chief Khalsa Diwan had always been confined
to conferences, resolutions and pamphleteering. When it came to
recovering possession of Sikh shrines from hereditary priests and a
clash with the government, which backed the priests in possession,
these methods were of little avail. The initiative passed from the
Singh Sabha to more radical elements, who organized passive

resistance and suffered torture and imprisonment in their cause. The diwan further antagonized the masses by its hostility to the Ghadr revolutionary group and in siding with the government in its coercive measures following the Amritsar shooting in April 1921. It never recovered from the discredit it suffered in popular eyes during this period.

The religious, literary and educational contributions of the Singh Sabha movement had a lasting effect. Sikh educational conferences were held annually under its aegis and a vast network of primary and higher schools, girls' and boys' colleges, were kept going. Vir Singh's Khalsa Tract Society and the weekly *Khalsa Samachar* and other works of a religio-literary nature did much to enrich Gurmukhi literature. Even in the realm of politics, however meagre its achievements, the name of the Chief Khalsa Diwan was always associated with an exemplary standard of honesty in pecuniary matters.

Chapter 8

AKALI AGITATION FOR SIKH SHRINES

The Sikh gurdwara is more than just a place of worship. It is also a school, a meeting place, and a rest house for travellers. Besides housing the Scripture, the Granth Sahib, and providing for secular and religious instruction, it has to give food to the hungry and shelter to the homeless and the itinerant. To meet all these demands a gurdwara is usually well endowed. It also has a handsome income by way of money offerings from the worshippers.

A gurdwara is an integral part of Sikh religious and social life. It was always meant to be so and Sikhs set great store by the traditions of sanctity and hospitality started by the Gurus. Those who have trifled with them have been punished. Those who suffered penalty for punishing wrongdoers have been given the martyr's crown. To contribute towards the construction or repair of gurdwaras is about the noblest form of charity recognized.

During the Sikh rule the gurdwaras were managed by priests (mahants) under the direction and control of the congregation. The incomes of the gurdwaras, which were meagre, were allotted to various charities, chiefly for providing food free of cost for all who asked for it. The priests were paid a nominal wage, and the office was not hereditary. Most of the priests were Sahajdhari Sikhs, being members of the sect of Udasies, who did not subscribe to the forms of Sikhism finalized by Guru Gobind Singh. The differences from orthodox Sikhism were, however, not emphasized during the Sikh rule.

With the advent of British rule, the position underwent a radical change. The introduction of canal irrigation increased the incomes from land enormously and several gurdwaras to which revenues of villages were assigned became wealthy institutions. The office of the priest consequently became one of importance, and the temptation to misuse gurdwara money for personal needs irresistible. Priesthood became hereditary and the incumbents began to assert their independence of the congregation by denying Sikhism and claiming the gurdwaras to be Udasi places of worship. Hindu idols appeared alongside the Granth Sahib and Hindu ritual replaced the Sikh.

British authorities took over the administration of the four important gurdwaras known as the Takhts (Amritsar, Anandpur, Patna and Nander in Hyderabad, Deccan). In the others, numbering about 260, the mahants continued in management, becoming more and more independent of the Sikh congregation with the passage of years.

Friction between the Sikhs and the mahants was inevitable. Corrupt expenditure of the offerings and sacrilegious misuse of sacred precincts became common. The Sikhs decided to free their places of worship from non-Sikh influences. Remedies provided by the law were found to be inadequate. Civil suits involved tremendous expense. The mahants were wealthy; the congregation, on the other hand, had to rely on voluntary contributions. In some cases, litigation went on for as long as thirty years with little result. When the Sikhs decided on direct action, i.e., taking forcible possession of the gurdwaras and ejecting the mahants, the strong arm of the executive came upon them. There were persecutions for criminal trespass, robbery and dacoity, and honest men fired with religious fervour were thrown into prison as common criminals. The Punjab Government, like all other governments, threw in its lot with the vested interests and in support of the status quo. The struggle for liberation of the gurdwaras had to be carried on on two fronts: against the mahants as well as against the government.

The first dispute with the government started early in 1914. In 1911 the capital of India was transferred from Calcutta to Delhi. In pursuance of its building plans, the government acquired the land of gurdwara Rikab Gunj in New Delhi from an accommodating mahant in order to drive a road across it to the Viceregal Lodge. The wall of the gurdwara was pulled down for that purpose. This action aroused resentment in the Sikh community, and plans were made to force the government to reconstruct the wall. Then the First World War broke out and the issue was shelved for some years.

During the war and the years immediately following it, the Sikhs were given more cause for conflict against the mahants and the government. The activities of the Ghadr Party (discussed in the next chapter) had bothered the government. This party consisted mainly of Sikh emigrants with a sprinkling of Hindus and Muslims. The passengers of the SS *Komagata Maru*, which brought them home from Canada and the United States, were mostly Sikhs. The victims of the firing at Budge Budge harbour (near Calcutta) were all Sikhs. In the conspiracy cases which tried the members of the Ghadr Party, most of the condemned men were Sikhs. The Ghadr Party became an emblem of national and communal consciousness. It won favour with most Indians, but to the Sikhs the nature of its personnel brought it closer to their hearts and it became a matter of pride. The mahants, under government inspiration, condemned these men as renegades and used the gurdwaras for pronouncing their excommunication.

The two years of political conflict following the first Great War of 1914–18 created a wider rift between the Sikhs and the government.

Sikh contribution to the war, both by way of men and material, had been considerably more than that of any other community in India. One Sikh out of every fourteen had enlisted. Sir John Maynard's estimate was that the Sikh contribution to the war effort was more than ten times that of any other community. Despite this, when it came to communal weightages in legislative bodies under the Montagu Chelmsford reforms, all they got was representation in proportion to their numbers. Their services during the war, their special position as landowners paying 40 per cent of the land revenue of the province, and the fact that at the time they formed 25 per cent of the voters on the electoral registers of the Punjab, were all ignored. The Muslims, on the other hand, got special weightage far in excess of their numbers in provinces where they were a minority, e.g., 33 per cent in Bihar with a population of 11 per cent.

While the Sikhs were agitating for the control of their shrines and for political recognition, the Indian National Congress under the leadership of Mahatma Gandhi launched a mass civil disobedience movement to compel the British to grant India self-government. The Muslims had grievances of their own – mainly concerned with the treatment of Turkey after the war. There was no identity of purpose between the Nationalists, who wanted freedom, and the Khilafatists, who wanted the restoration of the caliphate. They made common cause because both wanted to oust the British Government, one because it was foreign, the other because it was infidel. The Sikhs joined this nation wide movement with yet another motive. They wanted possession of their shrines, and as the government obstructed them, they willingly joined hands with those who were trying to remove the government.

The Amritsar Massacre

The dispute between the Indian National Congress and the British Government took a violent turn in the Punjab. At Amritsar unruly mobs, inflamed at the arrest of their leaders, tried to set fire to Christian mission schools. Four Europeans, including a woman, were murdered. The government banned meetings and the carrying of arms. On 14 April 1919 a mass meeting of the local residents, including women and children, was held in defiance of the ban at Jallianwala Bagh – a squarish plot of land surrounded on all sides by a high wall with a small exit at one end. This meeting was 'dispersed' by General Dyer and his Gurkhas who 'poured lead into the densely-packed sunken garden ... firing away all his ammunition'. Fifteen hundred people, according to the government estimate, were left dead or dying in the garden. A curfew order was immediately imposed, making it impossible for help to be brought to the wounded. Thereafter, for several days the populace were made to crawl on their bellies along the street where the European woman had been murdered. The world heard the news of the Jallianwala Bagh massacre with horror. Even the government, in whose interests General Dyer claimed to have acted, criticized his action. In the debate on the subject in the House of Commons, Mr Winston Churchill (who was then president of the Army Council) described it as 'an episode which appeared to be without parallel in the modern history of the British Empire'. It was, he added, 'an extraordinary event, a monstrous event, an event which stood in singular and sinister isolation'. Mr Asquith referred to it as 'one of the worst outrages in the whole of our history'.

The only people to applaud Dyer were the die hard English press and the mahants. The former presented Dyer with £28,000 collected by voluntary contributions and a golden sword proclaiming him as the defender of the Empire. The latter honoured him at the Golden Temple as the defender of the Sikh faith and presented him with a robe of honour. More than one-third of the victims of the shooting were Sikhs.

The inspiration for direct action in the matter of gurdwaras came from the Indian National Congress after its meeting at Amritsar in 1919. A body known as the Sikh League was formed. In May 1920 a Gurmukhi paper, *The Akali*, was started; several others followed, e.g., *Khalsa Advocate, Khalsa Sewak Punjab* and *Panth Sewak*. In a meeting in October 1920, which Mahatma Gandhi attended, the Sikh League adopted a resolution not to co-operate with the government.

Old leaders were cast aside. New men came to the fore. Prominent amongst them were Kharak Singh, Mahtab Singh, Master Tara Singh and Harbans Singh of Atari. 'A spirit of recalcitrance thus awakened', wrote Sir John Maynard, 'manifested itself in the first direct action by Sikh reformers.'

The issue of the gurdwaras agitated the Sikhs once more. The Rikab Gunj dispute was amicably settled through the good offices of Maharaja Ripduman Singh Nabha. The government restored the demolished wall at its own expense. It was, however, done under the threat of passive resistance, which was decided on at the Sikh League meeting in October 1920 and was to have started in December.

From the month of October 1920 onwards, the Sikhs started occupying gurdwaras all over India. In the beginning the mahants gave in and the government sanctioned the change of management which took place. A committee, known as the Shiromani Gurdwara Parbandhak Committee (usually referred to by its initials SGPC) was formed to organize the management of all places of worship which came into the hands of the Sikhs.

Early in 1921 the policy of the government changed and the trouble started. At the gurdwara at Turun Tarun (Amritsar District), a representative body of Sikhs who came to discuss the question of transfer of management with the mahants were assaulted. Two were killed and seventeen injured. Instead of punishing the mahants, the police started cross-cases against both the Akalis and the mahants. Fifteen priests and seventeen Sikhs went to jail. A fortnight later came the holocaust at Nankana (the birthplace of the founder of the faith).

The Nankana Massacre

Mahant Narain Das, the manager of the shrine at Nankana, had been accused by the congregation of being unfit to discharge the functions with which he was entrusted. A resolution demanding his resignation by the first week of March (1921) was handed to him. Narain Das did not bother to answer the charges but hired a large number of professional thugs and gave them shelter within the precincts of the gurdwara. (The commissioner of police admitted later in the Punjab Council that there were rumours that ever since October 1920 the mahant had been collecting arms.) The police force was too busy with arrangements in connection with the visit of the Duke of Connaught to take any preventive action in time. In the early hours of Sunday, 20 February 1921, a party of worshippers under the leadership of Lachman Singh, a well-known Akali, entered the gurdwara. The gates of the gurdwara were closed behind them. Narain Das and his hirelings butchered the worshippers in cold blood and proceeded to burn their bodies. Several hours later, when the police arrived on the scene, charred remains of 130 corpses were discovered. The gurdwara itself was one mess of putrefying human flesh and blood. The Scripture had been desecrated; its pages were bored with rifle shot and torn by the assassin's dagger. Lachman Singh had been killed while reading the Granth.

For some days local officials tried to belittle the incident by deliberately misinforming the people about the number of casualties. The Anglo-Indian press kept referring to it as an 'affray', a 'riot', a 'fight' – 'a disturbance of a sectarian character'. But the governor, Sir Edward Maclagan, took a different view. He came to Nankana accompanied by his executive councillors and publicly expressed sympathy with the relatives and friends of the victims of the outrage. The possession of the gurdwara was handed over to a committee of seven Sikhs, with Harbans Singh of Atari as president. Other gurdwaras in the town were also taken over. A few days later Mahatma Gandhi visited the shrine.

The result of the prosecutions which were started in connection with the Nankana killings was death sentence for three men and a term of life imprisonment for Narain Das. The Sikhs were further embittered by these judicial decisions.

In an official minute Sir Edward Maclagan wrote: 'The Nankana episode brought notice to the fact that the reforming party had some grounds of complaint in the difficulties which faced them in obtaining legal redress for the scandals in the shrines.'

The Keys Affair

By the time the excitement over the Nankana massacre had abated, the government stirred up another hornet's nest. On 7 November 1921 the keys of the treasury of the Golden Temple, Amritsar, were taken forcibly by the government. The committee which managed the affairs of the Golden Temple and several other shrines had been in possession of the keys for over a year. The government was at pains to explain that it was going to form 'a provisional advisory committee and that the object of the seizure was simply to institute a friendly suit and legalize the *status quo*'. The position became untenable and Sir Edward Maclagan did his

best to get out of it. Within a week he made a statement to the
effect that 'the Government intended withdrawing its control
over the Temple'. He hoped, however, that the Sikhs would
give him an opportunity to save face for the blunder committed
by the deputy commissioner of Amritsar 'by temporarily co-
operating with the Government nominee'. The Sikhs refused to
let the nominee enter the temple precincts. On 20 November
the superintendent of police arrested some of the Akali leaders,
including the president of the committee, Kharak Singh, the
secretary, Mahtab Singh, and Master Tara Singh. They were
sentenced to various terms of imprisonment varying from four
to six months. The governor stepped in once more. He offered
the keys back to the committee. The committee refused to accept
them unless the men imprisoned in connection with the affair
were released. By January 1922, all the leaders were released and
the keys handed back to Kharak Singh. The government even
acknowledged that the committee 'was representative of a large
section of Sikh opinion on the subject of Sikh gurdwaras'.

In spite of the fact that by now the government had had enough
opportunity to understand the situation and, in some cases, even
sympathized with the Sikh reformers, the attitude of the local
bureaucracy in the district did not change. Sikhs continued to be
arrested in large numbers for carrying kirpans that were too long
and even for wearing black turbans. The carrying of a kirpan had
always been admitted by the government to be the religious right
of every Sikh. The black turban was merely a badge of the Akalis
symbolizing sorrow over the fate of many of their co-religionists.
The Sikhs not unnaturally came to believe that the government
wanted to smash their religious fraternity and that the matter of
shrines was only one of the excuses for so doing. A semi-military
organization called the 'Akali Dal' (the Akali Army) was formed and
volunteers enlisted from all parts of the province. A large number

of retired soldiers gave up their pensions to join this voluntary militia, which was sworn to practise only passive resistance.

In May 1922 the government again made a faux pas and unwittingly challenged the entire organization in a test of strength. This was at Guru ka Bagh.

Guru ka Bagh

Guru ka Bagh was a piece of land connected with a shrine which had been in the possession of the Sikhs for some months. Wood had all along been cut from the trees on the land for the use of the temple kitchen. Then suddenly, Mahant Sunder Das, who had hitherto accepted the situation, lodged a complaint of trespass. He admitted having given up the temple but not the adjoining land. On 8 August 1922 the police started arresting Sikhs for criminal trespass. Then the Akalis launched a mass struggle and large batches of volunteers marched to Guru ka Bagh. They were stopped and mercilessly beaten. Leaders such as Pandit Madan Mohan Malaviya, Hakim Ajmal Khan and the Rev. C.F. Andrews, came to see the clash between passive resisters and the Punjab police. Rev. Andrews wrote: 'The brutality and inhumanity of the whole scene was indescribably increased by the fact that the men who were hit were praying to God and had already taken a vow that they would remain silent and peaceful.' In September 1922 the Indian National Congress constituted a committee under the chairmanship of Srinivas Iyengar to enquire into the atrocities committed by the police. After a thorough investigation the committee reported that 'the atrocity stories were true; that Akali volunteers were beaten till they were senseless; that they were drawn by their long hair or beards; that they were humiliated by acts of indignity offensive to their religious susceptibilities; that in no case did any Akali abandon passive resistance and retaliate'. 'Divesting ourselves of all political bias', wrote the members of the committee, 'we consider that the excesses committed reflect the greatest discredit on the Punjab Government and are a disgrace to any civilized government. We have no hesitation whatever to come to the conclusion that the force used, judged from all aspects, was altogether excessive. We are constrained to observe that the arbitrary and lawless way in which violence was resorted to was deliberate and in callous disregard of such humanity as even a government is bound to show. Lastly, we cannot help expressing our profound admiration for the spirit of martyrdom and orderliness which animated the Akalis and for their inflinching [sic] adherence to the gospel of non-violence and for the noble way in which they have vindicated themselves under circumstances of prolonged and unusual exasperation.' Even Sir John Maynard admitted that the Guru ka Bagh affair 'brought great odium upon Government ... All India rang with praises of the men who had submitted day after day to blows and arrests, without retaliation or resistance'. On 13 September Sir Edward Maclagan visited the spot and the beating was stopped. The arrests continued.

In an official minute Sir Edward Maclagan wrote: 'The Prabandhak Committee hoped to bring Government to terms by compelling them to cease the arrests, and the Government continued the arrests in the hope of wearing out the Committee.' By the time more than 5,000 Akalis had been imprisoned, the government and not the Sikhs wearied. Batches of hundreds continued to arrive every day to be arrested. On 8 March the Legislative Council, against the government's opposition, passed a resolution recommending the release of the prisoners. The government declined to act on it, but entered into negotiations. It offered to release the prisoners if the Parbandhak Committee expressed its disapprobation of violent action. The committee, which at no time had endorsed violent action, refused to be drawn into the trap and refused. Then the government released, first all prisoners who were under eighteen or over fifty, and then the whole lot. Sir Ganga Ram, a well-known business magnate and philanthropist, was made to buy the disputed site and hand it over to the Sikhs. The government saved face. The Sikhs triumphed. A remarkable compliment to the Akalis was paid soon after. Hindu–Muslim riots broke out in Amritsar and the Parbandhak Committee offered assistance in keeping order. The governor admitted that 'the Deputy Commissioner made use of them for a time'.

The Nabha Dispute

The next Akali-Government clash came a few months later. Maharaja Ripduman Singh of Nabha was deposed and exiled. The government gave several reasons for its action except the one the Sikhs knew, viz., he was friendly towards the Akalis.

Even prior to the Akali passive resistance, Ripduman Singh had made no secret of his sympathy with the Congress demand for independence. When he had taken over as maharaja, he had refused investiture by the English agent. In the years that followed there had been several incidents involving personal discourtesy towards him by the Governors Sir Louis Dane and, later, Sir Michael O'Dwyer. These incidents were bazaar gossip. The excuse to get rid of Ripduman Singh was provided by 'border' incidents between Nabha and Patiala and complaint by the latter about infringement of his territory. An enquiry was instituted. On 7 July 1923 the Government of India issued a communiqué stating that Ripduman Singh had agreed to abdicate. Two days later the communiqué was amended, deleting reference to his having agreed to the abdication. It was widely known that Ripduman Singh had been threatened with imprisonment (a European in his own service had warned him that if he did not agree he would be shot), and the maharanee had been insulted and locked up by an English colonel who had gone to serve government orders on the maharaja. Ripduman Singh's dismissal created commotion throughout India.

Resolutions demanding his reinstatement were passed in all the gurdwaras and prayers offered for his restoration. One such meeting was forcibly dispersed by the police while the congregation was still at prayer. This was at Jaito, just within the Nabha territory. Another mass movement was launched. A batch of 500 Akali volunteers marched from Amritsar and reached Jaito on 21 February 1924. They were stopped by the state police and, on refusing to disperse, were fired upon. Over forty were killed and nearly a hundred wounded. Other members of the band were arrested and sentenced to long terms of imprisonment. Leaders of the Indian National Congress, including Jawaharlal Nehru, who went to visit the spot, were also imprisoned. The Jaito passive resistance went on for some months till the state police gave in and allowed the seventeenth batch of 500 Akali passive resisters to enter the gurdwara.

But there was no change of attitude by the government. When the Nabha agitation was at its peak, it decided to settle the Akali question once and for all. On the night of 13–14 September 1923, fifty-seven leaders were arrested and charged with their misdeeds of the past three years. They were alleged to have conspired to overthrow British rule and set up a Sikh state. Sikhs who agitated against these arrests were also apprehended. The SGPC and the Akali Dal were declared illegal bodies. A trial, known as the 'Akali Leaders' Case', went on for three years. The conspirators were sentenced to various terms of imprisonment and all except four who appealed against their sentences were sent to jail.

The Gurdwara Act and the Akali Split

It took the government some time to realize that it could not continue an attitude of neutrality in the matter of Sikh shrines. Even when it did decide to act, there was no appreciation of the urgency of the problem. It took four years to produce an Act to regulate the management of Sikh temples. Meanwhile, arrests, beatings and shootings continued unabated.

Soon after the killings in Turun Tarun a communiqué was issued (16 February 1921) announcing that a committee of enquiry would be set up 'to consider the existing management of Sikh gurdwaras, shrines, etc., and the efforts being made to alter such management and to report the best method of settling disputes and of regulating future control of the institutions'. A preliminary conference representing the Sikhs and the mahants took place with the secretary of the Punjab Government in the chair. The conference proceedings were rudely interrupted by the tragedy of Nankana Sahib before it could make any progress. A month later (14 March) the government decided to issue an ordinance pending the passing of a comprehensive Act. A resolution to that effect was moved in the Provincial Council by Mian Fazli Hussain. But the Hindu members of the council, who had by then identified themselves with the interests of the mahants, succeeded in putting in amendments on which the Sikh members refused to vote. The government very wisely dropped the ordinance and decided to put in a regular bill. The Sikhs were asked to present their views on the form of legislation that would satisfy their demands.

On 20 March 1921 a meeting of the Sikh leaders took place at the Golden Temple. One section of those assembled were for refusing to co-operate with any government move while their co-religionists were still in jail and continued to be arrested. The more moderate elements, led by Harbans Singh of Atari, Mahtab Singh and Professor Jodh Singh, suggested a compromise whereby a committee of twelve would discuss the subject with the government, provided all the men imprisoned were released forthwith. This the government refused to do. On 8 April 1921 a text of the Sikh Gurdwaras and Shrines Bill was issued. Even the four Sikh members on the Select Committee, which issued the bill, disagreed with its provisions and wrote a minute of dissent.

The attitude of the Hindu members of the council had by now become definitely aligned with the mahants and against the Sikh point of view. On 11 April the SGPC constituted a working committee of seven to represent their views. Meetings with the mahants' nominees, now backed by advice of the Hindu members of the council, bore no results. A month later the working committee met again in an attempt to formulate its views and present them to the government. The majority of members were in no mood for negotiations while their colleagues continued to be under arrest. They passed resolutions criticizing the government and advocating the continuance of passive resistance. Two dissenters, Harbans Singh of Atari and Professor Jodh Singh, resigned.

No progress could be made for some time with legislative measures because of the arrests in connection with 'the keys affair', Guru ka Bagh and the Nabha agitation. The matter had to be restarted when the main fronts of passive resistance had been settled. The time to negotiate was well chosen. Although the Nabha ruler had been exiled, the government had conceded to the Sikhs the right to enter Nabha territory and meet in their temples. Passive Akali resisters, who had made the right of access to their shrines their main point, were no longer arrested and the agitation had quietened down. Most of the important shrines had already passed into Sikh hands. There seemed little point in keeping the Akali leaders in jail when what they had wanted had been given. All that was necessary was to persuade them (or some of them) to take over the management of their shrines. This the government decided to make the condition of their release. On the Akali side, too, there was the realization that their goal had been achieved. They had

had almost five years of uninterrupted political life, mostly spent in jails, and wanted to return to their homes and occupations.

The final text of the Sikh Gurdwaras Bill (it was passed into an Act in November 1925) was presented to the leaders in jail. It provided for the control of all historic Sikh shrines by an elected body, the SGPC. It also provided for the setting up of a tribunal which was to determine cases of disputed shrines and properties. Twenty-two Akalis, led by Mahtab Singh, who expressed satisfaction with the bill were released first and invited to take over the management of the shrines. The others had no objection to the proposed legislation either, but they nursed a sense of grievance against the government for the treatment meted out to them and refused to co-operate. The leaders of this group were Kharak Singh and Master Tara Singh. They were released later and, as expected, disputed the right of their erstwhile colleagues to the management of the shrines. In the first elections held in December 1926, Mahtab Singh's group was deprived of the control of the SGPC, Kharak Singh (who was still in jail) was elected president and Master Tara Singh, vice-president.

The Akali party underwent a further subdivision a couple of years later in its attitude towards the Indian National Congress. This division cut across the earlier one and produced a new alignment of party factions. An All-Parties' Conference convened by Pandit Motilal Nehru suggested proposals for communal settlement of India. Some Akalis were for accepting the Nehru report. They subsequently became the 'nationalist Sikhs', and included some well-known leaders like Gurdit Singh of the *Komagata Maru*, Amar Singh Jhabal and Hira Singh Dard. Other Akalis were for completely rejecting it and breaking all connections with the Congress. In this group were Kharak Singh and Mahtab Singh. A third group under the leadership of Master Tara Singh adopted the middle course. They condemned the Nehru report as derogatory to Sikh interests, but otherwise stuck to the Congress. Kharak Singh's party did not co-operate with the Congress Civil Disobedience Movement that came some years later. It lost ground as being anti-national and communal. The Congressites lost the confidence of the small community as being completely oblivious of its interests. Master Tara Singh's party gathered force. From its association with the Congress and participation in the Congress Civil Disobedience Movement, it gained prestige as a nationalist group. It won the sympathies of the Hindus and Hindu-controlled press, a factor of considerable importance in Sikh politics. From its constant reiteration of communal demands at Congress meetings, it continued to enjoy the confidence of the Sikh masses. Within a few years it emerged strong enough to claim the title 'Akali' exclusively for itself.

The Akali movement came to an end with the passing of the Sikh Gurdwaras Act and the release of Akali leaders. Protests against the treatment of the maharaja of Nabha continued for some time. Attempts were also made to start an agitation against the Patiala ruler, who had been instrumental in the removal of Ripduman Singh and was a notorious Akali-baiter. But these movements lacked the religious fervour of the earlier days. Besides that, there was no longer the unity in the Akali ranks, which had given it its dynamic force. Ripduman Singh's cause was soon forgotten and he died several years later in Kodaikanal (then in the Madras Presidency; now in Tamil Nadu) where he had been confined. The Patiala ruler continued his anti-Akali policy and arrested a large number of local Akalis. The Patiala passive resistance petered out without any results.

On the government side, positive steps were taken to reassure the Sikhs that there was no further cause for friction. The governor, Sir Malcolm (later Lord) Hailey, went on a tour of the province addressing Sikh meetings. Organizations of Sikhs who had remained aloof from the Akali movement, styled Sudhar Committees, were set up in several districts to counteract Akali propaganda.

It is estimated that in the five years of agitation over 30,000 men and women went to jail, 400 were killed and 2,000 wounded. Nearly 700 village officials were dismissed from their posts and over Rs 15 lac was realized in fines and forfeitures. The political results of the movement were far-reaching. The British lost the most loyal supporters of their regime in India: the nationalists won over a community whose contribution to the struggle for independence was thereafter far greater than that of any other.

Along with the passive resistance movement organized and conducted by the SGPC and the Akali Dal, there grew up an underground terrorist organization known as the 'Babbar Akalis'. The activities of the Babbars were inspired both by the Akali agitation and the Ghadr Party. A large number of its members had been abroad and in contact with the Gadrites. For three years (1921–23) the Babbars terrorized the central districts of the province. In the summer of 1924 ninety one were brought to trial on charges of conspiracy to overthrow the government, murder, dacoity and robbery of military stores, etc. On 28 February the trial concluded. Fifty-four men were convicted; of these, five, including the leaders Kishen Singh, Santa Singh and Nand Singh, were sentenced to death, eleven were transported for life, and thirty-eight sentenced to various terms of imprisonment ranging from three to seven years. The remaining thirty-four were acquitted.

Chapter 9

THE GHADR REBELLION AND MARXISM

In the last years of the nineteenth century, a movement to end British rule in India by violent means was started in Maharashtra and Bengal. In the beginning the movement was Hindu both in inspiration and membership. The chief apologist for the use of violence as a political weapon was Bal Gangadhar Tilak, the editor of the Mahrathi weekly, *Kesari*. The men who organized terrorism in Maharashtra were all Hindus, most of them belonging to the Chitpavan subsect of Brahmins. Even in Bengal, which became the main hotbed of terrorist activity from 1902 onwards, the movement remained confined to Hindus (Brahmins and Kayasths) and sought inspiration from Hindu religion. In Maharashtra, the cult of the Mahratta hero, Sivaji, who had fought and triumphed over the Muslims two centuries earlier, was revived and expressed in turbulent demonstrations at religious festivals. In Bengal the emphasis was on the worship of Kali, the goddess of destruction, and a reorientation of the teachings of the Hindu reformer, Vivekananda. In both these provinces and others like Bihar, Madras and the United Provinces, where the cult spread, texts of the

Bhagvad Gita were used to justify political crime. The movement was basically a revival of militant Hinduism. It remained confined to the educated middle class. It had more a religious than a political significance. In Maharashtra it was as anti-Muslim as anti-British.

In the Punjab the movement started later, and was initially directed by non-Punjabis like Rash Bihari from Bengal and Vishnu Pingley from Poona. But within a few months it became a purely Punjab affair, almost exclusively conducted by Sikh emigrants from Canada, the United States, China and the Malay States. From the very start it maintained a secular character and, at no time did it seek emotional inspiration from Sikh religion or manifest an anti-Muslim bias. It was the first to introduce Marxist concepts to India.

The circumstances that compelled a large number of Sikhs to leave their homes to go abroad go back to the last few years before the dawn of the twentieth century. Before the British annexation of the Punjab, most of the northern and north-western part of the province was a sparsely populated desert. In this region cultivation was largely confined to strips of land along river banks or, on a very small scale, beside wells. When the canals were dug to irrigate these lands, the government had to find people to farm them. Apart from the local population, which was largely Muslim, Sikhs were the only people enterprising enough to make the venture. Large numbers migrated from the East Punjab districts of Hoshiarpur, Ludhiana, Jullundur, Amritsar and Ferozepur, and moved north, north-west and south-west of Lahore to Gujranwala, Lyallpur, Sheikhupura, Sargodha, Sialkot, Montgomery and Multan. It brought them such prosperity as they had not known before and they became India's wealthiest agricultural community. For some years the pressure on the land in their original homes was eased and they were able to pay off their ancestral debts. As years went by, the contact between the settlers of the Canal Colonies and their

relations in eastern Punjab became fewer and fewer. The holdings
in the Canal Colonies were large and could provide for bigger
families. The holdings in the old homelands were small and the
land, which depended on rain for its crops, was less productive.
Here every increase in the family produced fragmentation of
holdings till, once again, the individual share became uneconomic.
Lands and livestock had to be sold to moneylenders and many had
to seek livelihood in other professions. The position was further
aggravated by a series of failures of monsoons between 1905 and
1910, resulting in famine in regions which depended on rain. It
was from these areas that emigration first started.

Most of the Sikh emigrants went east to Bengal. From there
they moved across the frontier to Burma, Malay States and then
China. Some occupations were readily open to them owing to
their excellent physique. They were employed as watchmen and
later as policemen in all the eastern outposts of the British Empire.
Those who had served in the mechanized units of the army took
to plying taxis or becoming electricians. The more enterprising of
the emigrants set up their own businesses or became contractors.

The spirit of pioneering did not spend itself in the neighbouring
countries. From Burma, the Malay States and China, Sikhs went to
Canada and the USA. Immigration to Canada and the US started
in 1887. That year Queen Victoria's jubilee was held in London.
Sikh troops attending the celebrations were sent to the other
Dominions on their way back to India. Canada impressed them
with its richness and prospect of good employment. These soldiers
returned home with tales of Canadian prosperity. Some of them
went out as policemen to Hong Kong and Shanghai and from
there on to British Columbia.

Within a few years stories of Canada's wealth had spread to
the impoverished Sikh peasantry. Steamship companies began to
publicize the prospects of employment in Canada and the United

States. Their advertizing was done in Punjabi and was thus directed
mainly to the Sikhs. Some of the ships went to Canada along
the Californian coast. Several emigrants stayed on in California
and fair-sized colonies grew up in San Francisco and Sacramento.
There are no official records of the emigration, but from 1904
onwards, the Canadian authorities started to keep a check on the
number of Sikh emigrants entering British Columbia. From July
1904 to June 1905 there were only forty-five. For the rest of the
year the figure rose to 587. 1906 and 1907 were the peak years of
Indian emigration, the figures being 2,124 and 2,623, respectively.

Large numbers went to other parts of the American continent,
and it is estimated that by 1910 the total number of Indians in
the Americas ran into five figures. Most of the emigrants, being
unskilled, were employed in mines and sawmills and as farmhands
or pickers in the orchards. Many were employed in the construction
of the Canadian Pacific Railway. The most popular areas of
settlement remained British Columbia in Canada and California
in the United States. There were prosperous colonies of Indians at
Vancouver and San Francisco, where they built their temples.

This infiltration of cheap foreign labour had unfavourable
repercussions in the American labour organizations. The Indians
were not conscious of the conflict between the workers'
organizations and the employers. They went to work when trade
unions struck for higher wages and better conditions. In the years
1906 and 1907 America was in the throes of an economic crisis.
To cope with the situation the employers demanded longer hours
of work with lower wages. The only group of labourers who fell
into line with their demands were the Indians, to whom even
these terms were better than those obtainable at home. Relations
between them and other workers deteriorated. Indians became
unpopular as strike breakers and blacklegs. They were ostracized
from American labour groups and frequently beaten up. Some

were kidnapped and put in cars which deposited them several miles away from the cities where they lived. Assaults on Indians became an everyday occurrence in factory areas. In Vancouver there were organized anti-Indian riots.

An American newspaper described their plight in the following words: 'It is really a sight to see them wandering daily here, there and everywhere, half starved, half naked, hording in wretched hovels, ordered here, excluded there and despised everywhere.'

In 1906 the Canadian Legislature passed the Immigration Act to control the influx of Asiatics. The Act and the various orders-in-council which followed were applied indiscriminately to all Asiatics including Indians who were British subjects. In 1907 the British Columbia Legislature deprived Indians of the right to vote in provincial elections. In 1908 municipal franchise was also taken from them. (By the Dominion Election Act of 1920, Indians in British Columbia were deprived of Dominion franchise.) Emigration to Canada was thus brought to a standstill. Then, the Canadian Government sought ways and means to rid itself of those who had already settled in the country.

Mr Mackenzie King (later prime minister of Canada) went to England in 1908 to settle the Indian problem with the British Government. He had conferences with Lord Elgin, the colonial secretary, Lord Wurley, the Indian secretary, and Sir Edward Grey, the foreign secretary. The Canadian representative and the British spokesman were of one accord regarding the Indians. Mr King stated that there was in England 'a ready appreciation that Canada should desire to restrict immigration from the Orient as natural; that Canada should remain a white man's country is believed not only desirable for economic reasons, but highly necessary on political and national grounds'.

In 1908 an attempt was made to persuade the Sikhs to leave Canada and settle in the Honduras. They were told that besides being the land of opportunity, its warmer climate would suit them more than the Canadian. A party of three Indians was sent to visit the Honduras. They returned dissatisfied. The Honduras were full of malarial marshlands already inhabited by disillusioned emigrants. It was common knowledge that the representatives had been offered bribes to make a favourable report.

In India, the government put into effect the agreement arrived at between Mr Mackenzie King and the British ministers, so that immigration could be checked at the source. An Emigration Act was passed which enabled the government to frame rules in accordance with the wishes of the Canadian Government. Warnings about the 'risks' involved in going to Canada were issued. Steamship companies were told that any attempt on their part to convey Indians abroad would be viewed with disfavour by the Governments of Great Britain, Canada and India. All these rules were said to have been made 'to protect the natives of India' and 'for safeguarding the liberty of British subjects in India'.

The emigrants found themselves in a quandary. All the governments concerned had refused to help them. The Canadian and the American Governments not only passed race legislation, but also took no action against whites who participated in race riots. British embassies had closed their doors to British subjects because they were brown. The Indian Government disapproved of foreign contacts because they bred sedition. Emigrants who returned home were treated as suspect and kept under surveillance. With this sense of helplessness came the realization that amongst the vast conglomeration of peoples in the American continent, only they were subject to such humiliation. Other governments came to the help of their nationals when they were ill-treated. The Japanese were particularly touchy about their rights. Even the Chinese occasionally protested against maltreatment of their nationals. The only reason they had to suffer indignities in foreign lands was obviously because they had no government of their own.

This sense of national consciousness found some sympathizers in America. Russian Communists who had fled from tsarist persecution came in contact with the Indians. Hitherto, the Indians had believed that the foreigners' treatment of them was the outcome of colour prejudice which would disappear with time. From the Communists they learnt that it was a part of the capitalist exploitation of workers of different nationalities and that race prejudice was only another facet of class snobbery where the exploiter and exploited happened to be possessed of skins of different colour. These ideas were eagerly grasped by the Indians.

Another factor which helped them was the impending war between the Kaiser's Germany and Great Britain. German spies had been in contact with anti-British elements in the British Empire and had given them financial assistance. Indian groups in America were not overlooked.

The Ghadr Party

In March 1913 first steps towards organizing a revolutionary movement were taken. Invitations were sent to Indian labourers and farmers to attend a conference at Washington. Amongst the sponsors of this move were Sohan Singh of Bhakna, Wasakha Singh, Jowala Singh, Kartar Singh Saraba, Karam Singh Chima, and Hardayal. Nearly 200 delegates attended the Washington conference, and its outcome was the founding of an organization known as the Hindi Association.

The aims and objects of the association were contained in the many resolutions passed at the inaugural meeting. The main object was the liberation of India from British rule, if necessary by force of arms. The associates pledged themselves to work for a government in India based on the principles of liberty, equality and fraternity. San Francisco was chosen as the headquarters not only because of the large Indian community in California, but also because, as a port, it provided facilities for contacts with foreign revolutionaries. The first president of the association was Sohan Singh of Bhakna. Santokh Singh Dharde was elected secretary and Pandit Kanshi Ram, treasurer.

The association's endeavours aroused immediate response. Within the first six months its membership ran into many thousands. It opened branches in Japan, China, Fiji and the Malay States. Handsome donations were sent and many whole-time workers engaged. In the summer of 1913 three of its members came to India to put the grievances of Indian emigrants before the government. They met Sir Michael O'Dwyer, the governor of the Punjab, and Lord Hardinge, the viceroy. They returned to Canada in the autumn of the same year to report that the Government of India was not willing to help them.

In October 1913 the Hindi Association met a second time in Sacramento. The office-bearers were re-elected. A month later the association brought out the first issue of the Ghadr (mutiny) in Punjabi, Hindi, Urdu and Mahratti, with Hardayal as its editor. From then onwards the association came to be known as the Ghadr Party. In March 1914 Hardayal was arrested as an 'undesirable alien'. His comrades had him bailed out and sent him away from America at the cost of the bail bonds. After that, Hardayal disappeared from the scene of Ghadr activities.

Early in 1914 the international situation had deteriorated and clouds of war cast their shadow on the globe. The British began feverishly to put their house in order. Amongst the many hostile elements they had to cope with were the Ghadrites in America. British spies infiltrated into the organization in order to discover and disrupt its activities. A few months later came the *Komagata Maru* incident.

The Komagata Maru

Reference has already been made to the emigration laws passed by the Canadian Government to prevent Indians from entering Canada. Not satisfied with just preventing new settlers from India coming in, the government devised legislation to eject those who were already settled on Canadian soil. Two orders-in council were passed in 1908 and renewed in May 1910. One of these required that any applicant for admission had to have $200 in his possession on landing in Canada. The other laid down that all immigrants seeking entry must have come to Canada by continuous journey and on through tickets from the country of their birth or citizenship.

Steps were taken to prevent Indian emigrants from having access to the courts against the decisions of the Canadian Immigration Department. A new section (23) was introduced in the Immigration Act which read: 'No court, and no judge or officer thereof, shall have jursidiction to review, quash, reverse, restrain or otherwise interfere with any proceeding decision or order of the Minister or any Board of Inquiry, or officer in charge, had, made or given under the authority and in accordance with the provisions of this Act relating to the detention or deportation of any rejected immigrant, passenger or other person, upon any ground whatsoever, unless such person is a Canadian citizen or has Canadian domicile.'

The practical effect of this legislation was to stop not only new workers coming in, but also even the wives and children of those already in Canada from joining their husbands or parents. The Indians protested against these discriminatory laws. Petitions were sent to the Imperial Conference, where members of the British Commonwealth of Nations met in 'equal partnership'. A delegation consisting of three British Columbia Sikhs with a Canadian missionary, the Rev. C.W. Hall, waited on Prime Minister Borden. Mr Robert Rogers, the minister of the interior, interviewed the delegation and told them that his government had no objection to their wives and children coming, but they must come in accordance with the regulations, viz., with $200 and by continuous voyage from the country of their birth. These conditions could never be fulfilled by Indians who had no ships of their own. The Canadian press aptly described the Indian delegation being handed a 'gold brick'. Attempts were made to enlist popular support amongst the Canadians, and Dr Sundar Singh, who was the editor of an Indian journal in British Columbia, toured the eastern cities addressing public gatherings.

The Canadian Government and their Immigration Department did not budge from their position. In January 1912 two Sikhs of Vancouver brought their wives and children with them when they returned from India. The women and children were refused permission to enter by the immigration officer. In April, the Dominion Government, by an order-in council, ordered their deportation. They were arrested and sent on board the SS *Monteagle*, on which they had come, but a habeas corpus was obtained for them from the Supreme Court of British Columbia and they were released. The Indians petitioned the authorites and, after some days, the minister of the interior ordered the immigration officer to let the women and children remain 'as an act of grace'.

In October 1913, a party of forty-six Indians came to Vancouver on board the Japanese vessel *Panama Maru*. Thirty-nine of them were refused admission and ordered to be deported. An application for the issue of a writ of habeas corpus was dismissed by Justice Murphy on the ground that under Section 23 of the Act he had no jurisdiction to hear the application. A similar application was made to Chief Justice Hunter. He did not agree with Justice Murphy and held that he was not barred by Section 23 from hearing and deciding the matter. He also held that both the orders in-council passed in 1910 were ultra vires, as not strictly complying with the language of the section of the Immigration Act under which they purported to be made. He granted the writ, the applicants were released and were enabled to enter Canada.

This pronouncement of the head of the judiciary was, however, not of much consequence to the Canadian Government or its Immigration Department. While the petitions were in the courts, an Indian whose application for habeas corpus had been granted by Justice Morrison was forcibly deported. The orders of a judge of the Supreme Court of British Columbia conveyed by telegram by the court registrar were ignored by the immigration officer. The officer was never tried for contempt of court. The government also upset Chief Justice Hunter's ruling by another order-in-council more drastic than the first. It made it illegal for artisans or labourers, skilled or unskilled, to enter Canada at any port of entry in British Columbia.

The news of Chief Justice Hunter's decision reached India while that of the Canadian Government's new order-in-council did not. Many families left their homes in the Punjab to join their menfolk in Canada. Some were prudent enough to conform to the provisions of the orders-in-council as well.

Gurdit Singh of Sarhali, who was a prosperous contractor, chartered a Japanese steamer, the *Komagata Maru*, and renamed it the *Guru Nanak jahaz*. The provision regarding 'continuous journey and on through tickets from the country of their birth or citizenship' was thus satisfied. He only took on board passengers who could pay the requisite $200. On his way Gurdit Singh consulted a well-known English firm of solicitors in Hong Kong

and got in writing that his act was constitutional both by English
and Canadian laws.

There were 165 passengers in the *Komagata Maru* when it left
Hong Kong. Another 111 were picked up in Shanghai, 96 in Kobe
and 14 in Yokohama, making a total of 386. All except 30 of the
passengers were Sikhs. On 21 May 1914, the boat reached Victoria
and anchored in the Burrard inlet off Vancouver harbour. Only
the Japanese captain, Gurdit Singh, his secretary, and a British
agent, Dr Raghunath, were allowed to land. No local Indians were
permitted to go on board to meet their relatives. The *Komagata
Maru* was cordoned off by patrol boats.

The passengers satisfied all the conditions on the statute book
of the British Columbia Legislature. But means were devised to
keep them out. At first the medical officer of the Immigration
Department pronounced ninety of the passengers to be medically
unfit. All the passengers had been examined and certified healthy
before being taken on board.

Gurdit Singh demanded permission for his passengers to land,
and put his case to a lawyer. Mr Bird, the attorney, was on strong
legal ground with the ruling of the chief justice behind him. He
could move for a writ of habeas corpus. From a writ granted there
was no appeal. From a writ refused, he could still apply to the
other judges, and failing that, go to the court of appeal. But, for
reasons best known to himself, he agreed with the Immigration
Department to allow his habeas corpus petition to be dismissed
by the Supreme Court without argument and then to move the
court of appeal. Gurdit Singh was indignant and described the
move as 'stupid'. But Mr Bird went ahead. An application was put
in as a test case, and allowed to be dismissed by the Supreme Court.
It was then taken up in appeal. The court of appeal pronounced
judgment on 6 July 1914. Section 23 was held to be valid. The
Immigration Department won.

While legal battles were being fought, the *Komagata Maru* passengers waited patiently. They ran out of food and fresh water. Men, women and children starved. The Immigration Department minimized the rumours about the state of suffering by spreading stories about nocturnal feasts aboard the ship. But the truth came to be known. While the Canadian press found the plight of the passengers of the *Komagata Maru* a good subject for humour, Indians in Vancouver decided to help their compatriots. The police were, however, too smart for them. Three members of the local Komagata Maru Committee were arrested with revolvers and ammunition.

On the night of Saturday, 18 July 1914, 120 Canadian policemen, with forty special immigration officers, led by the police chief and four police inspectors attempted to take possession of the ship. They were accompanied by Mr H.H. Stevens, Member of Parliament for Vancouver. The police were beaten back by unarmed, semi-starved Sikhs. The showdown of 18 July, described by the Vancouver papers as 'the battle of Burrard Inlet', brought the wrath of the Dominion Government on the hapless Sikhs. On the night of 20 July a 3,600-ton cruiser, the *Rainbow*, slipped quietly into Vancouver harbour and anchored alongside the *Komagata Maru*. Next morning the passengers in the vessel woke up to find the *Rainbow*'s two 6-inch and six 4-inch guns trained on them.

The plight of their countrymen inflamed the minds of Indians all over the world. In America Indian labourers and farm hands left their work and came to Vancouver. Within a few days several thousands had assembled in the city. News went round that if the *Komagata Maru* did not return to India immediately, the Canadian warship would fire on her. In the evening the Sikhs assembled in the gurdwara at Vancouver and took a solemn vow that if the ship were fired upon they would burn the city of Vancouver.

The *Komagata Maru* was not fired upon. But none of the passengers was allowed to land. On 23 July (after having been two months in Canadian waters), the ship left Vancouver on its homeward voyage. But its trials were not over. On reaching Yokohama, Gurdit Singh received a letter from the government at Hong Kong informing him that it was considered 'inadvisable' that any of the passengers should be landed there. They threatened to enforce a local vagrancy ordinance against any who might attempt to do so. No exception was made as regards former residents of Hong Kong who wanted to return to their earlier occupations. The British consul at Yokohama refused to supply additional provisions for passengers who were not travelling to India and the ship had to wait in Kobe harbour for supplies. Finally, on 3 September it left Kobe and reached Singapore on 25 September. Again no passengers were allowed to land, and people like Gurdit Singh himself, who had a flourishing business at Singapore, were compelled to go to India.

On 27 September the *Komagata Maru* reached Calcutta and was piloted to Budge Budge harbour, 14 miles away, to disembark its disillusioned cargo. Since war had recently been declared, the authorities were armed with additional powers. On 5 September 1914 an Ingress Ordinance had been passed to enable the movements of immigrants to be controlled. All the passengers on board the ship were subjected to a vigorous search, but no arms were found on their persons. They were then served with a notice forbidding them to proceed to Calcutta and were ordered into waiting trains that would take them straight to their villages in the Punjab. The few Muslims who were on board agreed to obey the order; the Sikhs refused. They had left their houses with all their possessions in the hope of earning a livelihood abroad. They could not return as paupers to villages where some had even sold their homes. They wanted to look for employment in

Calcutta or some other big city. The Sikhs formed themselves into a procession and, with the Granth Sahib in their midst, proceeded towards Calcutta singing hymns. The procession was forced back to the railway station by the police. A scuffle ensued and the police opened fire. Twenty-one Sikhs and two sightseers were killed. Most of the others were handcuffed and put in trains bound for the Punjab. On the way about thirty of them, including Gurdit Singh, overpowered the police guard and escaped. (Gurdit Singh foiled the Punjab police for seven years and then surrendered voluntarily in November 1921.)

A fortnight after the shooting at Budge Budge, another Japanese steamer, the *Tasu Maru*, docked at Calcutta carrying 173 Indian passengers, including some leaders of the Ghadr movement, notably the founder president, Sohan Singh of Bhakna. They were immediately arrested and sent to the Punjab. News of the treatment meted out by the Indian Government to the passengers of the *Komagata Maru* and the *Tasu Maru* spread in the countries along the Pacific coast. The Ghadr Party called for action. Many hundred emigrants decided to return to India, and Indian ports were besieged with those returning. On disembarkation they were faced with the Ingress Ordinance. The leaders were put in prison; the rank and file were restricted to their villages. Almost everyone was put under strict police surveillance. The numbers so dealt with were believed to be around 8,000. (The membership of the party was then over 10,000.)

Despite the measures taken by the government several members of the party escaped police vigilance and organized an underground movement to put their plans into action. Some ground had already been prepared by the activities of Lala Lajpat Rai (the Congress leader) and Ajit Singh. On the arrival of the Ghadrites, Rash Bihari of Bengal and Vishnu Pingley from Poona joined Parmanand (later on Bhai Parma Nand, the Hindu

Mahasabha leader) to co-ordinate their revolutionary activity in the Punjab. Indian troops were contacted and some persuaded to mutiny. Arsenals were attacked, bridges blown up, and lines of communication destroyed. But the major rising planned by the revolutionaries for 21 February 1915 went off badly. There were too many spies in their midst. Two days before zero hour, soldiers who had agreed to mutiny were arrested. Then followed several months of head-hunting in the Punjab. Ghadrites were tracked down relentlessly and the would-be mutineers court-martialled and shot. In a report dated 28 February, the Punjab Government described the revolutionaries as 'ignorant Sikh peasants who have been indoctrinated with crude ideas of equality and democracy in America and led to believe by Hardyal and his co-workers that India can be made into an Utopia'.

By March 1915, the Punjab Government assured itself that the Ghadr headache was over and they had all the men behind bars. But it could not risk an ordinary criminal trial for these revolutionaries. Sir Michael O'Dwyer, the governor, reported: 'It is not desirable at the present time to allow trials of these revolutionaries or of other sedition-mongers to be protracted by the ingenuity of counsel and drawn out to inordinate lengths by committal and appeal procedures which the criminal law provides.' He submitted the draft of an ordinance for speeding up procedure in cases by providing for the trial of offenders directly after police investigation had established a prima facie case. This trial was to be before a tribunal of three judges. There was to be no further appeal. Sir Michael O'Dwyer himself admitted that the methods proposed were exceptional. In April, a special tribunal of two English judges and one Indian judge was constituted to try the revolutionaries. Nine batches of conspirators were tried by special tribunals constituted under the Defence of India Act. In one of them, sixty-five men were charged with sedition, treason and waging war against the king. This was the First Lahore Conspiracy Case. Seven of the accused turned approvers.

Conspiracy Cases

The trial lasted nearly six months. The prosecution was represented by one of the ablest lawyers of the time, Bevan Petman, with many assistants. The conspirators were defended by nondescript junior counsel chosen by the government. The accused themselves acted as if they had no interest in the trial, and had to be frequently pulled up for interrupting the proceedings by singing and laughter.

On 15 September 1915 the revolutionaries were lined up in a barrack in the Lahore Central Jail to hear their sentences. Twenty-four were sentenced to death and confiscation of property; twenty-six to transportation for life; ten to various terms of imprisonment; five were acquitted (but rearrested immediately). The law provided an appeal for clemency but only one of the twenty-four condemned men (a non-Sikh) pleaded for mercy. The viceroy himself commuted the sentence of all but seven to that of transportation to the Cellular Jail in the Andamans. On 19 November 1915, seven men were executed. Amongst them were Kartar Singh Saraba, Bakhshish Singh and Pandit Kanshi Ram. Others, including Sohan Singh of Bhakna, Prithvi Singh Azad, Bhai Parma Nand, Pandit Jagat Ram, Baba Wasakha Singh, Gurmukh Singh, Baba Nidhan Singh and Harnam Singh of Tundilat, were sent to the Andamans.

The Ghadr Party's activities did not stop with the First Lahore Conspiracy Case. Stray instances of terrorism continued throughout the year 1915. Ghadrites were rounded up in small batches and tried in several conspiracy cases, such as the Second Lahore Conspiracy Case, the Mandi State Conspiracy Case, the Rawalpindi Bomb Case, but, by the end of the year, the authorities had complete control of the situation. A new method was devised to apprehend the conspirators. District committees of loyal Sikhs were appointed 'to enquire into the conduct and reputation of returned emigrants and their supporters and to advise the Deputy Commissioners as to the action to be taken under the Ingress Ordinance or the ordinary law'. Supporters of the government readily came forward with assurances of loyalty. Mahants of important shrines joined hands with the loyalists in excommunicating the revolutionaries as renegades from their faith. A government report acknowledged its gratitude to the 'committee of Sikh gentlemen who at the cost of much personal trouble and risk rendered loyal and valuable service in catching and controlling the movements of thousands of returned emigrants dispersed throughout the districts'. The government parted with 4,000 acres of land, Rs 29,000 in cash rewards and Rs 10,000 in remission of land revenue to pay for these services.

On the Indian scene this small-scale rebellion receded into the background due to the outbreak of serious communal riots in south-western Punjab in the districts of Jhang, Multan and Muzaffargarh. This diverted the focus of attention from the Ghadr Party and the Ghadr revolution faded into the realms of history.

In America and Canada, however, the torch of rebellion smouldered for some time. The British asked the United States Government to take action. In August 1917 the United States police rounded up the leaders of the revolutionary party and charged them with conspiring 'to set on foot a military enterprise to be carried on against India within the United States, the object of the enterprise being to incite mutiny and armed rebellion in India to obstruct Great Britain in the prosecution of the war against Germany'. All the arrested men were convicted. The trial ended on a melodramatic note. One Ram Chandra, a British spy, who had posed as a revolutionary, was shot in open court by Ram

Singh. Ram Singh himself fell to a hail of a police constable's bullets.

Soon after the departure of the *Komagata Maru* the Canadian Government engaged Hopkinson, an Anglo Indian police officer who had seen many years of service in India, to look into the Sikh organization in British Columbia. He succeeded in bribing one Bela Singh and two of his friends to report on their compatriots' activities. Bela Singh's friends were murdered. At the funeral service of the murdered men, Bela Singh ran amok and shot four Sikhs in the Vancouver temple. These men were known to be connected with the local Ghadr Party. Hopkinson turned up on the scene when the shooting was taking place (in the Vancouver temple several miles from his office). Bela Singh was tried for the murders. He pleaded that he had acted in self defence. Hopkinson was his only witness. When he came to give evidence, Mewa Singh – hitherto a quiet man of retiring habits – shot him dead in the court corridor. Feelings in Vancouver ran high, and the Indians had to barricade themselves in their homes for several days. Mewa Singh confessed to his crime, and said: 'I know I have shot Hopkinson and I will have to die. But it is for the others ... In Vancouver there are a few men who are Christian. Others have treated us like dogs ... I have given myself to stop this wrong.' On 14 October 1913 he was hanged. (Bela Singh was sent home at government expense. Several years later he was murdered in his village in the Punjab.)

The Ghadr Party's career of violence was stopped by the police in India, Canada and the United States. In India, Ghadrites who were not already in jail joined with the Akalis in their campaign to recover possession of their shrines. In Canada and the United States, their activities came to be restricted to supplying funds to co-workers in India. A Gurmukhi edition of the *Ghadr* continued to be issued from the head office at San Francisco.

By the time the Akali agitation was over, thousands of members of the old Ghadr Party had returned to their homes in the Punjab. They banded themselves into a separate political organization, which came to be known as the 'Babas'. (Some leaders of the Ghadr Party like Sohan Singh, Kesar Singh and Wasakha Singh were held in great esteem and addressed with the title 'Baba'— elder.) When the Akalis split into the Nationalists and the Akalis, the Baba group joined the Nationalists. Within the Nationalist parties, the Babas aligned themselves with the extreme left, and with the expulsion of the Communists from the Congress, they formed the Communist Party in the Punjab.

During the Second World War, the Communist Party of the Punjab was perhaps the most active provincial group in India. It was almost entirely Sikh – only a handful of Hindu and Muslim intellectuals were associated with its publicity and trade union sections.

Chapter 10

POLITICAL GROUPS

In the previous chapters we had occasion to refer to the historical background of the more important political movements and the antecedents of some of the men associated with them. In this chapter, we will endeavour to explain the pattern of Sikh politics as it existed before and during the Second World War. This will explain the attitude of the different parties towards the issue of the partition of the Punjab, which took place in 1947. A word of warning is necessary. Political alliances and fronts change rapidly – particularly when they are founded on personal considerations. This was largely true of the Sikh pattern. What is said in this chapter should not be taken as a guide for later developments.

There were many political groups influencing Sikh affairs at this time. In chronological order, they were the Princes, the Chief Khalsa Diwan, the Central Akali Dal, the Sikh Congressites, the Akalis and the Communists. Of these six, the influence of the Princes cannot be described as strictly political. They exerted their power through their coffers, and that followed the dictates of the Political Department under British rule and of the States Ministry after Independence. Of the remaining five groups mentioned, the

Chief Khalsa Diwan and the Central Akali Dal exerted only a very nominal influence amongst a following which was old and fast disappearing. There were only three political parties that were vital forces in Sikh politics. In order of importance, they were the Akalis, the Sikh Congressites and the Communists. We shall deal with them in more detail than the others.

The Princes

There were six Sikh states. In order of importance they were Patiala, Nabha, Jind, Faridkot, Kapurthala and Kalsia. Under British rule the external affairs of these states were controlled by the Political Department acting through a resident. After 1947 all these Sikh states along with Malerkotla, which was Muslim, and Nalagarh, which was Hindu, were grouped into one with the title Patiala and East Punjab States Union (PEPSU). Patiala was made president (*rajpramukh*) and Kapurthala vice-president (*uprajpramukh*) of the union. Patiala, Nabha and Jind traced their descent from a common Jat ancestor. Their relations with each other were more intimate than with the others.

Nalagarh, though a Hindu, was related by marriage to Patiala. The house of Kapurthala was not Jat, and only nominally Sikh. For almost half a century its heads evinced no interest in Sikh affairs. Kalsia was too small in size and income to be of much consequence.

The Princes had always exercised considerable influence on Sikh affairs. Their patronage was never limited to their domains. Their financial assistance to various gurdwaras and educational institutions in British India gave them a voice which was frequently decisive. There were, however, factors which checked their ability to dabble in Sikh affairs. First, the Political Department (and later the States Ministry) kept a vigilant eye on the internal affairs of the Princes and dictated their external policy. The more important posts in state services had to be approved by the Government of India and an ambitious ruler would frequently find his state saddled with ministers and heads of departments owing more allegiance to the Central Government than to himself. Besides, few, if any, of the Princes were trained to take part in civic life. All their English tutors succeeded in producing were semi-literate playboys who fell easy victims to the pampering and flattery current in Oriental courts. Despite these handicaps, some of the younger Sikh Princes were able to break with the corrupt tradition and catch up with the times. The ruler of Patiala played a prominent part in the political parleys that took place prior to the transfer of power. The raja of Faridkot had been involved in Sikh affairs from his teens and contributed generously to many institutions. His interest in the Sikh refugees who fled from Pakistan early in 1947 did much to ameliorate their plight. The young maharaja of Nabha likewise supported a large number of institutions and interested himself in community affairs.

In 1947 the States Ministry tried to set up a sort of popular government in the Patiala Union as a prelude to an elected government. The immediate effect was to do away with the influence of the Princes who were not members of the union and increase that of the president, the ruler of Patiala. He became the most important individual Sikh in the country.

The Chief Khalsa Diwan

The achievements of the Singh Sabha movement in the realm of literature and educational reform have already been mentioned. The Chief Khalsa Diwan was the political offshoot of the Singh Sabha. It was able to cash in on the popularity of the Singh Sabha amongst the Sikh middle classes at a time (1890–1914) when no other organized political party was in existence. It was successful in monopolizing the entire field of Sikh political activity when semi-democratic institutions were beginning to be introduced on a franchise that was favourable to the propertied middle class.

The Chief Khalsa Diwan was actively associated with the movement of separation from the Hindus, which, in political terminology, meant separate rights and reservation of seats in political councils and of posts in services. Since careers, both in services and politics, were a matter primarily touching the upper middle classes, its political programme was directed towards the preservation of the vested interests of the upper bourgeoisie. Its leaders, with certain exceptions, came from the landed aristocracy and the Sikh Princes had an important voice in its deliberations. Its relations with the British Government had therefore, of necessity, to be those of unquestioning loyalty. The Chief Khalsa Diwan made very little impression on the Sikh masses. As soon as political consciousness seeped down into these elements of society, the diwan gave way to organizations representative of their interests.

For about a quarter of a century preceding the First World War, the Sikhs were represented by just one political party, the Chief Khalsa Diwan. Its most outstanding political figure was Sir Sundar Singh Majithia. He was a minister in the Punjab Government for many years till his death in 1940. Majithia worked in close collaboration with other leaders of the Singh Sabha movement who were engaged in literary pursuits or educational activity. This close association of politicians and reformers saved the political aspect of the Chief Khalsa Diwan from discredit for a long time. What the politicians lost, the writers and reformers made up for. This lasted till the upheavals fermented by the Ghadrites and the Akalis forced the Sikhs to break the tradition of loyalty to the British Government.

After 1926, the Akalis along with the Nationalists practically monopolized Sikh politics. In the legislature, a few independently elected Sikhs joined the Chief Khalsa Diwan's legislative party known as the Khalsa Nationalist Party. It had no political programme apart from opposition to the Akali party. The leader of the Khalsa Nationalists was Sundar Singh Majithia. His most active assistant in the legislature was Ujjal Singh.

With the death of Sundar Singh Majithia, the political influence of the Chief Khalsa Diwan came to an end. An attempt was made to find a new leader in the person of his son, Kirpal Singh, a business magnate living in the United Provinces. Kirpal Singh's brief political career had an unfortunate start. He was beaten by the Akalis in the by-election caused by his father's death. Undeterred by the initial setback, he assumed leadership of the anti-Akali elements and successfully repulsed Akali attempts to oust Chief Khalsa Diwan control of the Khalsa College at Amritsar.

On Kirpal Singh's death, his younger brother, Surjeet Singh Majithia, resigned from his post in the Royal Air Force to step into his place. He was automatically elected to the control of all the institutions managed by the Chief Khalsa Diwan and, in 1946, was elected to the Central Assembly at Delhi. But he realized that the day of the diwan had long been past. He joined the Indian National Congress. Ujjal Singh, the only other individual who was connected with the diwan, went over to the Akalis on the eve of the election in 1946.

It could be said that by 1947 the Chief Khalsa Diwan was represented by some persons and institutions but no politics. Its leading figures were Bhai Vir Singh (a poet), Trilochan Singh (a banker) and Jodh Singh (principal of Khalsa College, Amritsar). Amongst the several institutions it controlled was Khalsa College.

The Central Akali Dal

The movement for the liberation of the gurdwaras (1919–26) was generally described as the Akali movement. It was conducted

under the leadership of Kharak Singh and all the volunteers who
joined in the passive resistance were described as Akalis. When the
gurdwaras were handed over to the Sikhs by the Gurdwara Act of
1925, the Akalis were divided into three groups. One group was led
by Kharak Singh (who was later joined by Mahtab Singh), another
by Master Tara Singh, and the third consisted of Congressite Sikhs.
(The causes which led to this division have been noted in Chapter
8.) They were, briefly, regarding the attitude to the government's
Sikh Gurdwara Bills and to the Indian National Congress. At the
time when the tripartite division in the Akali ranks took place,
the causes of the rift seemed to be of a temporary nature and of
little consequence. But with the establishment of the Shiromani
Gurdwara Parbandhak Committee, there was an economic stake
introduced, which perpetuated factionalism. The SGPC was put
in control of the finances and management of several hundred
gurdwaras. The power and patronage of the SGPC became the
prize for the contending groups. Kharak Singh's party was the first
to seize the SGPC and Master Tara Singh's party went into the
opposition.

Kharak Singh had a very short run as president of the SGPC.
He was succeeded by Master Tara Singh's party, which became the
official Akali Party. Kharak Singh's followers had to coin a new
name for themselves – the Central Akali Dal.

Despite Master Tara Singh's control of the SGPC, Kharak Singh's
party remained more popular for several years. This was because of
the prestige he had personally gained in Sikh eyes through many
years of courageous and relentless struggle in a great cause. But
Kharak Singh was temperamentally unsuited to lead a political
party or run an organization like the SGPC. He was a 'fighter'. He
had none of the tact and spirit of compromise essential for success
in politics. Petty disagreements were to him matters of principle
for which he defied law and courted imprisonment. Gradually,
his followers fell away and joined other parties. By 1947, he was

almost alone, a venerable hoary figure bent with age and suffering, but full of fire and fight, whom all Sikhs respected, many exploited, and but a few followed.

The Chief Khalsa Diwan was supported by two well-known journalists. Amar Singh (*d.* 1949), a veteran of the Akali movement, was the editor of the Urdu weekly *Sher-i-Punjab*, published from Lahore. He was held in some esteem as a writer and speaker, but his politics mattered very little. Labh Singh Narang, a younger man, wielded some influence through three journals which he owned, *Fateh*, *Pritam* and *Maya*. Other well-known supporters of the party were Bachittar Singh and Harbans Singh Sistani.

The Central Akali Dal had no political programme of its own. About the only constant feature of its political reactions was its anti-Akali attitude. Since the major group opposing the Akalis were the Congressites, the Akali Dal's endeavours frequently merged with the Congress. On the issue of Pakistan, this party was opposed both to the establishment of a Muslim state and the partition of the province.

The Akalis

Lieutenant-Colonel C.B. Birdwood wrote in 1945 in his book *A Continent Experiments* that 'modern Sikh political history is centred round the Akali party'. This was not an overstatement. The strength of the Akali party could be judged from the fact that, in 1946, four of the five Sikh members of the Constituent Assembly were Akalis: Baldev Singh, defence minister in Jawaharlal Nehru's Interim Government was an Akali; twenty out of thirty-three Sikh seats in the Punjab Legislative Assembly prior to partition were held by the Akali Party and the only Sikh minister in the Provincial Government was their nominee; of the 168 members of the SGPC, 140 were Akalis. The proportion of Akali to non-

Akali representatives was the same in other elected bodies like municipalities and district boards.

Akali monopoly of Sikh politics was due to the combination of several factors, of which the political acumen of the Akali leaders was only one. The Chief Khalsa Diwan, the predecessor of the Akali Party, had become practically extinct when the Akali movement began. The Sikhs were a community of small land holders and petty traders. The Akali movement was in some ways a bourgeois revolution by which effective political power passed from the landed aristocracy (backing the Chief Khalsa Diwan) to the middle class (backing the Akalis). It resulted in a change from feudal to a small–scale capitalist control.

The success of the Akali subgroup of Master Tara Singh in excluding its other Akali and Congressite rivals came through the initial control of the SGPC. Gurdwara fortunes running into seven figures per month were placed at their disposal. Thousands of posts – of priests, missionaries, managers and servants – were filled with judicious care, and influential men were given a stake in the future of the group which employed them. Along with these factors came the disruption of the rival parties. The Chief Khalsa Diwan had already become synonymous with toadying. Its chief spokesman, Sundar Singh Majithia, brought more unpopularity on it by his autocratic and uncertain temper. The Central Akali Dal floundered because of lack of leadership. Kharak Singh remained in jail most of the time and Mahtab Singh retired from political life to resume a lucrative practice at the Bar. The Congressite Sikhs got involved in national affairs and ignored gurdwara politics. The Communists, when they emerged as an independent party, kept aloof from religious matters. Akalis stayed in power because no other party tried to capture the gurdwaras from them and the gurdwaras gave them their strength and sustenance.

The Akali caucus consisted of about a dozen men led by Master Tara Singh. The party was divided into factions constantly angling for power in the party. One was led by Gyani Kartar Singh and the other by Isher Singh Majhail and Udham Singh Nagoke. The former was more powerful, the latter more numerous. Master Tara Singh himself belonged to neither, and keeping peace between them was a whole-time job for him. There were other Akalis who found it in their interest to keep neutral. We shall refer to these three groups as the Gyani group, the Majhail–Nagoke group and neutrals.

Neutrals

Master Tara Singh *(b.* 1885) was a Hindu (Malhotra) converted to Sikhism. He graduated from the Khalsa College, Amritsar, in 1907 and became a teacher in the Khalsa school at Lyallpur. The title 'Master' was attached to him at that time. He was one of the founders of the Akali Party. He was first arrested in 1921, and was imprisoned several times in connection with the Akali and Congress civil disobedience movements. From the time he became president of the SGPC, he was the most influential Sikh leader in India. His record in the service of his community was an enviable one and completely free from allegations in money matters. Despite his quick temper and unwillingness to compromise on small issues, he was always held in great respect both by his colleagues and adversaries.

Baldev Singh, defence minister in the Government of India, was the son of a wealthy steel magnate, Sir Inder Singh. He was an Akali backbencher during Sundar Singh Majithia's regime. Soon after Majithia's death, he became the leader of the Akali Party in the Punjab Legislative Assembly, and following an agreement between the Akalis and Sir Sikander Hayat Khan (then premier of the Punjab) replaced Dasaundha Singh (Majithia's successor) as a minister in the Punjab Government. He remained a minister until his nomination as defence minister in the Central Government.

Ujjal Singh was once a prosperous landowner in western Punjab. He lost most of his wealth as a result of partition. He started dabbling in politics during the Akali movement and later identified himself alternately with the Chief Khalsa Diwan and the Central Akali Dal.

He went to the Round Table Conferences held in London as a representative of the Sikh community. He was regarded as Sundar Singh Majithia's successor in the Punjab Cabinet, but was passed over as he was not a Jat by descent. After many years of opposition to the Akali Party, he joined it on the eve of the election in 1946. For a brief period he was minister in East Punjab. Ujjal Singh had the reputation of being the ablest Sikh parliamentarian, but his change of parties damaged his political career.

The Gyani Group

Gyani Kartar Singh was the most talked-of man in Sikh politics. By his admirers he was regarded as the brain behind the Akali Party, by his adversaries, its evil genius. Within the Akali group, he was the most cunning intriguer, and without it, its most constructive thinker. He had none of the fiery confusion of thought so prevalent amongst Sikh politicians. He had no political prejudices and was the leader of the group, always willing to come to terms with the Muslim League. He was the chief sponsor of the demand for an independent Sikh state as an answer to the Muslim demand for Pakistan.

The strength of Gyani's following in the Akali Party was probably less than that of his rival, Isher Singh Majhail. His predominance over the party despite numerical inferiority was due to the general recognition of his ability and support of the neutrals. His active assistants in interparty matters were Mangal

Singh, MLA (Central), Harcharan Singh Bajwa, and Hukam Singh, advocate of Montgomery.

The Majhail–Nagoke Group

This group consisted of a large number of semi-literate Akalis displeased with the Gyani group's monopoly of party affairs. It had the support of the rank and file who took part in the Akali passive resistance and vaguely expected to be compensated for it. They had no differences with the Gyani group on matters of principle. Leading figures of the party were Isher Singh Majhail, MLA (Punjab) and later minister in the East Punjab Government, Jathedar Udham Singh Nagoke, later president of the SGPC, Sohan Singh, Jalal Osman, Channan Singh Urara, Teja Singh Akarpuri and Babu Labh Singh.

The Gyani-Majhail friction had been usually restricted to gurdwara affairs with occasional repercussions in other communal matters. Master Tara Singh, who had been able to keep them from drifting apart, ceased to have much influence over this group after partition. Nagoke became president of the SGPC, with Master Tara Singh in the opposition.

The Sikh Congressites

Next to the Akalis, the Congress wielded the largest influence on the Sikh community. Their strength was probably more than could be estimated from the number of seats they held in elected bodies. Electioneering being as much a matter of organization and money as popularity, the issue was usually decided in favour of the Akalis, who had the gurdwara funds and organization at their disposal. The Sikh Congressites, on the other hand, had little money and

were at the mercy of the Punjab Provincial Congress Committee
and its bankrupt leadership. They continued to be spoon-fed by
non–Sikh leaders who were little concerned with their communal
problems. The policy of laissez faire in gurdwara affairs allowed the
Akalis to keep a hold of the Sikh electorate in religious as well as
secular affairs.

Sikh Congressmen never formed a separate communal group.
Some belonged also to the Congress Socialist Party or the Forward
Bloc. Others belonged to the orthodox Congress but divided their
loyalties to rival groups in the Provincial Congress Committee.
Sardul Singh Caveeshar was the leader of the All–India Forward
Bloc; Mota Singh was a Congress Socialist; Pratap Singh Kairon,
MLA (Member of the Congress Executive Committee and
later minister in the East Punjab Government), Kapur Singh,
MLA (Punjab), Gurmukh Singh Musafir (later president of the
Provincial Congress Committee), Darshan Singh Pheruman,
Surjeet Singh Majithia, MLA (Central), and several lesser lights
were just Congressites.

Notable additions to the Congress ranks immediately after the
Second World War were leaders of the Japanese-sponsored Indian
National Army, 'General' Mohan Singh, 'Colonel' Niranjan Singh
Gill and 'Captain' Gurbaksh Singh Dhillon. 'General' Mohan Singh,
for reasons of health and temperament, kept out of Sikh politics.
Dhillon failed to make an impression as he had removed his hair
and beard. He made an attempt to grow his beard and enter Sikh
politics, but within a few months gave up both. 'Colonel' Gill was
the only one of the Indian National Army who took advantage
of the popularity of the Azad Hind Government. His release from
prison early in 1946 coincided with the impending elections to
the Punjab Assembly. The Akalis, who had serious misgivings
regarding the strength of the Congress and the Communists,
seized upon Gill. A Panthic unity board was formed with Gill

as president. Congressite Sikhs joined the board with the Akalis. For themselves, the Akalis tided over a crisis arising out of the Gyani Majhail conflict by importing an unknown neutral. They also persuaded the Congressites to form a united front against the Communists. They won a majority of seats in the Central and Punjab Assemblies and swept the board in the gurdwara elections in the name of communal unity. When all that was achieved, 'Colonel' Gill was unceremoniously dismissed. Gill explained his 'resignation' in conventional phraseology as being due to 'reasons of health'. He 'retired' to active work with Mahatma Gandhi.

The Communists

An overwhelming majority of the Communist Party in pre-partition Punjab were Sikhs. The reason for this was chiefly historical. The members of the Ghadr Party who came from America were mostly Sikhs. Their travels and foreign contacts gave them an international outlook which neither the parochial Akali nor the narrow Nationalist could either appreciate or understand. As long as the Congress was struggling against British rule, the Akalis, Nationalists and the 'internationalist' Ghadrites worked together. The sufferings and sacrifices of the Sikh émigrés from America gave them enormous prestige with the masses. Hundreds of them were hanged or shot in the rebellion. Their properties were confiscated and thousands spent the best of their lives in jails. These Ghadrites, popularly known as the Babas, were the founders of the Communist Party in the Punjab. When the Congress made headway, differences between its many constituents became manifest. The final break came in 1942 when the Congress under the inspiration of Mahatma Gandhi launched the 'Quit India' Movement. The Communist Party of India supported the war against the Fascist powers as a people's war and looked upon the

Congress attitude as sabotage. In pursuance of that policy, the
Punjab Communists broke away from the Congressites and Akalis.

On the termination of the war, the Congress came down
on the Communists as 'traitors'. The Congress attitude was
not really determined by the Communist support of the war
because several other parties, e.g., the Akalis, who also actively
sponsored recruitment to the army, were not dubbed as traitors.
The Communists supported the Muslim League demand for an
independent Muslim state (not the same as Pakistan) which the
Congress condemned. The Congress desired to crush the pro-
League non-Muslims and utilized all the means it could muster.
The 1942 movement was glorified as a fight for liberty and those
who kept aloof were decried as quislings. The Indian National
Army, which the Congress leaders had themselves at one time
condemned as Japanese sponsored, was acclaimed as an army of
liberation. With these weapons, Communists, who had spent their
lives working in the Congress and had made the name of the
Congress great, were temporarily squashed.

In the Punjab, Congress disparagement of the Communists
helped the Akalis to power. All over the province the peasants,
who had looked upon the Communists as just Congressites with a
socialist bias, were told that they were really godless traitors. In the
1946 elections not one Communist was returned to the Punjab
Legislative Assembly. It was an Akali triumph with the aid of a
Congress truncheon.

The Communists suffered further setbacks with the partition
and the communal massacres which took place in the winter of
1947–48. Communal hatred overwhelmed all reason. The Akalis
took an active part in the killings – the Congressmen just looked on
passively and even excused them as 'retaliation'. The Communists
who tried to hold out against the wave of hatred were submerged

in the tide. Their support of the Muslim League made them special targets of the anti-Muslim elements.

A peculiar feature of the Punjab Communists was that they were mainly recruited from the small peasant proprietors rather than the landless tenant. The reason again was that the Ghadrites who formed the nucleus of the party were small land-holders and their following remained largely their own class.

The central districts of pre-partition Punjab were Communist strongholds. Their leaders consisted mainly of the Babas, most of whom were in their eighties. Babas Jawala Singh, Wasakha Singh, Rur Singh, Midhan Singh and Sohan Singh Bhakna were old revolutionaries. The younger Communists were divided into two groups of *kirti* (labour) and *kisan* (peasant). The two together were led by Sohan Singh Josh, MLA (Punjab), one of the members of the famous Meerut Conspiracy, the first large-scale trial of the Communists in India. The two groups functioned together under the guidance of the Communist Party of India. They had their own weekly organ, the *Jang-i-Azad*, which was printed in Gurmukhi.

After 1946, the Punjab Communist Party disintegrated like the Central Party itself. Josh's chief rival, Teja Singh Swatantra, MLA (Punjab), was suspended on charges of corruption. He decided to form a rival party in the province. Internal rivalries went underground, as did the party itself when the Congress Government imprisoned most of the leaders, including the nonagenarian Sohan Singh Bhakna.

Chapter 11

PARTITION HOLOCAUST AND THE EXODUS

On 23 March 1940 the Muslim League at its annual session at Lahore passed a resolution demanding 'such territorial readjustment that areas in which the Muslims were numerically in a majority, as in the north-western and eastern zones of India, should be grouped to constitute Independent States, in which the constituent units would be autonomous and sovereign'. This came to be known as the Lahore resolution for Pakistan. The provinces concerned were the North-west Frontier Province, Punjab, Sindh and Baluchistan at one end, and Bengal at the other.

The demand for a separate Muslim state was not new. Almost from the time of the introduction of semi-democratic institutions in India, the Muslim middle class had felt that its rights could only be safeguarded in a state purely Muslim and free from domination by a Hindu majority. A line of prominent Muslim leaders had voiced this opinion, starting with Sir Syed Ahmed Khan, the poet Sir Mohammed Iqbal, Sir Sikander Hayat Khan and finally M.A. Jinnah. As more and more power began to pass from British to Indian hands, the demand gathered momentum. This was neither unexpected nor unreasonable. The Indian national movement had, in many ways, been mixed up with a renaissance of Hinduism. At no time did many Muslims join it. Even when they co-operated with the non-co-operation movements, as during the Khilafat agitation of the 1920s, there was no identity of purpose. The Nationalists wanted Britain out of their homeland. The Khilafatists only protested against the treatment given to the Caliph and wanted to migrate to Muslim lands.

During the Second World War it became apparent to everyone that the transfer of power from British to Indian hands only awaited the conclusion of hostilities. The transfer, in terms of class, was, of necessity, to be to the Indian middle class. If the Muslim middle class were to benefit at all, there would have to be a double transfer, viz., from British to Indian and Indian to Muslim hands. This sense of urgency was reflected in the phenomenal rise in the popularity of the Muslim League between the war years. Whereas the first formal demand for Pakistan in 1940 could have been dismissed as another stunt in political blackmail by a party which scarcely mattered amongst even the Muslims, after the 1946 elections, it had to be taken seriously. In these elections, the Muslim League gained every Muslim seat in the Central Legislative Assembly and came into power in the provinces of Bengal and Sindh. The only stumbling blocks to League's aims were the North-west Frontier Province, where anti-League forces were able to hold their own, and the Punjab, where they were kept out by a combination of Unionists and non-Muslim members. But in both these provinces, the League had made much headway. Being robbed of power in what was to be the heart of Pakistan caused a sense of frustration. As transfer of power became imminent, the League leadership became frantic in its attempts to seize it.

The position in the Punjab was tricky. Here Malik Khizr Hayat Tiwana led a coalition government, formed by 18 Unionists (10

Muslims, 8 Hindus), 51 Congress Hindus, and a combination of Sikh members numbering 23 – making a total of 92. The other 78 Muslims were members of the League and formed the largest single party in the house. It should be remembered that even Khizr Hayat and his Muslim colleagues in the Unionist party supported the League demand for Pakistan. Their differences with the League were purely regarding the position of non-Muslim minorities and the ways of bringing about Pakistan.

A few months after the elections, communal riots broke out in Calcutta and thereafter spread to other parts of India. They changed the political pattern of the country and had an important bearing on the Sikh attitude towards Pakistan. We shall therefore interrupt our narrative to say a few words about them.

In August 1946 the Muslim League decided to celebrate a 'Direct Action' day. The nature of the proposed celebration is not known, but on that day (16 August) the first of the series of communal riots was started in Calcutta, ending in the Punjab massacres a year later. It would be hazardous to give an answer to the question as to who started the killing. Three things should, however, be borne in mind: (1) Bengal was then governed by a Muslim League ministry; (2) an overwhelming majority of the police force in Calcutta was Muslim; and (3) the Sikh population of the city, consisting largely of taxi drivers – numbering less than a thousand – and a handful of businessmen, was in no way connected with the killings. On the other hand, the Muslim premier of Bengal, Shaheed Suhrawardy, in a public speech, expressed his appreciation of the work this small community had done in helping the victims of the riots.

The number of people killed in Calcutta at this time is said to have been over 4,000 and those wounded around 10,000. In all probability, the numbers of Hindus and Muslims killed were roughly equal.

By October the riots had spread through Bengal to Noakhali in East Bengal. In this area, the population was predominantly Muslim, the victims all Hindu. There were no Sikhs in Noakhali.

Two weeks later the pendulum swung back and this time the Hindus struck in Bihar, where they outnumbered the Muslims by nine to one. The victims were Muslim. In Bihar also there were no Sikhs.

By the winter of 1946–47 atrocity stories of the Bihar killings reached the Punjab and the North-west Frontier Province. In the order of things, the Muslims in these parts might have wreaked vengeance on the Hindus. But in these areas Hindus lived in towns where there were police stations and units of the army. Besides, it was not easy to tell a Hindu from a Muslim. Sikhs were a rural people living in isolated villages and were easily identifiable by their turbans and beards. For the first time in the series of communal killings, the Sikhs were involved as victims. In all the districts affected, Hazara (North-west Frontier Province), Rawalpindi, Campbellpur and Multan, the Sikh proportion of the population to the Muslim was two to ninety. Within a few days hundreds of prosperous Sikh villages were looted and burnt, men murdered, women and children abducted and raped – unless they forestalled their ravishers by mass suicides. A number of Muslims were also killed by the defenders and the police.

Although it would be foolish to attempt to estimate the number of people killed, in judging the subsequent trend of Sikh politics, it should be remembered that after January 1947 the one factor which coloured the Sikh outlook was a sense of insecurity from associating with the Muslims. Atrocity stories were circulated amongst the Sikhs all over the Punjab and the number of victims, no doubt, vastly exaggerated. But the Sikhs could not get away from the feeling that the reason for the assaults on them could not be retaliation for the killings in Bihar – because there were no

Sikhs in Bihar – but because the Muslims did not want them in what was going to be Pakistan. It is also significant that amongst the victims of the killings were close relatives of the Sikh leader Master Tara Singh. Mr Justice Teja Singh, the only Sikh member of the Punjab High Court and unofficial adviser to many Sikh politicians, lost several members of his own and his wife's family.

Now we return to affairs at Lahore. On 24 January 1947 the Unionist Government made a perfectly legitimate, but in the inflammable situation that prevailed, an ill-timed decision to ban private armies, and declared the Muslim League National Guards and the Hindu RSS (Rashtriya Swayamsewak Sangh) unlawful. The League pounced upon this opportunity to launch an agitation against the government and thousands of League volunteers went to jail. At last, Khizr Hayat Tiwana threw in the sponge and his ministry resigned on 2 March. The League, however, failed to get any non-Muslim support to form a government and the governor, Sir Evan Jenkins, took over the administration.

The resignation of the Unionist Ministry set the second round of communal killings in the Punjab going.

Outside the Assembly Hall, where thousands of Muslim League supporters had gathered and were shouting 'Streams of blood will flow, we will get our Pakistan', Master Tara Singh unsheathed his kirpan and shouted 'Death to Pakistan'. Then the fat was in the fire. Stabbing and arson became the order of the day in Amritsar and Lahore. Civil life came to a standstill. When all this had been going on for nearly three months, the British Government announced the plan to partition India (on 3 June 1947). Opinions of Sikh leaders had already been ascertained. They had agreed to the division of the Punjab.

In his broadcast on the plan Lord Louis Mountbatten said: 'We have given careful consideration to the position of the Sikhs. This valiant community forms about an eighth of the population of the Punjab, but they are so distributed that any partition of this province will inevitably divide them. All of us who have the good of the Sikh community at heart are very sorry to think that the partition of the Punjab, which they themselves desire, cannot avoid splitting them to a greater or lesser extent. The exact degree of the split will be left to the Boundary Commission.'

In a press conference Lord Mountbatten referred to the subject again. He said: 'I find that the Congress had put forward a resolution on the partition of the Punjab at the request of the Sikh community. I sent for a map with the population of the Sikhs marked and I was astounded to find that the plan which they had produced would divide the community into almost two equal halves. So I spent a great deal of time finding out a solution which would keep the Sikh community together. I have not been able to see any solution. But whatever steps are taken are based on the Congress resolution on the subject which was passed at the insistence of the Sikhs.'

The answer to the question 'Why did the Sikhs want partition when it would inevitably divide the community into two?' lies in the riots of the winter of 1946–47. Prior to that, the only section of the community that talked of partition was the Communists. They supported the Muslim demand for Pakistan and the setting up of a 'Sikh homeland' in the districts of Amritsar, Ferozepur, Jullundur, Ludhiana, Hoshiarpur and the Sikh States. The Akali Party, under the inspiration of Gyani Kartar Singh, had put up a a demand for an 'Azad Punjab' Sikh State, i.e., East Punjab including the Sikh States but excluding the Hindu-majority areas of Gurgaon, Hissar and Rohtak. This was more a move to counter the Muslim demand for Pakistan than a serious proposition. But by the beginning of 1947 all Sikhs had come to the conclusion that, since they could not prevent Pakistan, the best they could do was to save as much of the province as they could from going into Muslim hands. It was with this in mind that the Akali party passed a resolution on 8 July which read: 'The Sikhs declare in unequivocal terms that the partition of the Punjab should be effected in a manner whereby their integrity and solidarity [sic] is maintained and they get an adequate share in the canals and canal colonies and their sacred shrines are included in Eastern Punjab. Any partition which does not secure this for the Sikhs will be unacceptable to them.'

When the Boundary Commission was constituted (on 26 June), thirty-two Sikh members of the Punjab Assembly presented a memorandum on behalf of their community. It was prepared by an eminent Sikh lawyer, Harnam Singh (later a judge of the East Punjab High Court), who also argued the Sikh case.

The terms of reference of the commission were to demarcate the boundaries of the two parts of the Punjab on the basis of ascertaining the contiguous majority areas of Muslims and non-Muslims. In doing so, the commission was also to take into account 'other factors'. It was on the last two words that the Sikh community pinned its hopes.

The following facts were brought to the commission's notice: inaccuracy of population statistics, which had changed the Muslims from a minority to a majority community in the Punjab between 1901 and 1911; the floating character of a section of the Muslim population; the colonization of all the richest lands in western Punjab by Sikhs; the existence of some of their most important historical shrines, including the birthplace of the founder at Nankana and the site of the execution of the fifth Guru at Lahore; payment by the Sikhs of over 40 per cent of the land revenue and water rates and many other state charges of the province. The Sikh demand was that the boundary line should be fixed at the river Chenab, which would, with certain minor modifications, bring about 95 per cent of the Sikhs into eastern Punjab.

On 18 August Sir Cyril Radcliffe gave his boundary award. The Canal Colonies and over 150 historical shrines, including those mentioned in the previous paragraph, went to Pakistan. The Sikhs accepted the award with resignation and were willing to take what fate had in store for them. Their spokesman in the Central Government, Baldev Singh, said: 'It is not a compromise. I prefer to call it a settlement.'

If Pakistan was to mean anything by way of prosperity for the Muslim middle classes, the Sikhs had to go. The Sikhs owned land and used Muslim peasants to till it for them. The Hindus were largely city dwellers and were in trades and professions which the Muslims did not know much about, e.g., money lending, stockbroking, shopkeeping. Their remaining in Pakistan was useful, in the earlier stages, even necessary. So began the drive to get Sikh land-holders out from the Canal Colonies. If there was opposition it was countered with murder. Within a few days millions of Sikhs, and with them terrified Hindus, were on the march out of Pakistan to India. Andrew Mellor of the *Daily Herald* (London) wrote in his *India since Partition*, that 'in 42 days from September 18th to October 29th, 24 non-Muslim foot columns ... 848,000 strong, with hundreds of bullock carts and herds of cattle, crossed the frontier into India ... Some, from Pakistan districts like Lyallpur and Montgomery, had to make marches of up to two hundred miles. During September many were inadequately protected and were attacked on the roads by one community or the other.'

In continuing the narrative from the Sikh point of view, we have, perhaps unjustly, overlooked the fact that by this time anti-Muslim riots had spread all over East Punjab and the refugee movement had become a two-way traffic. There were atrocities on either side, each more diabolical than the other. No one was spared – sick or aged, women or children. By the time the transfer of populations was over, almost 10 million people had changed homes. Perhaps 100,000 had fallen victims to marauding bands, fatigue, disease and floods.

Both the Pakistan and Indian Governments issued versions of these communal massacres casting blame on the other side. There is little doubt that the politicians in both countries have much to answer for. Several of the leading Akalis and, more notably, men of the Indian National Army were actively associated with the killings in East Punjab. Since participation in these crimes was not a matter of shame but of pride, there is no need to labour with proof. On the other side, the entire Muslim League organization, including women members of its executive committee, were members of a devilish conspiracy to organize stabbings and arson. This was amply proved in an enquiry conducted by the Pakistan Government in 1949 against the nawab of Mamdot, who had been president of the provincial Muslim League and, subsequently, prime minister of the Pakistan part of the Punjab. The case for the prosecution was that the nawab had received funds for the purchase of arms for use in communal riots as early as October 1946 but had used them for private purposes. His defence was that arms had, in fact, been purchased, distributed and used. The nawab was acquitted. We shall quote at some length from the official organ of the Muslim League, *Dawn,* dated 22 October 1949:

Answering questions by defence counsel in the Mamdot Enquiry on Thursday, Chaudhri Mohammed Hassan, ex-MLA affirmed that in October 1946 members of the working committee of the Punjab Provincial Muslim League and prominent Muslim League writers met in a secret meeting at Mamdot Villa. Amongst those who attended were the Khan of Mamdot, Mian Abdul Bari, and the witness.

The meeting was held at a time when communal riots in Calcutta and Bombay had not yet completely ended. It was decided at the meeting to raise secret funds to be called 'secret Sanduq' for the purchase of jeeps, trucks, iron jackets, arms and ammunition, and blankets.

'Consequently', the witness continued, 'another secret meeting was called and Khan of Mamdot directed Rana Nasrullah Khan to arrange for the purchase of one hundred iron jackets through his brother Rana Zafrullah Khan. At the same meeting Begum Shah Nawaz was asked to arrange for the purchase of hand grenades through her daughter, the late Miss Mumtaz Shah Nawaz.'

Replying to further questions, the witness deposed that 'it was true that Sardar Rashid Ahmad and Mohamed Azam Khan, who is the son-in-law of Begum Shah Nawaz, were also directed to purchase arms and ammunition from the Frontier Province to bring them here for distribution ... The respondent provided the requisite money with which seven thousand steel helmets were purchased directly from military stores.'

By the spring of 1948, practically every single Sikh had been evacuated from Pakistan. They had changed places with landless Muslim tenantry from East Punjab. The number of refugees on either side was roughly the same, the difference in prosperity enormous. The Sikhs, whose property consisted largely of agricultural land, were compensated with less than one tenth of their previous holdings. Thus were the former rulers of the Punjab deprived of their homes and hearths and humbled in their pride.

PART III

Chapter 12

THE CULTURAL HERITAGE

The Language

The language of the Sikhs, as that of all other people living in the Punjab in both the Pakistani and the Indian provinces, is Punjabi.

The origin of Punjabi has been the subject of much speculation. Most linguists have agreed that it is one of the many offspring of the language of the Aryan settlers of northern India. To anyone travelling across the Indo-Gangetic plain it is apparent that Kashmiri, Punjabi, Sindhi, Hindi, Urdu, Gujarati, Maharathi, Maithili and Bengali are only local variations of one common language. F.E. Keay and Grierson, both well-known Orientalists, are of the opinion that Punjabi is of greater antiquity than any of those mentioned and place its origin at A.D. 1000. Punjabi is spoken by a larger number of people than many of the other Indian languages. According to the census of 1931, 21,893,000 spoke Punjabi – which was more than either Gujarati, Maharathi, Rajasthani, Oriya and many South Indian languages.

The chief difference between Punjabi, Kashmiri and Sindhi and other languages of Aryan origin is the preponderance of Persian and Arabic words in the languages of the northern regions and that of Sanskrit in the others. This was due to the stronger Muslim domination in Kashmir, the Punjab and Sindh. In the case of Punjabi, there was another factor, the contributions of Muslim poets of the seventeenth and eighteenth centuries who introduced Persian and Arabic phraseology and literary concepts into it.

Although Punjabi has always been the language of the peoples of the Punjab, the sophisticated have all along disdained it as too rustic to be a cultured man's medium of expression. For several centuries, Persian was recognized as the language of the upper classes. Even during the period of Sikh ascendancy, the ruling class set great store by the knowledge of Persian, in which all official correspondence was carried on. After the annexation by the British, Urdu replaced Persian as the language of the law courts and littérateurs. In the early years of the twentieth century, when there was a renaissance of Punjabi literature and attempts were made to have it officially recognized, they were countenanced by giving Punjabi a communal label as the language of the Sikhs, just as Hindi was of the Hindus and Urdu of the Muslims.

The result of this move was that whereas Punjabi remained, as before – the spoken language of all Punjabis, whether Hindu, Muslim, Sikh or Christian – its literary output came to be largely confined to Sikh writers.

The partition of the Punjab in 1947 made the position even more incongruous. In the Pakistan half of the province, while Punjabi continued to be the spoken language of the people, Hindustani of the type spoken in and around the cities of Delhi and Lucknow was officially recognized as the medium of instruction in the universities and as the language of the law courts. The only explanation for this peculiar official decision was that, whereas

Hindustani or Urdu was usually written in Arabic characters, Punjabi was not. This gave Urdu some sort of merit in Islamic eyes. Punjabi on the other hand, despite its debt to Muslim writers, largely derived its literature from Sikh sources and was written in Gurmukhi characters. Urdu is likely to continue its hot-house existence in Pakistani Punjab until the zeal for everything Muslim, Arabic and Persian peters out, and the people's language becomes the language of the land

In the Indian part of the Punjab also, the language controversy assumed a communal aspect. In the Patiala and East Punjab States Union, where the Sikhs predominated, Punjabi in Gurmukhi script continued to be the official language and was being rapidly adapted to forensic and bureaucratic usage. In the provinces of East Punjab and Himachal Pradesh, emphasis was placed on Hindi although Punjabi was also recognized as a medium of instruction. Here too, the position became as incongruous as in Pakistani Punjab. The people were almost entirely Punjabi speaking (except in the more eastern regions), but in spite of that the study of Hindi written in Devanagri script was made compulsory in schools. This was done although the literary output in Punjabi had always been considerably more than that in Hindi. According to the 1931 census, 7,248 books in Gurmukhi were published in the preceding ten years: the corresponding figure for Hindi was 1,577. The number of journals printed in 1931 was fifty-six in Gurmukhi (more than double the number published in 1921); the corresponding figure for Hindi was twenty-four.

Perhaps the solution will be to recognize Punjabi as the only spoken language of the Punjab and allow it to be written in Gurmukhi, Devanagri and Urdu characters.

Punjabi has many dialects. Some writers have tried to evolve a standard form based on the dialect spoken in and around the central districts of Lahore and Amritsar. This standardized Punjabi, with a bias towards Hindi, is used by newspapers and broadcasting stations. Although it has the obvious advantage of creating a uniform diction, it has serious shortcomings. For one, literature tends to break away from the spoken language and writers use a vocabulary which is more often than not unintelligible even to an educated Punjabi. For another, the strong point of the Punjabi language has been its rustic simplicity. Dialects are always a rich storehouse of spontaneous expression, and if they are ignored Punjabi, like Urdu spoken in the Punjab, will lose contact with the common people who give it its natural charm and masculine vigour.

The usual script for writing Punjabi is Gurmukhi. This was not always so. At one time the number of Punjabi books written in Arabic characters outnumbered those written in Gurmukhi. The writings of the Muslim poets of the seventeenth and eighteenth centuries were all in Arabic characters and were later transcribed into Gurmukhi. Some of the younger writers have had their novels produced in Devanagri script.

The origin of Gurmukhi is still a matter of controversy. The alphabet has much in common with Lunda, the script used by the moneylenders of northern India. It has also some letters in common with the Kashmiri and Devanagri scripts. Some people believe that it is older than either of these. The Sikh Gurus made it popular and gave it form and finish.

Punjabi Literature

Some students of literature trace Punjabi literary writing to the twelfth century, to the works of Sheikh Farid Shakargunj. Others deny the authenticity of the writings ascribed to Farid and his contemporaries and disagree that the language used was Punjabi. In the absence of reliable records, the only certain starting point is the writings of Guru Nanak contained in the Adi Granth. But Guru

Nanak's compositions show a standard of technique which leave no room for doubt that he must have inherited some sort of tradition in the form of literary expression. The identity and achievements of Guru Nanak's literary predecessors remain to be established.

Early Punjabi writings were exclusively religious, being closely connected with the Bhakti movement (fifteenth to sixteenth centuries), of which the Sikh religion was itself an offshoot. The writers of this period fall into two main groups – the Sikh Gurus and Mussulman Sufis. They had much in common in their thought content, form and expression. Sufism was a revolt against the narrow bigotry of early Islam and insisted on the acceptance of certain Hindu doctrines. The Bhakti movement, particularly Sikhism, was, on the other hand, a revolt against the anti-Muslim prejudices of the Hindus and demanded recognition of Islamic values. This resulted in the birth of a system of philosophy half Islamic and half Hindu. It also brought about a literature in which Arabic and Persian mixed with Sanskrit and Hindi with such facility that it became difficult to tell which language was basic and which the addition. This was the Punjabi of the Sikh Gurus and their contemporary Sufi writers.

The Sufis came to India with their co-religionist invaders. For several centuries their doctrines of religious tolerance and understanding were submerged under the rulers' zeal for forcible proselytization. Sufi centres at Multan, Pakpattan and Kasur came into prominence only when the iconoclast gave way to the ascetic. Where force failed, persuasion succeeded, and the Sufis carried the gospel of Prophet Mohammed to the people. They had to speak and write the language of the people and use similes and metaphors intelligible to them.

The most outstanding of the Sufi writers was Sheikh Farid Shakargunj, whose verses were incorporated in the Adi Granth. Other notable Sufi poets were Madhu Lal Hussain (1539–93),

Shah Sharaf Sultan Bahu (1639–91), Bulhey Shah (1680–1758), Ali Haidar (1690–1785) and Hashim Shah (1753–1823).

Most of the Sikh Gurus were given to versification and the writings of Nanak, Angad, Amar Das, Ram Das, Arjun, and Tegh Bahadur are preserved in the Granth Sahib. The two outstanding contributors to the Sikh scriptures are the first Guru, Nanak, and the fifth Guru, Arjun.

Guru Nanak preached through his poetry, and consequently his works have a didacticism explaining his philosophy of life and exhorting others to a particular way of living. Most didactic poetry suffers from a cramping narrowness imposed by the purpose for which it is written, but Guru Nanak's poetry displays a remarkable freedom of expression. The beauty of pastoral Punjab, the ripening cornfields, the break of dawn, and the awakening of birds, the graceful flight of deer in the woodlands, the majesty of monsoon clouds and the music of rainfall – all aroused him to religious and poetic frenzy. The commonplace was for him pregnant with symbolism of moral significance. Domestic situations, relations between husband and wife, and all the intricate relationships-in-law peculiar to the joint Hindu family, became his similes. Household duties of a rural home, gleaning of corn, picking of cotton, weaving and spinning, milking of cattle and churning of butter gave him his metaphors. The best known works of Guru Nanak are his *Babar Vani* (which also depicts the tyranny and lawlessness at the time of Babar's invasion), *Asa di War* (hymn of the morning) and *Jup Sahib*, the morning prayer. Examples of his poetry have already been quoted in Chapter 2. The following three verses from the morning prayer are typical of his style and method of conveying his message:

As a beggar goes a-begging,
Bowl in one hand, staff in the other,

Rings in his ears, in ashes smothered,
So go thou forth in life.

With earrings made of contentment,
With modesty thy begging bowl,
Meditation the fabric of thy garment,
Knowledge of death thy cowl.
Let thy mind be chaste, virginal clean,
Faith the staff on which to lean.
Thou shalt then thy fancy humiliate
With mind subdued, the world subjugate.

Hail! and to thee be salutation.
Thou art primal, Thou art pure,
Without beginning, without termination,
In single form, for ever endure.

(Verse 28)

From the store-house of compassion,
Seek knowledge for thy food.
Let thy heart-beat be the call of the conch shell
Blown in gratitude.

He is the Lord, He is the will, He is the creation,
He is the master of destiny, of union and separation.

Hail! and to thee be salutation.
Thou art primal, Thou art pure
Without beginning, without termination,
In single form, for ever endure.

(Verse 29)

If thou must make a gold coin true
Let thy mint these rules pursue.

(Verse 29)

In the forge of continence
Let the goldsmith be a man of patience,
His tools be made of knowledge,
His anvil of reason;
With the fear of God the bellows blow,

With prayer and austerity make the fire glow.
Pour the liquid in the mould of love,
Print the name of the Lord thereon,
And cool it in the holy waters.

(Verse 38)

Guru Arjun's poetry expresses the same deep sentiments as Guru Nanak's. His verse abounds with jewelled phrases and has a haunting melody produced by the use of alliteration and repetition of words. *Sukhmani* is Guru Arjun's greatest composition.

The Granth is the greatest work of Punjabi literature. Most of the labour involved in its compilation was done by Guru Arjun and a contemporary writer, Gurdas. It is a voluminous book containing nearly 6,000 verses. Besides the writings of the six Gurus mentioned, it has in it selected verses of several poet-saints associated with the Bhakti movement.

Guru Gobind Singh was perhaps the most erudite of all the Sikh Gurus and was familiar with Hindu mythology as well as Islamic theology. He was a patron of art and letters, and had fifty-two poets in his own court. He wrote mainly in Sanskrit and Persian (and just one couplet in Punjabi). Unlike his predecessor, he did not restrict himself to expressing the glory of God in his verses. Guru Gobind Singh's writings have a moral as well as a political significance. The martial spirit which he infused amongst his followers is expressed in the vigorous poetry of his famous *Zafarnama*, the 'Epistle of Victory', addressed to Emperor Aurangzeb. His *Jup Sahib* is to this day a source of inspiration to his followers. Guru Gobind Singh's works were compiled and edited by his contemporary, Mani Singh.

The writing in the Adi Granth is the best that Punjabi literature has hitherto achieved. It has a form and finish not equalled by subsequent writers. The beauty of its composition has a powerful appeal, and large numbers of Punjabi-Hindus read the Sikh scripture. The entire non-Muslim population of Sindh read and worship the Granth together with their own deities.

After the passing of the ten Gurus, a spate of literature was produced on the lives of the Gurus by their contemporaries and others who were able to glean information on the subject. These biographies are known as *Janam Sakhis* and are valuable historical records. The more well-known historians of the period were Seva Ram, Ram Koer, Santokh Singh, Ratan Singh Bhangu and Gyan Singh.

No literature was produced by the Sikhs during their struggle for power. But while they were busy fighting, two Muslims, Bulhey Shah (1680–1752) and Warris Shah (1735–1798), wrote verse which is the finest example of romantic and mystic Punjabi poetry. Bulhey Shah's *Kafis* and Warris Shah's epic *Heer Ranjah* are most popular and are recited and sung in every village in the province. They have also influenced subsequent generations of Punjabi writers.

Punjabi Literature after Annexation

For nearly half a century following British occupation, there was little literature produced in India. It took many years to recover from the effects of the political change and in sizing up Western values. The early English rulers were convinced that all Oriental culture was worthless and the best thing that the Indians could do was to adopt the European. One generation of Indians agreed with this opinion and anglicized themselves till they lost all contact with Indian tradition and learning. The next generation discovered the folly and proceeded to blow away the dust off the archives housing the achievements of ancient India. This process took place all over the country. Since the Punjab was the last to be subjected to these Western complexes, it was the last to shake off their effect. The renaissance in Punjabi writing was consequently somewhat later in time than in the rest of the country.

Post-annexation Punjabi writing corresponded roughly to the social and political movements, which have already been dealt with in the earlier chapters. The Nirankari and Namdhari movements did not produce any literature of their own, but the Singh Sabha, the Akali and the Communist did. In each case, the literary output bore the impress of the problem that faced the different movements. The classification is admittedly open to objection because it does not account for the writers who were oblivious to social and political problems and wrote, as it were, for the sake of writing. We shall make reference to them wherever necessary.

Singh Sabha Writers

The literary output of the Singh Sabha movement is the most important part of its contribution to Sikhism. The person to whom it owes most is Vir Singh *(b.* 1872).

Vir Singh's literary works have to be viewed with reference to social and political conditions at the end of the nineteenth century, when he wrote. Without that background most of his prose appears insipid. His novels, which made his name known in all Sikh homes, were written at a time when the Sikhs were beginning to doubt the achievements of their ancestors. English historians harped on the crude and corrupt Sikh rule, which they had replaced by an 'enlightened' one. Sanskrit scholars belittled the religion of the

Sikhs as a poor imitation of the Hindu and ridiculed its forms and symbols as barbarous. Vir Singh's novels, *Baba Naudh Singh*, *Sundri*, *Vijay Singh* and *Satwant Kaur*, had as their central theme the heroism and chivalry of the Sikhs and the ethical excellence of their religion. This was set in contrast to the servility of the Hindu masses and the oppression of the Mussulman rulers. The Sikhs devoured Vir Singh's novels with enthusiasm and gratitude. But with the passing of that peculiar state of mentality, the novels lost their appeal. To the present-day reader, they appear somewhat dull. Their place is not in literature but in history.

Vir Singh himself gave up writing fiction and took to translating and explaining the Scriptures in a series of pamphlets, which were published by the Khalsa Tract Society, and in his weekly paper, the *Khalsa Samachar*. Along with these appeared his poems, which gave him first place amongst Sikh poets.

Vir Singh first experimented in blank verse. A long poem, *Rana Surat Singh*, was published in 1905. The theme, as usual, was religion. His technique and mastery over the language were impressive. No one had successfully written blank verse in Punjabi before, and Vir Singh had turned out a work of sustained excellence where alliteration and onomatopoeia, rhythm and repetition, produced a lilting melody with all the languor and sensuousness of a summer afternoon. Thereafter, Vir Singh set himself to writing about the lives of two Sikh Gurus, the founder Nanak and the last Guru, Gobind Singh. *Kalgidhar Chamatkar*, the life of Gobind, appeared first and was followed three years later by *Guru Nanak Chamatkar*.

In between these biographies, Vir Singh published several anthologies of verse employing a short metre hitherto not used in Punjabi poetry. The more popular of these were in the form of *rubayat*s (familiar to the readers of Omar Khayyam). In these he expressed his philosophy and mysticism, where the love of God and human beings, the spiritual and the sensual, mortal and divine, move in a colourful kaleidoscope, beautiful and baffling. There is always an underlying sense of humility which is at times almost masochistic:

> Thou didst pluck and tear me from the branch,
> Held me, breathed the fragrance,
> And – cast me away.
> Thus discarded,
> Trodden underfoot and mingled with the dust,
> All I remember – and with gratitude –
> Is the memory of the touch.

And again:

> In a dream you came to me.
> I leapt to hold you in my embrace.
> It was but fantasy I could not hold
> And my arms ached with longing.
> Then I rushed to clasp your feet
> To lay my head thereon.
> Even these I could not reach
> For you were high and I was low.

In another verse, Vir Singh expresses his belief in the superiority of faith over reason:

> I made my mind a beggar's bowl,
> I begged the bread of learning door to door;
> With crumbs that fell from houses of learning
> Did I cram it.
> It was heavy,

I was proud,
I was a pandit.
I strove to walk in the clouds
But even on the earth I stumbled.
One day I went to my Guru

And placed the bowl before him as an offering.
'Dirt', he said, 'dirt',
And turned it upside down.
He threw my crumbs away,
Scrubbed the bowl with sand,
Rinsed it with water,
Cleansed it of the filth of learning.

There is little in the way of honest literary criticism of Vir Singh's work. His personality intrudes on his poetry. His admirers do not tolerate anything but laudatory appreciation of his work. Others, particularly the non-religious modernists, criticize him for his dogmatic restatement of platitudes and lack of appreciation of nature, and tend to underrate his achievements. This is further complicated by bias in judging a man who has a political past. He was an important figure in the Singh Sabha movement and never gave up his interest in its fortunes. But he has none of the qualities associated with politicians. He is shy and retiring. He has never been known to make a public speech, nor does he easily allow himself to be photographed. Political adversaries do not find the usual material to run him down. Only his writings come in for pre-judged criticism or grudging appreciation, punctuated with ifs and buts. Like all great writers, Vir Singh will have to await recognition.

Other writers who fall in the group of Singh Sabha writers are Kahan Singh, Puran Singh and Charan Singh Shaheed.

Kahan Singh was a senior contemporary of Vir Singh. He is best known for having compiled an encyclopaedia of Sikh culture and religion. Professor Puran Singh wrote both in English and Punjabi and translated some of Vir Singh's poems. His excursion into blank verse was the subject of much literary comment. In two of his published anthologies, *Khule Ghund* and *Khule Maidan*, he experimented with a new vocabulary and an unconventional style to expound unfamiliar themes. His poems are emotionally surcharged and erratic. Puran Singh also published a collection of essays called *Khulilekh*. Charan Singh Shaheed edited a weekly paper called the *Manji* and published a collection of his poems. He was the first to write humorous prose and verse in Punjabi.

Before passing to the next set of writers, reference must be made to the Hindu poet Dhani Ram Chatrik, who is considered second only to Vir Singh. His better known anthologies are *Chandan Vari*, *Kesar Kiari*, *Nawan fahan* and *Sufi Khanan*.

The Akalis

The feature that distinguished the Singh Sabha school from that of the Akalis is that, while the former laid stress on religion, the latter emphasized tradition. The Akali school was a school of writers who were connected with the Akali movement. Journals which came into prominence with, the movement were *Akali Teg Purdesi*, *Phulwari* and *Pritam*. In the columns of these journals many new writers made their debut. Some wrote poetry (such as Gurmukh Singh Musafir and Hira Singh Dard) and others fiction (Master Tara Singh). But most of them stuck to political writing and their style remained journalese. The Akali movement's literary output is more notable for its quantity than quality.

'Progressive' Writers

Punjabi writing, which is often labelled as progressive or rationalist, is chronologically associated with the growth of the Kirti Kisan (Communist) Movement. Several of its most important figures were associated with socialist politics. Hira Singh Dard, who edited *Phulwari* for some time, was connected with both the Akali and the Communist parties; so also was Sohan Singh Josh, who wrote for the Communist weekly *Jang-i-Azad*. Others, though non-political, abandoned the emphasis on religion and tradition and described themselves as progressive. The central figure amongst the progressives is Gurbakhsh Singh.

Gurbakhsh Singh started life as an engineer and his studies took him to the United States. Soon after his return the urge to write and propagate modernism got the better of his professional pursuits. His magazine *Preet Lari* had quick success and, within a few years, came to be the most widely read magazine in Punjabi. He put his schemes of communal living into practice by founding an institution known as Preet Nagar, halfway between Lahore and Amritsar. Preet Nagar became a centre of academic activity. But its popularity amongst the younger generation of Sikhs was more than offset by the animosity aroused amongst the orthodox elements. Gurbakhsh Singh himself became a symbol of revolt against traditionalism in writing. Even his adversaries admit that he is much the best essayist and prose writer that the language has produced. His most popular book of essays is *Sanvin Padhri Zuidgi*. Gurbakhsh Singh is also the inspiration behind many writers with leftist tendencies.

The break with tradition initiated by Gurbakhsh Singh produced a crop of young writers. Amongst the writers of stories, Kartar Singh Duggal, Rajinder Singh Bedi, Nanak Singh and Prem Singh of Hoti-Mardan deserve reference. Duggal has produced a spate of short stories, some of which would find a place in the best of collections anywhere. Duggal's forte is his knowledge of the dialect of Rawalpindi District, which he uses with remarkable effect in all his story telling. He first produced several collections of short stories, of which *Sver Sar* and *Pippa/ Puttian* were noteworthy. After the partition of the Punjab he wrote a large number of stories dealing with the communal riots and transfer of population. He also wrote two novels on the subject, of which *Andran* is the most outstanding work in Punjabi fiction. It has a masterly portrayal of character and a skilful handing of a situation where pastoral peace moves into a tragic climax. Duggal's excursions into the field of playwriting and poetry have been less successful. Bedi has written very little in Punjabi. His short stories, some of which have been translated from Urdu, have given him an enviable reputation in the literature of both languages. Although Nanak Singh is not progressive in the sense his contemporary writers are, nor is his writing of a high literary calibre, he can claim to have made the Punjab fiction-conscious. He has written more than three dozen novels and every year more appear. Prem Singh of Hoti-Mardan has written several books on Sikh history where the borderline between history and fiction is somewhat blurred. But his 'history' has the merit of being readable.

Contemporary Punjabi poetry of the progressive variety has not achieved a very high standard. Although almost everyone with literary pretensions has tried to write poetry, barely half a dozen of the moderns have been able to produce anything which is of any merit. The two outstanding figures in this sphere of literary activity are Mohan Singh, editor of the monthly magazine *Punj Darya*, and Amrit Kaur. Mohan Singh's earlier poems, compiled in his *Save Patr, Kusumbra* and *Adhvatey,* gave him the first place amongst the moderns. His later works, particularly those produced to fill columns of the *Punj Darya*, savour of writing written to order. In his last work *Kucha Sucha*, written after 1947, Mohan Singh expresses a strong left-wing bias where political emotion is given precedence over poetical form. Mohan Singh enjoys a well-deserved reputation for being an able exponent of Punjabi literature and its most discerning critic. Amrit Kaur has steadily produced poetry that is very popular and has been consistently improving. Her youthfulness and lack of erudition have proved to be both her making and her shortcoming. Her poems have a naiveté and charm of simplicity. She writes about everyday events in life with an ease that makes her poetry eminently readable. Her last two anthologies of poems, *Lamian Wattan* and *Sehrgi Vela*, deal with the trials and tribulations following the partition of her province and were very well received. But her work rarely rises above the commonplace.

Playwriting is the most neglected part of Punjabi literature. Some comedies written by Professor I.C. Nanda attracted public attention. After him several plays have been published, but they have not achieved any high standard. Gurdial Singh Khosla has produced several one-act plays and is actively associated in developing a Punjabi theatre.

Several Sikh writers have written in languages other than Punjabi. Most of their works consist of translation of the scriptures or are interpretations of certain aspects of Sikh history and religion. The most successful of the translators is Professor Teja Singh.

Sir Jogendra Singh's ventures into English novel writing are only known in the Punjab. His novels *Kamla*, *Nurjehan* and others were widely read in the province. In all of his books the theme was religious and it struck a discordant note in the setting that he created. He also published some books on the lives of the Gurus.

Architecture

After the decline of the Mughals, most of the styles of architecture evolved were hybrid products of earlier ones. Sikh architecture (if indeed the term can be used) is a typical example of this evolution. All the most important Sikh shrines have a pattern of their own very much in line with the style of the Golden Temple at Amritsar – with a large dome shaped like a squashed onion surrounded by smaller ones fashioned after the Mughal style. The domes adorn the central shrine, which is usually in the middle of an open courtyard where the congregation sits. This design was used in buildings other than temples. A notable example is Ranjit Singh's mausoleum in Lahore.

Painting

The schools of painting which flourished in northern India during and after Sikh rule were the Sikh, Rajput and Kangra. Large numbers of the paintings of these schools executed by Sikh artists are still in existence in museums and private art collections. There are panels of wall paintings in Ranjit Singh's mausoleum and in some buildings round about the Golden Temple. These and other pictures illustrating books and manuscripts resemble the Kangra style. Of the later artists, one Kapur Singh, who lived during the last days of Sikh rule, is the only one known by name. Some of his miniature portraits are preserved in the Lahore Museum, but details of his life and works are not available.

Modern Indian painting has not yet shaken off the cramping weight of tradition. The pioneers of the renaissance, Abanendra Nath Tagore and Nand Lal Bose, looked to the Ajanta frescoes as their inspiration. The inspiration soon became the model, which never changed its form. As a reaction, a school of artists sprang up at Bombay completely removed from Indian tradition and taking the European, mainly Italian, masters as their model. Some efforts to assimilate the two were made (e.g., at Lucknow). The only Indian artist to resuscitate the Indian tradition and yet be modern, to accept the Ajanta and modern European schools and yet stamp them with her own individuality, was Amrita Sher-Gil, the daughter of a well-known Sikh scholar of Sanskrit, Umrao Singh Sher-Gil (brother of Sundar Singh Majithia, referred to in the earlier chapters).

Amrita Sher-Gil (1913–41) started painting at the age of eleven. She was sent for training first to Florence and then to Paris at the academy of the Grande Chaumerie of Pierre Vaillant. She was later admitted to Lucien Simon's École des Beaux Arts, where her artistic talent was nurtured into maturity. She was much influenced by the French impressionists, particularly by Gaugin. On her return home, the Indian tradition claimed her and she became at once, according to the Indian art critic Khandalawala, 'the most vital force in modern painting'. Some of her canvases show the spirit of Ajanta, others the simple beauty of the Rajasthani and Kangra schools. In no case is there any imitation. Her work bears her personality whatever the subject of her painting.

Amrita Sher-Gil aroused a storm of controversy. Traditionalists condemned her work as an outrage on Indian tradition; the moderns hailed her as the first Indian artist who was traditional with modern upbringing. Amrita did not live long enough to justify the hopes of her many admirers. She died at the age of twenty-eight with just seven years devoted to painting. Most of her pictures have been acquired by the Indian Government.

Other well-known Sikh painters are S.G. Thakur Singh, a painter of landscapes who has veered between the Bengal and the

Lucknow schools, and Sobha Singh, who has done a large number of portraits and pictures of episodes in Sikh history. A young Sikh artist who has been attracting a good deal of attention of art critics is Sarabjeet Singh *(b.* 1923). His landscapes have an extraordinary feel of space and perspective.

PART IV

Chapter 13

THE FUTURE

The Sikh community is going through a process of profound change. While some of the changes are disintegrating and threaten the community with extinction, others are in the opposite direction and make towards the elevation of the Sikhs from a religious community to a nation with its own psychological make-up and traditions. A student of sociology would be in a better position to trace the causes of these trends and indicate the consequences. A layman can only detect their existence and present them for scrutiny and judgement.

There are two factors which make for the extinction of the Sikhs as a separate community. The more important of these is the rapid decline in the observance of the forms and symbols of the faith. Those who maintain that the only dividing line between Sikhs and Hindus is the external emblems of Sikhism believe that this tendency will result in the Sikhs merging back into Hinduism.

The other disintegrating tendency is the appearance of a new form of caste system, as anti-social as the one which the Sikh Gurus tried to abolish. The Hindu division of society into four castes

191

corresponded to the economic structure of early Hindu society. With the disappearance of that economic structure in the cities, the caste system began to break up. In the villages, where feudal economy remained untouched, the caste system continued as rigid as ever. This was as true of the Punjab as of the rest of India. The Sikh crusade against caste was an urban phenomenon. In the villages, higher caste converts did not intermarry, interdine or even admit lower caste converts into gurdwaras built by them. The introduction of modern methods of cultivation will inevitably affect rural economy in such a way as to abolish caste structure and conventions. But the last fifty years have produced another caste system with a new economic basis which permeates the entire Sikh social fabric, urban and rural. This is the division between what are known as agriculturalists (Jats) and non-agriculturalists (non-Jats). At one time this division threatened to divide the community into two distinct groups, almost like the Muslim divisions of Shia and Sunni. But with the abolition of communal and caste privileges after 1947, there is reason to hope that Jat–non-Jat differences may also disappear.

A move in the opposite direction from the one mentioned above and allied to the problem of the forms and symbols of Sikhism is the new phase in relations between the Sikhs and the Hindus. Whereas the disappearance of forms and symbols is an inclination to merge back into Hinduism, the political bias of the orthodox elements of the Sikh community is to emphasize independence of the Hindu associations. The Sikhs are today more insistent than ever in emphasizing their 'nationality' and 'race' as distinct from those of the Hindus. Only time will tell which of these opposing tendencies will ultimately triumph.

Forms and Symbols

In our chapters on the history of the Sikh religion, we mentioned the five *kakka*s (unshorn hair, comb, steel bangle, shorts and sword) which were incorporated as integral symbols of the Sikh faith. These were introduced by Guru Gobind Singh on the Hindu new year's day in 1699, when he raised the militant Khalsa from the pacifist Sikh. It is certain that none of the forms and symbols was observed or enjoined as a matter of principle by Guru Gobind Singh's nine predecessors (a fact incorrectly assumed by some Sikhs). The first nine Gurus probably wore their hair long as had been customary amongst ascetics in India. Guru Gobind Singh was the first to introduce external symbolism as an essential part of the Sikh religion. Those who did not accept his innovations but stuck to the teachings of the other Gurus were separated from the rest. Sikhs were divided into two groups, the Sahajdhari and the Khalsa.

For a long time, the distinction between the two kinds of Sikhs was of as little consequence as that between Sikhs and Hindus. But as the latter division, that is, Sikh-Hindu, became pronounced, the position of the Sahajdhari Sikhs became an anomalous one. The only way the Sikhs asserted their independence from the Hindu community was by emphasizing the importance of forms and symbols. The move had its economic and political advantages and these were given precedence over the sociological disadvantages. The Sahajdharis, who were Sikhs in all but the forms, were cold-shouldered by the Khalsa. Those who cut off their hair or shaved their beards were not even considered Sahajdharis but were disowned as renegades or *putits*. The Sahajdharis were too few to form a community of their own. In any case, the distinction between Hinduism and non-symbolic Sikhism was very slender. The Sahajdharis merged back into the Hindu fold and came to be referred to as just Hindus believing in Sikhism.

The process of relapsing back into Hinduism is gathering speed. The tendency was noted by the earliest Sikh historians, particularly those writing at the time of Ranjit Singh. With the end of Sikh rule the process would have been accelerated but for army regulations introduced by the British insisting on observance of symbols. In 1896 J.N. Bhattacharya, the author of *Hindu Castes and Sects*, wrote that 'under British rule it [i.e., Sikhism] is fast losing its vitality and drifting towards amalgamation with the Hindu faith properly so called.... In the course of a few more years it is likely to be superseded by one of those forms of Vaishnavism which alone have the best chance of success amongst a subject nation in times of profound and undisturbed peace.' Professor Bhattacharya overlooked the effect of the army regulations and the revivalist movements, Nirankari and Namdhari (which were before his time), and the Singh Sabha and Akali (which followed). These movements checked the process of lapse and had limited success in persuading more people to accept forms and symbols. But on the whole the professor was right. The revivalist movements referred to had only temporary influence and the general move towards Hinduism has continued.

Strict adherence to the code of Guru Gobind Singh is now more the exception than the rule. In the Sikh states only the rulers of Patiala and Faridkot had, since infancy, refrained from cutting their hair. The young maharaja of Nabha was persuaded to become a proper Sikh after his return to India. The rulers of Kapurthala, Jind and Kalsia were only nominally Sikh. With the Sikh upper classes trimming of beards and smoking are not uncommon. Amongst the Sikh peasantry, the position is much worse. In the districts of Ludhiana and Jullundur, most Sikh Jats trim their beards and smoke hookahs or cigarettes. Sikhs of Lahore, Amritsar and Sheikhupura have not yet taken to smoking, but trimmed beards are by no means rare. The only class of Sikhs to observe strictly the forms and symbols of Sikhism are the lower middle class from northern Punjab.

The practice of trimming in one generation almost invariably leads to the complete removal of the beard and cutting the hair in the next. From generation to generation the process of relapse may be summed up in four successive stages, viz., orthodox–non-orthodox–Sahajdhari–Hindu.

The leaders of the Sikh community have hitherto paid little attention to this grave problem. In 1926 a young Sikh student sent a circular to several leading Sikh politicians and theologians asking them to state their views on the necessity of growing long hair and beards. These views were published later. One contributor, a clean-shaven Sikh and member of the Indian Civil Service, stated categorically that he believed Sikhs should abandon these symbols, which were an anachronism. He did not answer the next question as to whether the Sikhs would then be able to maintain an identity distinct from the Hindus. (The answer was provided by his own daughter, who married a Hindu.) The trend of most of the other replies to the questionnaire was disappointing. Sir Jogendra Singh wrote: 'When you belong to a society or a club, you have to observe its rules, till these rules are changed.'

Most of the others said the same thing in insisting on observance as a matter of *espirit de corps*.

Jats and Non-Jats

Another sociological and political problem which faces the Sikh community is the growing division between the agriculturalists and non-agriculturalists.

The caste system was inherited by the Sikhs as a legacy from their Hindu forefathers. Abolition of this system of grading human beings on the simple criterion of birth was the most important part of the teachings of the Sikh Gurus. The Gurus themselves were all Kshatriyas (now a non-agriculturalist caste), but most of their followers then were Jats, who belonged to the lowest of the four Hindu castes (Sudras). There are no records to elucidate to what extent they succeeded in their own lifetime in removing these distinctions. But it is almost certain that soon after them their injunctions against caste practices were relegated to realms of theology and the system itself came back to its own.

During Sikh rule and the early years of British occupation, large numbers of Hindus living in northern Punjab, mainly Kshatriyas and Aroras (non-agriculturalists) were converted to Sikhism. The illiterate Jats of Lahore, Amritsar, Sheikhupura, Ferozepur, Ludhiana and Jullundur Districts were now brought into religious fraternity with educated Kshatriyas and Aroras. The difference was not merely one of literacy. The Jats were entirely agriculturalist by occupation, the newcomers mainly petty businessmen and moneylenders. The problem got an economic background and the economics perpetuated the problem.

The distinction was given statutory recognition by the government, and certain tribes were declared agriculturalist irrespective of the actual occupation of the individuals comprising them. Non-agriculturalists were forbidden to buy land from statutory agriculturalists (but not vice versa). In the services similar measures were undertaken. As long as appointments in the services were made by open competition, the Jat stood very little chance against the non-Jat, who had the tradition of learning for several generations behind him. Consequently, the Sikh personnel of all higher services, civil or military, had become predominantly non-Jat. Later on, specific provisions were made reserving a large percentage of the Sikh posts for Jats. The scales were reversed. A Sikh got a job reserved for a Sikh not because he was a Sikh but because he was a Jat Sikh. Caste proportions had to be maintained within the community. As in other spheres of life in India, efficiency became only one of the many criteria for selection and, most frequently, the least important of all the requisite qualifications.

Amongst the Sikhs themselves some attempts were made to combat this growing evil by encouraging intermarriage between Jats and non-Jats and re-emphasizing the teachings of the Sikh Gurus. But the attempts were all one-sided, i.e., on the part of the non-Jats. At one time the Akali Party led the movement against this schism. Later on, it not only accepted it but actively sponsored its growth by choosing ministers on this basis.

As already stated, the problem is an economic one and religion is a poor argument against money. The Jat middle class has benefited enormously. Non-Jat moneylenders have been replaced by Jat landlord moneylenders. Jats have got away with all sorts of jobs, from those of peons up to that of minister in the cabinet, on the strength of their caste. The Jat is beginning to appropriate the title Sikh exclusively for himself and accept all the privileges attached to it. The fact that the ten Gurus themselves and some of the most important figures in Sikh history, viz., Banda, Jassa Singh Ahluwalia, Jassa Singh Ramgarhia, Hari Singh Nalwa, Ram Singh (Namdhari), and a host of others were non-Jats, is glibly forgotten. Even later, the more important figures in the community were non-Jats, e.g., Vir Singh (the poet), Kharak Singh (the veteran Akali leader), and Master Tara Singh (leader of the Akali Party).

Sikh versus Hindu

Guru Nanak, the founder of the Sikh religion, was a Hindu; so were the nine succeeding Gurus. Guru Nanak tried, like his contemporary reformers, to prune Hinduism of the many pernicious practices which were corroding Hindu society. His inspiration was essentially Hindu. The ideas were, of necessity, borrowed from Islam, the only other religion available for scrutiny. There is little evidence to support the belief that Guru Nanak planned the founding of a new community synthesizing Hinduism and Islam. He simply planned to reform Hinduism. He did so by reference to Islam. His emphasis on certain Islamic beliefs, e.g., the unity of God as opposed to Hindu pantheism, the equality of mankind as opposed to the Hindu caste system, the condemnation of asceticism, etc., aroused enthusiasm amongst Muslims. Many legends grew up about his being a Mussulman and going on pilgrimage to Mecca. All these are at the best wishful compliments from a community to which he owed so much.

Whatever the intentions of Guru Nanak, the newness of his teachings and his own powerful personality created a new sect properly described as a sect of Hindu dissenters. Almost all the members of this new branch were recruited from the Hindus and, even in later years, conversion to Sikhism was largely from this community. But within a few years after the death of Guru Nanak, certain factors making towards a schism were introduced. A new script, Gurmukhi, was invented. A new religious literature was epitomized in the Adi Granth. New centres of worship and social intercourse (gurdwaras) were erected. New customs and conventions were introduced. Thus, for the Sikh the language was Punjabi not Hindi; the script Gurmukhi not Devanagri; the scripture the Granth Sahib and not the Vedas; the place of worship the gurdwara with the Holy Book and not the temple with its stone idols. Hindu children shaved their heads and celebrated *mundan*. The Sikhs were baptized and swore an oath not to clip their hair. The Hindu was married round a sacrificial fire to the chanting of the Vedas. The Sikh was married round the Adi Granth to the singing of hymns. The dead Hindu had his skull smashed and his ashes cast into the Ganga. The Sikh was cremated with different ceremonial and his ashes thrown into the Beas.

In themselves these differences were unimportant and, for nearly four centuries, neither the Sikhs nor the Hindus thought much of them. They were united in a common struggle against

Muslim persecution. As the Sikhs were the spearhead of the assault
on the Mughal Empire, what they stood for and did was emulated
and applauded by the Hindus. When the Sikhs became the ruling
class, their practices were imitated as a form of flattery. But with
the disappearance of the unifying factors, viz., Muslim persecution
and the Sikh temporal power, separatist tendencies which had lain
dormant began to manifest themselves.

The Hindu-Sikh schism in its active form dates from the British
annexation of the Punjab. The Nirankari, Namdhari and the Singh
Sabha movements, in turn, emphasized the independent entity of
the Sikhs and warned them of the consequences of merging with
the Hindus. The Akali movement, which was primarily a political
movement, accelerated the process. Since it was directed against
the priests, who were more Hindu than Sikh, this was perhaps
inevitable. But it was accentuated by the lack of imagination on
the part of the Akali leaders who became the masters of the Sikh
shrines where the Hindus were also wont to worship. The advent of
Akali predominance in Sikh affairs brought in a certain amount of
rancour and bitterness in the relationship of the two communities,
which had hitherto been unknown. Before the Akali movement,
Punjabi families with one set of brothers brought up as Sikhs and
another as Hindus were the normal feature of Hindu society in
northern Punjab. Intermarriage between the two communities
was common and the reading of Sikh scriptures in Hindu houses
was not unknown.

After the Akali agitation, the position changed. Whereas clean-
shaven Sikhs were accepted by the Hindus, intermarried with them
and finally became Hindus, social intercourse between orthodox
Sikhs and Hindus continued to decrease. With the partition of the
province, the gulf widened even more. One of the major unifying
factors – fear of Muslim domination – had gone. It was replaced
by rivalry for possession of property left by Muslim refugees and

for jobs in services. There were Hindu-Sikh riots, never heard of in the Punjab before.

One of the reasons for the demand for a separate Sikh state made by Akali leaders was this hostility between the two communities. In the Sikh state the Sikhs would not only be free of Hindus and Hindu influences, but the Sikh youth could also be persuaded (if necessary compelled) to continue observing the forms and symbols of the faith.

AFTERWORD

My father's book, *The Sikhs*, a classic, was first published in 1952. In this epilogue, I will take the narrative to the present, 2019. 'Operation Bluestar', the storming of Amritsar's Golden Temple, the holiest shrine of the Sikhs, by the army in June 1984, was a pivotal, albeit tragic, event in recent Sikh history. Therefore, I have written, in some detail, of 'Bluestar', and its aftermath, which was the assassination of Indira Gandhi and the ensuing anti-Sikh riots. Shamefully, the government has failed to bring the guilty to justice, thirty-five years after the tragic event.

With particular emphasis on Punjab and the Sikhs, I have tried to fill the gaps by doing some research (partly in London's wonderful British Library), so as to make this edition as up to date as possible.

The surprise Congress Party victory in the General Election and the even more surprising appointment, in 2004, of Dr Manmohan Singh as Prime Minister, the first Sikh to hold that position, need mention. And I have elaborated on Dr Manmohan Singh's tenure, first as Finance Minister, under Narasimha Rao, when the reform and liberalization of the Indian economy really took off, to his two terms as Prime Minister, between 2004 and 2019.

The other subject I have looked at is the Sikh diaspora in foreign lands, mainly the USA, Canada and the UK. This had some political ramifications on the Khalistan movement. Then, there is the continuing drug problem in Punjab, which has got more severe over the years. In fact, with Sikh militancy declining in the last three or four decades, the drug problem has taken its place. Why and how it can be tackled is a priority issue facing the Sikhs today. Indeed, how has a state that symbolized progress and prosperity, in the wake of the Green Revolution, degenerated into a land of despair, corruption and lack of any meaningful economic growth?

The 'Dera' phenomenon, exemplified by that criminal charlatan, Gurmeet Ram Rahim Singh, now mercifully in jail, is also fascinating and deserves a closer and more detailed look. How did he get such a vast following of Sikhs, including cricketers Yuvraj Singh and Harbhajan Singh? Were the followers of these deras mainly low-caste Sikhs, rejected by the organized, orthodox gurdwaras? Clearly, characters like Gurmeet Ram Rahim Singh had an appeal that the existing religious establishments, including Hindu ones, lacked. The caste system, which Guru Nanak's teachings were meant to abolish, evidently exists, perhaps even thrives, amongst the Sikhs.

My father's book ends on the issue of Sikh identity. He felt very strongly about the need for Sikhs to maintain their outward symbols, namely their long hair, beards and turbans. I have added some thoughts on this touchy issue.

And, finally, Kartarpur, which has been very much in the news in connection with the 550th birth anniversary of Guru Nanak, the founder of the Sikh faith. Five kilometres across the Wagah border into Pakistan is where Nanak spent the last seventeen years of his life. The Kartarpur Gurdwara will probably see millions of

Sikhs from India and elsewhere making a pilgrimage when this updated edition of my father's book is published.

Operation Bluestar and Its Aftermath

Indira Gandhi's seventeen years as Prime Minister of the country had its ups and downs. Here, I shall only cover her relationship with Punjab and, in particular, the Sikhs. When she was first made Prime Minister in January 1965, by the old guard of the Congress Party, 'The Syndicate', they thought they could easily manipulate her. But they were wrong. She showed them she was no '*goongi gudiya*' (dumb doll), as she was once described. She outsmarted them, emerging as her own person, unrivalled and supreme. But after her great moment of glory, the Bangladesh liberation, came her notorious 'Emergency' rule, followed by a couple of years in the wilderness. But she bounced back and rose phoenix-like as the Janata Party imploded. Then came perhaps the biggest tragedy in her personal life when Sanjay, whom she was grooming to succeed her, was killed while flying a stunt plane. Something seemed to snap within her. She lost her once-sure political touch.

'With the death of Sanjay Gandhi, the uncanny sense of timing political action, an instinct that enabled Indira to act with precision and power had diminished,' wrote her close friend and confidant, Pupul Jayakar. 'She was a woman who in the past would listen intently to her advisers and political comrades but acted on her own instincts; an intuitional skill had enabled her to feel into a political situation and plan her electoral strategy with formidable strength.'

In 1980, I was covering the Punjab state election. Indira Gandhi was riding on the crest of a popular wave. The fact that Sanjay had married a Sikh, Maneka, added to Indira's appeal to Punjabis. The Congress triumphed over the formidable Sikh-dominated

Akali Party, clearly indicating that a large number of Sikhs had voted for her. Then, after Sanjay's death, things began to unravel. Indira Gandhi's 'intuitional skill' somehow began to desert her. She began to listen to unprincipled and opportunistic advisers. Worse, she took their advice. Punjab, where the Congress had done so well, posed a major challenge. An obscure, fundamentalist Sikh preacher, a school dropout, Jarnail Singh Bhindranwale, was thrust on to centre stage by the Congress Party. He had a supporter in Giani Zail Singh, a former Punjab Chief Minister and then Home Minister in Indira Gandhi's Cabinet (he would later become the nation's President). Zail Singh's intention was to sow confusion in the Akali Party's ranks. He succeeded in doing exactly that but at huge cost. The Congress puppet – Bhindranwale was allegedly in the pay of the Punjab government and allowed to go scot-free even when there were serious charges against him – severed his strings and became an uncontrollable Frankenstein monster. He moved into Amritsar's Golden Temple complex, the holiest shrine of the Sikhs.

Here, an explanation why many Sikhs responded to him, is called for. Sikhs were facing an 'identity crisis'. Quite a few of them, especially the younger generation, were discarding the outward, distinctive symbols of the faith, i.e. the long hair, the beard and the turban. Though this was part of the process of modernism, it was not how some orthodox Sikhs saw it. They felt their faith was in danger and that some kind of Hindu conspiracy was behind making them 'second-class citizens' and discriminating against them. Only an independent Sikh state, where Sikhs would be in a majority and where the true faith would be preached and followed, could save Sikhism. Thus was born the notion of 'Khalistan'. Unrealistic and mad though it may sound now, the notion had its fanatical adherents, with Bhindranwale fanning the flames of communalism and separatism. Ominously, his followers began to grow. Those who

openly opposed him 'disappeared'. Dead bodies began to be found
in the sewers of the Golden Temple complex. Hindus were pulled
out of a bus by Sikh terrorists and shot. Editors of newspapers
critical of Bhindranwale were assassinated. My father had to be
given round-the-clock security after he condemned Bhindranwale
in his columns and was issued threats. Bhindranwale's malevolent
intent was clear: To instil so much fear into Hindus in Punjab
that they would be forced to leave the state, while the backlash
against Sikhs elsewhere would make the latter flee to Punjab for
safety. In other words, a forced transfer of communities would
take place, just as had happened during the Partition of the Indian
subcontinent in 1947. Shamefully, the Akali leaders, also ensconced
in the Golden Temple complex and scared out of their wits by
Bhindranwale's violent tactics, did not have the guts to oppose
him. The neighbouring Haryana government made matters worse.
It singled out Sikhs at the state border and humiliated them by
detaining and searching them. Even army generals and senior
government officials were not spared.

Amongst them was Major General Shabeg Singh, a war hero
and the man who trained the Mukti Bahini, the Bangladesh
guerilla force. He was later stripped of his rank and dishonourably
discharged from the army, a day before his retirement, for alleged
corruption (the charges were never proved). He claimed that the
discharge was because he was a Sikh, a feeling that was reinforced
by the humiliating way he was treated when he tried to enter
Haryana on his way to Delhi. An embittered General Shabeg
became an ardent follower of Bhindranwale and, as will be related
later, the main thorn in the side of the Indian armed forces
when they entered the Golden Temple complex. Meanwhile, the
complex was being converted by Bhindranwale into a veritable
armed fortress. A variety of deadly weapons were being smuggled
into the holy shrine, while inflammatory and seditious speeches

were being given with impunity. Communal killings continued unchecked. It is believed that over 100 civilians and security personnel were killed between 1981 and 1984. Fear and foreboding pervaded the state. The stage was set for perhaps the darkest chapter in independent India's history.

A flashpoint came on 25 April 1984, with the murder of deputy inspector general (DIG) of police, Avtar Singh Atwal, a Sikh, who was leaving the Golden Temple after having offered prayers in the shrine. Several policemen said they had seen the murder suspect run into the shrine after shooting Atwal at point-blank range. It was the perfect opportunity for the police to enter the shrine and go after the killer, and at the same time apprehend Bhindranwale. Inexplicably, nothing was done and the opportunity lost. Referring to the inaction of the authorities and their allowing him the freedom to say what he liked, even to spew communal hatred and preach sedition, Bhindranwale commented, 'The government has done more for me in a few days than what I could have achieved in years.' On 26 January 1983, Republic Day, a Khalistan flag had been raised on top of a building in the Temple complex.

By end May it was abundantly clear that the government had lost all control over the complex and that Bhindranwale was calling the shots. The decision to call in the army was probably taken when Akali leader Harchand Singh Longowal announced the launching of a state-wide 'morcha' (agitation) on 3 June 1984, to prevent the movement of food grains. The government also realized that the piling up of weapons in the Golden Temple complex included sophisticated ones, like rocket-launchers, against which police action would be inadequate. Only the army could now overcome Bhindranwale and his armed followers. Major General Kuldip Singh ('Bulbul') Brar, a Sikh, though clean-shaven, related that he was about to go on a holiday to the Philippines with his wife when he was summoned from Meerut, where he was stationed, to Chandimandir, a military base on the outskirts of Chandigarh, for a conference on 'internal security'.

Brar was ushered into the Operations Room and received his first instructions from Lieutenant General Krishnaswamy Sundarji, General Officer Commanding, Western Command (he would later become Chief of Army Staff). Present with him was Lieutenant General Ranjit Singh Dyal, Chief of Staff, Western Command. The fourth key person was army chief General Arunkumar Shridhar Vaidya (he would years later be killed by two terrorists in Pune). Brar was told he would be in charge of all the forces, including the police and the para-military. The objective was to oust Bhindranwale and his followers from the shrine and to prevent any uprising in the surrounding countryside. The action in the Golden Temple complex was code-named 'Operation Bluestar' and the sealing of the border with Pakistan and the securing of the area, 'Operation Woodrose'. Minimum force was to be used and damage to the complex, particularly the Harmandir Sahib (sanctum sanctorum), avoided.

'We did not go in anger, but with sadness; with a prayer on our lips and humility in our hearts,' said Sundarji eloquently.

According to R.K. Dhawan, personal secretary to Indira Gandhi, Vaidya assured her that there would be few casualties and no damage to the Golden Temple complex. With a General Election looming, she would be seen as upholding national unity against secessionist forces. The reality turned out to be entirely different – and unbelievably tragic. Shabeg, a master tactician of urban warfare, had fortified the five-storey Akal Takht, the second holiest building in the complex, bricking up the windows and balconies and placing machine-gun nests there, as well as in other places in the complex. The open ground between the entrance of the Golden Temple and the Akal Takht was turned into a

killing field, with machine-guns targeting it from all sides. The
'intelligence' outputs that the army received were completely off
the mark, grossly underestimating the extent of the fortifications
prepared by Shabeg and the fighting prowess of the militants
he had trained. The timing of the Operation was also strange
(according to some Sikhs, deliberate): 3 June, the day of the army's
assault, also happened to be the martyrdom day of one of the Sikh
gurus, Arjun Dev, when thousands of pilgrims would be in the
temple. Though many were able to leave after announcements
were made, quite a few, probably several thousand, stayed behind
in the confusion. They were caught in the crossfire between the
army and the militants.

Brar's first targets were two 18th century watchtowers and an
elevated water tank. They overlooked the Golden Temple and had
been converted into sniper nests with sandbags. They were all blown
up with a 106-mm recoilless gun and a 3.7-inch howitzer. 'Shells
hit sandbags and sent them flying, with flailing limbs,' reported an
eyewitness. Brar evidently hoped that such shock-and-awe tactics
would persuade the militants to surrender without any more loss
of life. Unfortunately, no such luck. Hence, the decision was made
to send in specially trained, heavily armed commandos equipped
with gas canisters. The time of the assault was 10 p.m. on 5 June.
The commandos immediately came under withering fire from
above and along the ground. Most of them were mowed down,
the survivors finding shelter behind some pillars. More waves
of commandos were similarly killed and the infantry forces sent
behind them were unable to make much progress, while suffering
heavy casualties.

With daylight approaching, the decision was taken to bring in the
tanks, after an Armed Personnel Carrier (AMC) was immobilized
by an anti-tank missile. 'We never imagined the militants had anti-
tank weapons in their inventory', Brar admitted later. At 5.21 a.m.

on 6 June, three Vijayanta tanks brought their heavy arsenal to bear down on the Akal Takht, shattering its defences and reducing it to a fiery ruin. That is probably when Bhindranwale and Shabeg, along with most of their followers, died. At 11 a.m. a large group of militants rushed out of the Akal Takht in an attempt to escape. They were all gunned down. Mopping up operations continued over the next two days.

When President Zail Singh visited the complex on the morning of 8 June, a sniper fired at him. Though he was not hurt, an officer accompanying him was seriously wounded. Zail Singh was visibly shaken when he saw the damage to the complex, especially to the Akal Takht which was a smouldering wreck (the Sikh Reference Library had also been completely gutted and the Golden Temple was pock-marked where bullets had struck). According to the military, 136 army men died and 220 were injured in the operation. Civilian casualties were 492. These figures have been hotly disputed, with the number of civilians (mainly pilgrims) being killed said to be as high as 5,000 to 20,000. As for the army, even Rajiv Gandhi, Indira Gandhi's elder son who was prime minister, claimed, in one of his speeches, that '700 soldiers' were killed. In 2009, the CNN–IBN channel reported that the army lost 365 commandos. Whatever the true figures, Operation Blue Star was the bloodiest confrontation of the military with a section of its own people in India since Independence. Strangely, the army carried out no inquiry, though it is customary for it to minutely and critically examine every action it undertakes. 'Bluestar' traumatized the Sikh community. And the trauma still continues. At least 4,000 Sikh soldiers mutinied. Indira Gandhi paid for it with her life. On 31 October, four months later, she was gunned down by two of her Sikh bodyguards. This was followed by anti-Sikh riots in which over 3,000 Sikhs were butchered in the capital alone. By then, her elder son, Rajiv, had taken over as Prime Minister. Virtually justifying the riots, he stated infamously, 'When a big tree falls, the earth is bound to shake'. Some years later, an army Colonel who had been posted then in the outskirts of Delhi revealed to me that word of the riots had got to his unit.

'We were itching to get orders to go to Delhi and restore peace,' he said to me. But the orders never came until it was too late and the rioters had done their worst.

It was clear that the powers that be felt that the Sikhs had to be taught a lesson. Various inquiry reports came to nothing and the main culprits have not had to answer for their crimes. No closure has yet taken place. It has been difficult for the Congress to point fingers at Modi for the anti-Muslim communal killings of 2002 in Ahmedabad, when its own record in Delhi in 1984 has been highly questionable. The massacres led to a decade of Sikh terrorism, aided and abetted by Pakistan. Tens of thousands died in that terrible decade – terrorists, security forces and innocent civilians. The Punjab police became a law unto themselves, often extorting money from innocent people.

I recall N.N. Vohra, then Punjab's Home Secretary and in direct charge of the police (he later went on to serve a long term as Governor of Jammu and Kashmir), telling me that his driver had once been held up at a police check-post and asked for money. When he refused and said that he was the Home Secretary's driver, he was thrashed. 'I could not do anything,' related a helpless Vohra. 'The police would have planted drugs in the car and said that the car was carrying them.'

In March 1986, Julio Ribeiro, who had been head of police in Maharashtra, was brought in as Punjab's Director General of Police. It was an inspired move. When he was in Bombay earlier, following Indira Gandhi's assassination, he had immediately ordered the rounding up of goondas and other troublemakers. No Sikh was harmed in the city. The Sikhs have much to thank him for. Instead, there were two attempts on his life by the terrorists. In Punjab, he followed the same tough policy, 'bullet for bullet'. The terrorists were put on the back foot. A trio mainly ran the state then: Chief Secretary P.H. Vaishnav, an outstanding Gujarati civil servant who was fluent in Punjabi, Chief Minister Surjit Singh Barnala, perhaps one of the best chief ministers Punjab has ever had, and Ribeiro. A Roman Catholic, a Hindu and a Sikh, a stirring example of Indian secularism at its best, tackling perhaps the worst internal problem faced by India post-Independence. Sadly, though, the police often went too far. According to a Human Rights Watch report on Punjab: 'State security forces adopted increasingly brutal methods to stem the insurgency, including arbitrary arrests, torture, prolonged detention without trail, disappearances ... members of the police force, federal paramilitary troops of Central Reserve Police Force (CRPF) and, to a lesser extent, the Indian army, engaged in summary execution/killing of civilians and suspected militants.' K.P.S. Gill, who had taken over from Ribeiro, was in charge of the Punjab police at the time.

By the end of 1995, Sikh militancy more or less came to an end. The overwhelming majority of Sikhs, who had never been sympathetic to the Khalistan call, were somehow able to put aside the bloodshed and bitterness, and return to the mainstream. That took courage of a different kind and showed that the bonds binding Hindus and Sikhs, though strained, had not been irretrievably broken. The proof of that was the elevation of a Sikh, Manmohan Singh, as Prime Minister, and another Sikh, General J.J. Singh as the army chief. Nevertheless, Operation Bluestar and its aftermath will remain an ugly, defining moment in independent India's history.

From Prosperity to Decline

Punjab used to be India's most progressive and prosperous state, the envy of the rest of the country. At the time of Independence, it also comprised what is now Haryana and Himachal Pradesh.

Then came the short-sighted Akali Party-led 'Punjabi Suba' agitation. Many Hindu-Punjabis, whose mother tongue was Punjabi, declared their language to be Hindi, fearful of Sikh domination. It was the start of a rift between Hindus and Sikhs in Punjab, which was unimaginable earlier. Hence, a new state of Haryana was carved out of erstwhile Punjab in 1966, followed by Himachal Pradesh in 1971. A truncated but Sikh majority state was left. Nevertheless, it prospered, thanks mainly to the Green Revolution which transformed Indian agriculture. Over 90 per cent of Punjab's farmers were Sikh, since most of Punjab's Hindus were concentrated in the towns and cities. Hence, the Green Revolution was essentially the achievement of Sikhs. High-yielding variety of seeds for both wheat and rice, which had been developed in research institutes abroad, in Mexico and Manila, were imported into India. Under a collaboration agreement between the Indian government and the Ford Foundation, Punjab, because of its reliable water supply, was selected as the first site to try out the new crops. (In 1961, India was on the verge of mass famine, hence the added urgency to try and increase food production.) M.S. Swaminathan, who was Adviser to the Indian Ministry of Agriculture, invited Norman Borlaug (who went on the win the Nobel Prize) to helm the experiment. The results were spectacular. Thanks to a semi-dwarf variety of rice, which produced more grains per plant when certain fertilizers were used, rice production went up a phenomenal ten times, from one ton per acre to ten tons. Naturally, the cost of rice also came down and independent India became one of the world's most successful rice producers, and is now a major rice exporter. Punjab, which had earlier hardly produced any rice, became the country's main production centre. Similarly, the introduction of new high-yielding varieties of wheat led to the soaring of production from ten million tonnes a year in the early 1960s to 75 million in 2006. India became a food-surplus country and was able to stop the food grain imports from the USA under PL 480. Under Nehru and then Indira Gandhi, the country was ostensibly following a 'non-aligned' policy. To be so heavily dependent on the USA was humiliating for a proud nation. India was derisively described as living a 'ship-to-mouth' existence. However, later on, excessive use of chemicals, pesticides and fertilizers, along with water, led to a rise in underground water levels, pushing salts to the surface and making large tracts of once fertile land barren and unproductive.

Nevertheless, the 1960s and 70s were indeed Punjab's golden years. A state ravaged by Partition lifted itself up from its bootstraps to become the most go-ahead and wealthy in the entire country and the Sikhs were admired and liked.

This period roughly coincided with the chief ministership of Partap Singh Kairon. The civil servants Mohinder Singh Randhawa and Edward Nirmal Mangatrai served under him. Historian, arts-and-culture promoter Randhawa played a major role in the establishment of agricultural research in India which was pivotal for the Green Revolution. He and Kairon were also instrumental in the resettlement of refugees from west Pakistan, who were mainly Sikhs, a stupendous task, since there were about three million of them. Jawaharlal Nehru decided that as Lahore, which had been the political and cultural capital of undivided Punjab had been lost to Pakistan, another city should come up in India's new Punjab to replace it. That was the origin of Chandigarh and the key players were Kairon and Randhawa, along with the great Swiss architect-cum-town planner Le Corbusier (who was a friend and admirer of Nehru's). In fact, Randhawa, a keen horticulturist, was largely responsible for planting a variety of trees in Chandigarh, many of them fruit-bearing. An enchanting rose garden in the heart of the city was his doing and has a bust of him. Chandigarh is probably the greenest and cleanest city in India, a haven for the retired, thanks mainly to this remarkable renaissance man. Writer Gulzar

Singh Sandhu called him '*Punjab da chhewan dariya*' (the sixth river of Punjab), an apt description. Kairon and civil servants like Randhawa were the architects of the rebirth and then prosperity of post-Independence Punjab. A state shattered by Partition rose up from the ashes, phoenix-like.

Kairon established the pioneering Punjab Agriculture University (PAU) in Ludhiana and put Punjab once again on the economic map of India. Apart from resettling the Sikh refugees flooding across the border from Pakistan, he also resettled many of them in Ganganagar in Rajasthan, and in the Terai region, where they thrived. In addition, he helped establish the industrial township of Faridabad and opened three engineering colleges. Punjab's basic infrastructure, like roads and electricity, were expanded by him. On the social side, primary- and middle-level school education was made free and compulsory. There were corruption charges against him but the courts cleared him. However, he was killed, in 1965, over a family dispute. A sad end to a true son of Punjab and the main founder of its prosperity.

The downturn came towards the end of the seventies. The 1965 and 1971 wars with Pakistan had already scared away investors from outside Pakistan. Who wants to put their funds in a state where wars tend to break out, or where there is constant tension and unrest? Only a few large industries came up and unemployment rose. Many Sikh farmers' sons, perhaps lured by the bright lights of the big cities and the attraction of modern lifestyles, did not want to live in the countryside and toil on the farms. The policies of the Indian armed forces also changed. It was decided that other states and communities in the country, which had been relatively neglected in the recruitment of soldiers, would be given greater and more proportionate representation. Punjabis, and particularly Sikhs, had constituted an entirely disproportionate share of the armed forces, ever since Sikhs were inducted in the

British Indian army in the mid 19th century. The Sikhs had sided with the British during the 1857 Indian Mutiny (also called the First War of Indian Independence) and Sikh troops had been a key factor in quelling the Mutiny. In gratitude and in tribute to the fighting prowess of the Sikhs, more of them were taken into the British army. It is estimated that during the First World War (1914–18), around 20 per cent of the soldiers in the British Indian army were Sikh, even though they constituted less than 2 per cent of the Indian population. In 1947, at the time of Independence, Sikh officers constituted 50 per cent of the Indian army, and 38 per cent of the Indian Air Force. Of the combat soldiers, Sikhs made up 33 per cent of the military. After Independence, these percentages steadily declined. The armed forces had been a major source of employment for Sikhs. That source began to dry up. With fewer retired Sikh soldiers and officers drawing pensions than before, many Sikh families did not have the financial cushion that they had before. In brief, there was less money to go around. The Green Revolution, which had brought so much employment and funds to Punjab, and particularly to the Sikhs, had plateaued by the early 1980s. A 2015–16 study by Punjab University revealed that 86 per cent of the farmers in the State faced various levels of indebtedness, with a third living below the poverty line. From having the highest per capita income in the country, after the 1980s, while India's economic growth picked up, Punjab's started to decline. By 2012, six states – Maharashtra, Haryana, Gujarat, Himachal Pradesh, Kerala and Tamil Nadu – had overtaken Punjab. A report in 2018 by the rating agency Credit Analysis & Research (CARE) says that Punjab is the most indebted state in India, with 26.7 per cent of its revenue going towards interest payments. Little wonder, then, that hardly any new investment has come into Punjab. The only businesses that seem to be thriving are those run by politicians, or those with political connections. The Badal family, which has ruled the state and controls many businesses, is a case in point.

A survey in 2015 by Punjab Agricultural University (PAU) and Guru Nanak Dev University reveals that since 2000, nearly 16,000 farmers and agricultural workers have committed suicide. In the 1960s and 70s, small and medium enterprises, like the manufacture of bicycles, hosiery and sports goods, did well in Punjab. No longer. On the contrary, a disclosure made by the Punjab Department of Industry and Commerce, under the Right to Information Act, showed that as many as 18,770 factories had been forced to shut shop between 2007 and 2014. Asit Jolly, writing in *India Today*, has this telling description of a major industrial hub:

> Mandi Gobindgarh, located prominently along the Grand Trunk Road (National Highway 1) between Ambala and Ludhiana, starkly demonstrates the malaise that seems to be afflicting Punjab's industrial sector. One of the oldest iron and steel hubs, in operation since the 1930s, and still counted among the most important ferrous metal markets in south Asia, Mandi Gobindgarh essentially comprised a dense cluster of some 450 induction furnaces, coal-fired foundries and rolling mills that churned out everything from ingots, construction steel, specialized high carbon steel, to every known description of angles and channels. Motorists on the GT road had routinely cribbed about the smog in the area but business was great and the Mandi, as locals call their town, had innumerable rags-to-riches stories to tell. All that has changed.

He quotes a mill owner as saying that the air has become cleaner but the mills are being literally 'choked out of existence', and that he faces a daily challenge in keeping his father's two steel rolling mills going. It is the same story in Amritsar, Ludhiana, Jalandhar, Batala and Kapurthala. Thousands have lost their jobs.

An idle mind, it is said, is the devil's playground. If a person is busy, he tends to stay out of trouble. Drugs had earlier never been a problem in Punjab, and smoking tobacco was taboo amongst the Sikhs. My grandfather usually popped a plug of opium in his mouth after a hard day's work because it relaxed him and brought on a feeling of contentment. Many other Punjabis did that, but very few were drug addicts. All that started to change. Joblessness and the easy availability of all kinds of drugs, not just the relatively harmless opium plugs my grandfather used to take, made a deadly mix. There was another factor. Huge sums of money were offered to farmers where development works were being undertaken. For instance, Rs 1.5 crore an acre was the price of land where the international airport and aerocity came up, on the outskirts of Chandigarh. In Rajpura, further away, the rate was Rs 35 lakhs an acre for the building of a thermal plant and Bathinda Central University. A flood of cash came into quite a few idle hands.

It was around this time that Sikh militancy under the malevolent and hate-spewing preacher, Jarnail Singh Bhindranwale, bared its fangs. Pakistan, especially Pakistan's 'deep state', the Inter State Intelligence (ISI), seeking revenge for India's hand in the break-up of their country and the creation of Bangladesh, felt this was an ideal opportunity to weaken India. In the chaotic conditions in Afghanistan and the withdrawal of Soviet troops, the country had once again become a source of heroin, which is derived from opium and perhaps the most addictive of all narcotics. This was smuggled across the Indo-Pak border border. Even though it was heavily guarded, our Border Security Force (BSF), sadly, was known for its rogue elements who, in collusion with the Pakistani Rangers, their counterparts, could be bribed to let the stuff cross the border. When I was posted in Chandigarh in the 1980s, the BSF was derisively known as the Border Smuggling Force. Opium was also grown legally in various parts of north India, especially in Madhya Pradesh and Rajasthan (it can also be turned into morphine, used widely for medical purposes as a pain-reliever) but there was clandestine growth of the poppy as well, as well as leakage. The poppy husk and sap were turned into heroin in illegal laboratories and found its way into various parts of the country, including Punjab.

I have some frighteningly sad statistics before me on drug use in Punjab, along with the bewildering array of drugs smoked, ingested and injected commonly in that State. The Punjab government itself informed the Punjab and Haryana High Court that a staggering 75 per cent of the state's youth is addicted to drugs and that one out of three college students takes drugs. Almost a third of all those who are in jail have been arrested under the Narcotic Drugs and Psychotropic Substances Act. A large number of Sikh youngsters trying to enroll for the army found it difficult to qualify. Earlier, they could easily pass the test. The usual healthy and strapping Punjabis had given way to emaciated youngsters, thanks mainly to the constant use of various narcotics. Apart from marijuana, heroin and their various derivatives, there were synthetic drug formulations such as methamphetamine which also has derivatives. These were sold at pharmacies. Though they needed prescriptions, it was widely known that they were sold by chemists freely, to get the votes of Punjabi youths. There was clearly political involvement in the drug trade and it was rumoured that a senior minister in the Badal Cabinet was directly involved in the highly lucrative business.

There was another factor at work, to explain why there was so much joblessness in the state: The poor quality of education that did not equip even graduates to qualify for high-level jobs. I was once staying at one of the best hotels in Ludhiana on an assignment for an NGO. Some foreigners were with me. They were unable to communicate at all with senior members of the hotel staff, because the staff could not speak English, a consequence of the then Punjab government's foolish and short-sighted policy of promoting Punjabi and downplaying English which, as anybody knows, is essential for jobs in the service industry. Hence, the flight of Sikhs to more favourable climes – they found it easier to escape the country and find jobs abroad. The lucky ones found legal means but many others took the illegal route through touts who, at a hefty price, promised they could get them employment in the Gulf, even western Europe and the USA. Most of the promises evaporated into thin air and they were dumped in countries with much lower level jobs than had been promised, or left stranded at an international airport, with a fake passport and false papers. They were left having to fend for themselves or were deported. Some tried to get to their desired destinations by hazardous land or sea journeys, a few perishing along the way. Perhaps the saddest cases were of single women who were inveigled, through fake marriage bureaus, into marrying men living abroad. When they got there, some found that the man they had earlier 'married' was already married and that he expected her to be virtually a maid. She was trapped, unable to return home. Cultural troupes invited abroad would take along members for a hefty fee. Once they were in the invited country, they would simply slip away. But with US President Donald Trump cracking down on those who have overstayed beyond the period permitted by their visas, and those who have gone illegally, their days abroad may be numbered. The same policy of being tough on those who overstay and go to the UK illegally is likely to be followed after Brexit comes into effect.

The Sikh Diaspora

The Sikh diaspora has been compared to the Jewish one. Both were religious, perhaps the only diasporas based on religion. But there is one major difference. The Jews dispersed to various parts of the world, mainly due to persecution; the Sikhs, for better opportunities (except some who fled abroad, following the crackdown on Sikh militants, after 'Bluestar'). There are presently an estimated 27 million people of Indian origin living abroad, the largest diaspora, except for the Chinese. Emigration of Indians began in significant numbers only in the 19th century, following the abolition of slavery, in 1833–34. There was also the 'convict diaspora', whereby Indian convicts were sent to the British colonies in South-East Asia for developing the infrastructure by clearing forests, building roads and bridges and constructing buildings. This also helped reduce the large number of convicts in overcrowded Indian jails. However, migration in the true sense only began with the introduction of what is called the 'indentured system'. This was essentially to get over the ban on slavery and meant that the migrant would have to serve a term of so many years, after which he was free to do what he wanted. The Indian diaspora, from about 1830 to the 1920s, spread to colonies like Mauritius, Malaya, Burma, Ceylon, Jamaica, Trinidad, British Guyana, Martinique, and Natal in South Africa. Not too many Sikhs went abroad under this system because they did not like the idea of working under labour contractors but some of them, because of their formidable appearance and fierce looks, went as security guards.

Punjab was the last of the major areas to be taken over by the British, following the Anglo-Sikh wars. After their defeat, the Sikhs were quickly inducted into the British Indian army. Their numbers continued to rise and some were sent to serve in combat zones like central and South-East Asia, the Middle and Far East. The British favoured them not just because of their fighting prowess but also because their religion was egalitarian and not governed by caste, as was that of the Hindus. After the 1857 Mutiny, in which the Sikhs played a vital role on the side of the British, John Lawrence, Governor of Punjab, wrote: 'The discovery of the valour of the Sikhs coincided with the 1857 Mutiny. I am lost in astonishment that any of us are alive. But for the mercy of God we must have been ruined. Had the Sikhs joined against us, nothing humanly speaking could have saved us.' High praise indeed from an outstanding figure of British colonial rule. Sikhs who got into the army were not only permitted to retain their beards, long hair and turban but encouraged to keep these outward symbols of their religion. As a result, many 'sehajdhari' (shorn) Sikhs became 'keshdhari' (with hair). There was another factor at work, which in its own way contributed to the Sikh diaspora. Sikhs had got used to movement, being uprooted, and starting life anew. After all, they lived in an area which saw repeated invasions and incursions. Their resilience saw them through. Guru Nanak himself travelled in and outside India. Hence, the tradition of movement amongst the Sikhs was an old one. Much of the migration came from the 'doab' region, between the five rivers of Punjab. This had the highest population density in Punjab. Migration relieved the pressure of numbers. Land holdings, too, were becoming smaller due to the increase in population, making migration even more attractive.

The first Sikhs to go overseas were policemen to soldiers on duty abroad. In June 1867, a hundred Sikhs arrived in Hong Kong to join the police force on the recommendation of their superiors. Reports of better opportunities in North America and Australia led to a wave of migration to these countries. A second wave came after the First World War when citizenship laws were liberalized in many countries, making it easier to migrate there. However, there were aberrations, such as the expulsion of Indians from Uganda by its dictator, Idi Amin. In Kenya and Nigeria, too, Indians faced problems in the newly independent countries and many of them decided to migrate to other countries.

Today, Canada has close to half a million Sikhs (and also the most number of Sikh ministers in its cabinet outside India). In the 2015 Canadian elections, as many as seventeen Sikhs were elected Members of Parliament. The UK has 342,000 Sikhs, the USA 180,000, Australia 126,000 (making Sikhism the fifth-largest religious group, after Christianity, Islam, Hinduism and Buddhism), Bangladesh 23,000, and lesser numbers in Belgium, France and Germany. Almost a decade ago, Sikh soldiers in the US army, who had been compelled to cut their hair and shave off their beards, won the right to retain these symbols of their faith. Against this minor victory was the setback in France in 2004, where Sikhs with long hair and turbans were denied admission to State-funded schools. France has, since the French Revolution, had an entirely secular policy. Christian girls cannot wear necklaces with a cross and Muslims aren't allowed burqas or scarves. If you want to dress that way, the State says in so many words, go to your own private schools, not to government-funded ones. I, for one, entirely agree with the French government, but the matter is before the authorities who have yet to make a final decision.

Of the Sikh diaspora, perhaps the most pernicious are those in Canada and the UK. A few misguided Sikhs have taken up the cause of Khalistan, or an independent Sikh country. They make up for their lack of numbers with aggression and intimidation. Whatever resonance they had during and after 'Bluestar', particularly fanned by the anti-Sikh riots, has long gone. Yet, they continue to support – and fund – a lost cause. And, of course, commit violent acts. Strangely, both the British and Canadian governments have done little to curb the activities of these Sikhs, or bothered to check the accounts of the Gurdwaras they control.

As part of the Press party, I once accompanied Rajiv Gandhi on his first major tour abroad, after he became Prime Minister in 1984. In Washington, he met members of the American Press. Amongst the audience was a group of vociferous Sikhs raising Khalistani slogans. During Rajiv Gandhi's interaction with reporters, he addressed the Sikhs, pointing out that the Khalistan they wanted was basically the kingdom over which the Sikh emperor, Ranjit Singh, had ruled. It was now most of Pakistan, with its capital in Lahore. The Sikhs had no answer to this rather sly observation of Rajiv Gandhi's except more shouting.

Sikh Identity and the Dera Phenomenon

Perhaps the most transformative part of Guru Nanak's teachings was his stress on equality and, in particular, his rejection of the Hindu caste system, especially the practice of untouchability. It is likely that this philosophy was borrowed from Islam which also stresses equality and is anti-caste. In any case, he must have noticed during his extensive travels that many of the coverts from Hinduism to Islam came from the lower Hindu castes. Be that as it may, the tradition of the 'langar' in gurdwaras, whereby free food is distributed to everybody who comes – no matter from which religion, caste, or class – embodies this vital aspect of Sikhism and of Nanak's philosophy. However, over 500 years later, caste divisions, even the practice of untouchability, exist in Sikhism, particularly in the rural areas, where in some villages there are separate wells for the Dalits who are barred entry into the regular gurdwaras. This is a terrible blot on the current practice of Sikhism. Punjab has the highest percentage of Dalits amongst all the states in the country, at 31 per cent.

I once appeared on a television programme (conducted by Barkha Dutt) on this very subject. There were several turbaned and bearded Sikhs in the audience. When I mentioned how Dalit Sikhs were discriminated against by the orthodox Sikhs, despite Nanak's teachings, there was an angry uproar from them. Barkha had to calm them down during a break in the programme and threatened to throw them out if they did not behave. After order was restored, I asked the audience, 'How many of you know that

Kanshi Ram (the founder of the Bahujan Samaj Party and mentor
of its present leader, Mayawati) was a Sikh?' There was a stunned
silence, followed by more shouting from the Sikhs. At another
point in the programme, when we were discussing Sikh identity,
I held up a picture of Guru Gobind Singh (the last of the Sikh
gurus), on horseback, looking very martial. It was from a book
and was a print of a painting hanging in a well-known museum.
Though the Guru was shown bearded and turbaned, his beard
was clearly a trimmed one. More angry shouting erupted. The
simple point I was trying to make was that, though they may have
retained their long hair and turbans, most Sikhs trimmed their
beards. After the programme ended, the group had collected in
the foyer, intending to beat me up. One of them tried to snatch
the book in which the offending Guru Gobind Singh picture had
been reproduced. Alarmed, and fearful for my safety, Barkha had to
summon the police to escort me home. I should add that my father
had 'coached' me before the TV show. He, like other thoughtful
Sikhs, felt that the continuing discrimination between high-caste
and low-caste Sikhs was a shame, and that it marred the practice
of the faith.

A more heinous – and criminal – example of such discrimination
came to light at one of the Khushwant Singh Litertature festivals
that is held annually in Kasauli, Himachal Pradesh. Nirupama
Dutt, who had written a book on a folk singer, Bant Singh, '*The
Ballad of Bant Singh*', urged us, the organizers, to invite her subject.
Bant Singh arrived in a wheelchair for a simple reason: He had
just one limb on his entire body, a leg. A horrified and spellbound
audience listened as he related his tragic saga and his continuing
fight for justice. When he was thirty-six, his daughter, who was still
a minor, was gang-raped by some higher caste Jat youngsters. This
was a common occurrence in the part of Punjab he came from. If
the victim dared to complain to the authorities, she and her family

were either threatened or bought off. Despite the Panchayat telling Bant Singh to keep quiet, as his daughter would not get married otherwise, and resisting offers of large sums of money, he decided to fight back, and went to the police. Fortunately, he also had the backing of a left-wing organization he belonged to. He even managed to get a few of the perpetrators convicted of the rape, the first time in the region that a Dalit Sikh in the area had dared to complain against upper caste violence and had secured conviction. The perpetrators of the crime sought revenge. They ambushed and savagely assaulted Bant Singh, leaving him severely injured and bleeding. By the time he was taken to hospital and treated, gangrene had set in and his two arms and a leg had to be amputated. You would have thought that after this terrible ordeal and warning, he would be cowed down. But not Bant Singh. He continues bravely to try and bring more of the perpetrators – two of whom were the sons of the sarpanch of his village – to justice, a continuing uphill task, given the prevailing mood and prejudice against Dalit Sikhs. I have mentioned Bant Singh's courageous saga in some detail because this shamefully remains the norm in many areas of Punjab. With organized Sikh religion having failed to break through these barriers of discrimination, to allow all Dalit Sikhs entry into whichever gurdwara they might want to enter, little wonder that they have started looking elsewhere to fulfill their spiritual needs and for leadership. This partly explains the phenomenal rise and huge popularity of the so-called 'deras'. These are curious socio-religious organizations, usually with a charismatic guru. Many of them pre-date the birth of Sikhism, some of them being Sufis and followers of the Bhakti movement. However, the deras have increased in number in more recent times, amongst the Sikhs as well as the Hindus in Punjab, even in the adjoining states, like Haryana, Rajasthan and Uttar Pradesh. According to a ten-year-old study, there were some 7,000 Sikh and non-Sikh deras in rural

Punjab, testifying to their appeal and popularity. The newer deras became rallying points for Dalits who, despite having embraced the Sikh faith, were excluded by Jat-dominated bodies like the Shiromani Gurdwara Prabandhak Committee (SGPC), the so-called highest spiritual authority of the Sikhs but which has had a tradition of caving in when faced by a challenge to its authority, like the one that Jarnail Singh Bhindranwale posed when he took over the Golden Temple in 1984. Perhaps the most successful of the deras is the one called the 'Radha Soamis', which attracts both Hindus and Sikhs, owns vast tracts of land and has centres all over north India. It also has a 'guru', the present one having got into dubious financial transactions with a prominent Sikh business family.

But the most fascinating, outlandish and talked-about of these dera leaders of our times has been the man who headed the 'Dera Sacha Sauda' for several years, Gurmeet Ram Rahim Singh. Ostensibly a Sikh, he was a school drop-out but obviously a glib talker with marketing abilities. Note the name he adopted, a clever ploy to attract people of all denominations, Muslims, Hindus and Sikhs. He set out to be a 'guru' at a fairly young age and succeeded, probably more than his wildest imagination, in acquiring a huge following, estimated at some 70 million at its peak, not just in Punjab but adjoining states as well, even abroad. Two famous cricketers, Yuvraj Singh and Harbhajan Singh, were amongst his devotees. With the growing followers came untold wealth. He set up 40 ashrams in India, and more in the USA, Canada, the UK, UAE, Singapore, and Australia. His dera owned large amounts of land, covering hundreds of acres, and many properties. Some 150 products were manufactured under the name he gave himself, 'MSG' (Messenger of God), with sales of Rs 1 crore a day. He produced five thoroughly bad films, yet apparently earned Rs 1,000 crore from them. To give his empire a veneer of respectability, his dera ran thirteen schools and colleges, and three hospitals. Needless to say, with so much wealth and so many followers came political clout. Well-known politicians, even chief ministers, courted him, attending his functions, knowing that his support could swing an election one way or another. His lifestyle and tastes were unbelievably garish and downright vulgar, with expensive flashy cars and over-the-top outfits. Yet, his followers worshipped him and his decidedly weird antics. Looking back, it seems incredible that so many people found him and his simplistic teachings so appealing and profound. Little did they know that beneath the glitz and bombastic talk was a crumbling foundation of deception and lies—and criminality. Gurmeet Ram Rahim was a serial rapist and a double-murderer, who ordered the castration of 400 of his disciples. It was only the dogged perseverance of two of his *sadhvi*s whom he had raped – one of them a minor at the time – that finally nailed and convicted this criminal charlatan. His sentence? Twenty years of imprisonment with hard labour, with probably more to follow for the murder charges. How could such an obvious fake get worshipped as some kind of god and be given so much power that he felt he could do whatever his perverse mind took a whim or fancy to? What was the management of the dera doing all this time? These are questions that not just Sikhs alone, but also other Indians need to ask themselves. He is certainly not the first, neither will he be the last 'godman' to hoodwink so many gullible people and take them for a ride. As mentioned earlier, the blame lies partly with organized religion and bodies like the SGPC. They have clearly been oblivious of the needs and desires of so many Sikhs, particularly of the Dalit Sikhs, leaving them to be lured by the likes of Gurmeet Ram Rahim.

My father has written about how Sikhs need to retain their outward symbols of long hair, beard and turban if they are not to be overwhelmed by the much larger number of Hindus around them and hence merge into Hinduism. I tend to disagree, as the reality is that the unstoppable forces of modernity are too compelling for most of us Sikhs to retain these symbols, even though we remain proud Sikhs. The SGPC has not addressed this vital issue of Sikh identity. On the contrary, it has sometimes supported measures that define Sikhs in the narrowest possible terms. A little over three years ago, the Gurdwara Act of 1926 was amended to bar Sehajdhari Sikhs (those like myself who do not have long hair or a turban) from voting in the SGPC elections. This was a shocking amendment which has not received the attention it deserves. A decade ago, another regressive judgment was passed by the Punjab and Haryana High Court defining Sikh identity. An SGPC-run medical institute denied admission to a Sikh student, Gurleen Kaur, for an MBBS course because she had plucked her eyebrows and hence was 'no longer a Sikh'. The august High Court agreed with the SGPC, evidently using a 'true' Sikh's definition as somebody who left their hair unshorn, or unplucked. Actually, the SGPC has another category of Sikhs apart from 'Sehajdhari' and 'Keshdhari', which is 'Patit', namely apostate or degenerate, one who is initiated into the Sikh faith but then violates its precepts. There is also the 'Amritdhari', those who have been anointed at a special ceremony. Though the SGPC bars sehajdhari and patit Sikhs from its elections, it is only too happy to receive their donations when they go to gurdwaras. No wonder then that Sikhs are confused about their identity.

The number of Sikhs in India and abroad seems to vary from 18 million to 25 million. According to the 2011 census, there are some 14 million Sikhs in Punjab, which is 60 per cent of the state's population. According to the SGPC, only 5.5 million are keshdhari, or 'real' Sikhs. I would contest even this figure. How many of the men trim their beards and women pluck their eyebrows? I suspect most do, hence a great many of them are not 'real' Sikhs, going by the rigid definition of the SGPC. In fact, by this definition, Sikhs are actually a minority in Punjab. It is time the SGPC confronted the reality and, instead of examining plucked eyebrows, set about bringing all Sikhs together, shorn and unshorn, into one vibrant, progressive community.

Not so long ago, there was a tradition in Punjabi Hindu families to bring up the eldest son as a Sikh. That increased the number of Sikhs perceptibly. It also furthered good relations between Sikhs and Hindus. The practice under British rule of taking in keshdhari Sikhs into the army made many Sikhs who had cut their hair grow it long again, just to be able to enlist in the army, with its good pay and benefits. But the changes in army enlistment after Independence meant that the number of Sikhs in the army declined steeply. And the growing rift between Sikhs and Hindus, thanks to the Punjabi suba movement, and the onset of Sikh militancy in the 60s, 70s and 80s, also witnessed the virtual end of Punjabi Hindus bringing up a Sikh son. The space for Sikhism got narrower. On top of that came the SGPC's short-sighted 'real' Sikhs stance, and it became narrower still.

A few words are needed on an unusual and exceedingly enterprising community: the Sindhis. As the name indicates, they are from Sindh, the area around the river Indus, which is now part of Pakistan. Most of the Hindu Sindhis came to India as refugees after Partition but even after Partition, an estimated 3.5 million stayed on (the Pakistan Hindu Council states the figure as eight million which is probably an exaggeration). In any case, the vast majority of Hindus still in Pakistan are Sindhis. The mid-19th century British writer and traveler Richard Burton described them as 'heterodox Sikhs,' which is as good a description as any. He writes, 'They show a general tendency towards the faith of Nanak and that many castes have so mingled the religion with their original Hinduism that one can scarcely discern the line of demarcation.' That is true of non-Muslim Sindhis even today. Most of them are worshippers of the first Sikh Guru, they frequent gurdwaras and some of them even have long hair and turbans. Their enterprising nature and eye for business opportunities has taken them to various parts of the world.

Dr Manmohan Singh

Dr Manmohan Singh was the first and only Sikh prime minister India has had, a matter of great pride for the community. The appointment was also symbolic of the fact that Sikhs were finally back in the mainstream, after having been looked at with suspicion during the two decades of Sikhs militancy.

My father liked and admired Dr Manmohan Singh. In fact, Dr Singh is the kind of person most people cannot not but help warming towards. Humble and unassuming, he was cut out to be an academic, not a politician. But politics was thrust upon him, and I don't think he was fully able to adjust himself to its demands. Somehow, he looked unhappy during much of his political career, rarely smiling or cracking a joke. Yet, my father was his fan throughout, in good times and bad. When Dr Singh became Prime Minister, my father took a vow that he would never ask him for a favour for anybody. Asking for favours and having them granted has been an age-old tradition in India. It's called '*sifarish*' and is considered normal. My father knew that some of his friends and acquaintances were bound to ask him to 'put in a word' for them – as they did. But he refused them every time.

Once, Dr Singh's wife, Gursharan, came to my father to ask him whether he had recommended somebody, since her husband had received a signed letter on my father's letterhead. Astonished, my father said that he had sent no such letter to the Prime Minister. It was later found that my father's signature had been forged on a fake letterhead!

When Dr Singh was standing for election to the Lok Sabha, his brother came to see my father, requesting him to give a donation to help in meeting the expenses of Dr Singh's campaign. My father willingly gave a couple of lakh rupees. After the election, which he lost, Dr Singh rang up my father, asking to see him. When my father said, 'Come whenever you like,' Dr Singh turned up with a packet in his hand.

'I believe my brother asked you for some funds for my election campaign,' said Dr Singh. 'Here, I am returning the amount to you.' And he handed the packet over to my dumbfounded father.

Later, when he used to be asked by people what he thought of the Prime Minister, my father would relate this incident. 'Which politician in India would do that?' he would reply rhetorically.

When Rajiv Gandhi was assassinated on 21 May 1991, Narasimha Rao, a seasoned politician, who had earlier been Chief Minister of Andhra Pradesh, was all set to retire from the political scene when he was surprisingly chosen as Prime Minister, even though there was a stronger candidate, Arjan Singh, former chief minister of Madhya Pradesh, keen on the job. Rao's first move was to find a suitable Finance Minister, as the Indian economy was rapidly going downhill. He astutely chose an outstanding economist, Dr Manmohan Singh. It was an inspired move. Dr Singh would turn out to be the right man at the right moment.

The process of dismantling the 'licence permit Raj', as it was mockingly called, was urgently called for. Rajiv Gandhi had initiated the dismantling, but under Rao it was accelerated. The overvalued rupee had made exports uncompetitive, hence it had to be devalued. This was done in two stages. The next step was to abolish industrial licensing and drastically reduce the number of industries reserved for the public sector. The public sector, which in Nehru's and Indira Gandhi's time 'commanded the heights of the economy', had to be cut down. Some of the public-sector units had served their purpose, others had outlived their time, or should not have been there in the first place. The earlier rigid rule for foreign direct investment had to be loosened, which was done. This is also the period when the newly set up information technology (IT) industry took off and then soared in the late 1990s. Personal and corporate tax was reduced to 20 per cent and 40 per cent respectively. As a result, tax compliance and collection went up significantly. Civil aviation was opened up to the private sector.

At around the same time, a seismic global event took place which helped swing the public and political mood towards economic reform, namely the break-up of the Soviet Union. A highly regimented government-driven economy had failed, so it was time to try something else. There were aberrations, of course, during this changing era, such as the Harshad Mehta scam, when Dr Singh had offered his resignation, which Rao turned down. Nevertheless, Dr Singh played a stellar role as Finance Minister and made the economic reform process irreversible, salvaging the Indian economy from the hole that it had found itself in after years of thoughtless and populist-driven 'socialism'.

In 2009, when the Congress Party won a surprise victory over the BJP, Sonia Gandhi was expected to become the new Prime Minister as she had master-minded the Congress electoral campaign. Wisely, she turned to the trusted, reliable and self-effacing Dr Singh. Her choice shocked many, since there were other heavyweights jostling for the coveted seat, but when one looks back on her choice, it was a sensible one, at least from her perspective. With no mass political base of his own, and no guile either, Dr Singh was no threat to the Gandhi family. The public perception was that he would keep the seat warm until Rahul Gandhi was ready to occupy it. In any case, Dr Singh was undoubtedly the most academicallyqualified Prime Minister, with an Oxford university doctorate behind him. Apart from having been a Finance Minister, he had also been Governor of the Reserve Bank of India and Deputy Chairman of the Planning Commission.

However, the new Prime Minister headed a shaky coalition called the United Progressive Alliance (UPA) that also consisted of the DMK's Karunanidhi, Lalu Prasad Yadav's Rashtriya Janata Dal (RJD), with outside support from the left. The consensus is that during UPA's first term (2004–2009), Dr Singh was given a fairly free hand, especially over foreign affairs. His main achievement was undoubtedly the signing of the Indo-US nuclear deal in the face of fierce opposition from the leftist supporters of the Congress (they eventually withdrew their support but it did not matter). Called the 123 Agreement, nuclear materials and technology that had been denied to India following the 1974 Pokhran test were resumed once again. Dr Singh and US President Bush warmed towards each other and Indo-US ties enjoyed a much-needed boost. Japan, an important trading partner for India, was also given favourable treatment, and a dispute with Bangladesh over river waters was partly resolved.

Then, in a momentous breakthrough, for greater transparency and better governance, the Right to Information Act (RTI) came into force in 2005, whereby an individual could seek information from the government and the public sector, a lacuna in the earlier 2002 Right to Information Act. The initiative for the Aadhar card was taken by the Manmohan Singh government, followed up more rigorously by its originator, Nandan Nilekani. The controversial General Sales Tax (GST), as a nation-wide tax, was proposed initially by the UPA government and, ironically, opposed by the BJP, though the latter changed its stance after coming to power. Similarly, the Mahatma Gandhi National Rural Employment Guarantee Act (MGNREGA) was made effective by February

2006, and though it was criticized as being populist and a massive drain on the exchequer, it has now become indispensable, even for the BJP. The GDP growth rates of 8 per cent in the first seven years of UPA1 and UPA2 compare very favourably to the performance of the BJP. Exports, too, went up from 11.8 per cent of GDP to 17 per cent.

Sadly, these major achievements and breakthroughs of UPA1 and UPA2 have been almost forgotten under the Modi wave and the debacle of the UPA in the 2014 and the 2018 general elections. Allegations of corruption and widespread wrongdoing began doing the rounds at the time of the 2005 Commonwealth Games and continued through the allocation of coal mines, and the auctioning of 2G spectrum on a 'first-come-and-first-serve basis'. A. Raja, the then Telecommunications Minister, and Kanimozhi of the DMK were arrested but eventually acquitted. The credibility of the CBI took a severe beating from which it has yet to recover. It was called a 'caged parrot' by the highest court in the land. When confronted with the allegations, Dr Singh dismissed them as 'coalition dharma' and the 'compulsions of coalition politics'.

There are many supporters of Dr Singh – and I am one of them – who feel that he should have handed over his resignation before UPA2's term ran out. Be that as it may, the anti-corruption mood reached a crescendo with the agitation by the crusader Anna Hazare in New Delhi. Though it was centred in the Capital, it had repercussions all over the country, and was a crucial factor in the 2014 BJP victory. Dr Singh was called an 'accidental Prime Minister' by his Media Adviser, Sanjaya Baru, and in a film made by that title, which was a very unfair and belittling depiction of Dr Singh. In the midst of press criticism, he once said that history would perhaps see him in a better light. I am sure it will. He was the kind of leader India had never seen before and I doubt will see again.

Navjot Singh Sidhu

Navjot Singh Sidhu, former cricketer, television commentator and comedy show host, is the new face of Sikhs and of Punjab. Sidhu entered the political arena on a BJP ticket from Amritsar in the 2004 elections. In December 2006, he was found guilty of culpable homicide in a case of road rage dating back to 1991. He resigned as Member of Parliament in January 2007 and appealed to the Supreme Court which stayed his conviction and allowed him to contest (and win) the Amritsar Lok Sabha seat in February.

In 2009, Sidhu won again, but was not nominated from Amritsar in 2014. In 2017, he joined the Congress and won a resounding victory in the Punjab Assembly Elections that year. He resigned from the Punjab Cabinet in June 2019. His resignation was accepted in July.

It is no secret that the Punjab Chief Minister and former Maharaja of Patiala, Amarinder Singh, and he do not like each other (even though Sidhu served briefly in Amarinder's Cabinet). Sidhu covets Amarinder's position and Amarinder knows that Sidhu is immensely popular, a true crowd-puller and a riveting orator.

I had witnessed him during his days of cricket commentary and on TV comedy shows. Though I thought he behaved like a buffoon, the audience loved his witticisms, his turn of phrase and Urdu couplets. With some trepidation, we invited him to the Kasauli Literature Festival and he accepted. He was a huge hit and the hall was absolutely packed. For the first time, I saw his serious side and some of his concerns for his state and the Sikhs. My assessment of him changed from that of a lightweight to somebody who should be taken more seriously. It was clear that he would play a major role in the Punjab political scene, and perhaps later in the Centre.

He quickly grasped a key issue as an opportunity, namely the coming 550th birth anniversary of the founder of the Sikh faith, Guru Nanak. When the new Pakistan Prime Minister invited him to his inaugural ceremony, he promptly accepted, the only major Indian political figure to do so. After all, he and Imran had played cricket together. He was widely criticized for it. But as a votary of better Indo-Pak ties and more people-to-people contact, I supported him entirely. He also talked about how north Indians had more in common with Pakistanis, in language, food and culture, than they did with south Indians, which is the truth, however unpalatable it may be to the ultra 'nationalists' amongst us, a growing tribe.

Kartarpur

A gurdwara on the Indian side of the border is where Guru Nanak was born. Another gurdwara, a short distance away on the Pakistan side, in Kartarpur, is where Nanak spent the last seventeen years of his life and also where he died. Both places are sacred to the Sikhs, and on 12 November, Sikh pilgrims in their millions, from India and abroad, will probably try to make their way from one gurdwara to the other, along a corridor that Islamabad and New Delhi are working on. It will be one of largest pilgrimages made in recent times. Navjot Singh Sidhu has made it his mission to facilitate it, even though it poses a security nightmare for both the India and Pakistan governments. It could be a shining moment for Sidhu that may catapult him on to the national stage and be a welcome turning point for closer relations between the two countries.

Rahul Singh

INDEX

Abbot, Captain James, 73, 76
Abdali, Ahmed Shah, invaded
    India, 48, 58; invasion of India
    and Sikh resistance against,
    43–46
Abdus Samad Khan, 42, 43, 44
abstinence from alcohol and
    tobacco, 19
Adeena Beg Khan, 45
Adi Granth (Granth Sahib),
    23, 172, 173, 177, 198;
    compilation of, 15, 30;
    contents of, 30–32
Afghan
    armies, 46
    possessions in India, recovered
        by Ranjit Singh, 59
Afghanistan, 6, 43, 51, 54, 57, 60,
    68, 217
Afghans, 5, 43, 45–46, 51, 53, 56,
    58–60
Afridis, 59

Ahluwalia, Fateh Singh, 57
Ahluwalia, Jassa Singh, 44, 46, 47,
    48
Ahluwalias, 47, 50
Ahmad, Sardar Rashid, 165
Ahmed, Syed, 59
Ajanta frescoes, 186
Akal Purukh (timeless), 24–25
Akali Dal/Akali Party, 111, 115,
    118, 120, 145, 146, 147–49
    and Anandpur Resolution,
        169–70
    Central Akali Dal, 145–46,
        148–50
Akali Teg Purdesi, 182
Akalis, 109
    agitation for Sikh shrines,
        103–20
    and Ghadrites, 144
    Gurdwara Act and the Akali
        split, 115–20

Guru ka Bagh incident,
  112–14
Gyani group, 149, 150–51
Majhail–Nagoke group, 149,
  151
monopoly of Sikh politics,
  148
Nabha dispute, 114–15
Nankana massare, 113–14
and Nationalists, 140
Akarpuri, Teja Singh, 151
Akhand Path, 31
Alexander, Czar, 4, 54
Allard, French General, 57
All-Parties' Conference, 118
Alwars, 8
Amar Das, third Guru, 15, 28, 174
Ambala, 54, 71, 73, 254
Amrit Kaur, 184, 185
Amritsar massacre. *See* Jallianwala
  Bagh
Anandpur, 21
anarchy and persecution, 43–44
Andrews, C.F., 112
Angad, second Guru (1504–1552),
  15, 33
Anglo-Sikh wars, 57
  First, 72
  Treaty of Lahore, 72–75
  Second, 75–77
anti-Sikh pogrom (1984), 37, 98,
  201, 209, 222. *See also* Gandhi,
  Indira. Operation Bluestar
Arabs, 5
architecture, 186

Arjun, fifth Guru (1563–1606),
  15–16, 17, 27, 30, 32, 174, 176
  Sukhmani, 176
Aryans, 4
asceticism, 11, 12, 35, 42, 198
Asquith, 107
Attock, 48, 53, 58
Atwal, Avtar Singh, 206
Auckland, Lord, 69
Aurangzeb, Mughal Emperor, 16,
  21–22, 177
Avitabile, governor of Wazirabad
  and Peshawar, 57
Azad, Prithvi Singh, 137
Azizuddin, Fakir, 57

Baba Kharak Singh (1867–1963),
  66, 67, 108, 111, 118, 119, 146,
  148, 197
Babar, 10–11
Babbars, 120
Bactrians, 4
Badal, Prakash Singh, 216, 218
Bahadur Shah Zafar, 22
Bahadur, Banda Singh (1708–
  1726), 40–43
Baluchistan, 156
Bandei Khalsa, 42–43
Bangladesh, creation of, 203, 205,
  217, 233
Barakzai, Azim Khan, 58
Barakzai, Fateh Khan, 58–59
Bari, Mian Abdul, 164
Barnala, Surjit Singh, 211
Barnes, Captain, 69

Baru, Sanjaya, 234
Bedi, Rajinder Singh, 183
Bhakti movement, 8–10, 173, 176, 225; and Punjabi literature, 170, 172
Bhangis, 47–49, 50, 51
Bhangu, Ratan Singh, 177
Bharatiya Janata Party (BJP), 232, 233, 234, 235
Bhindranwale, Jarnail Singh, 204–09, 217, 226
Bingley, Major, 89–90
Bird, Mr, 132
Birdwood, Lieutenant-Colonel C.B., *A Continent Experiments*, 147
Bonaparte, Napoleon, 54, 61
Boorea, 55
Borden, Robert Laird, 130
Border Security Force (BSF), 217
Borlaug, Norman, 212
Bose, Nand Lal, 186
Bose, Rash Bihari, 122, 135
Boundary Commission, 161, 162
Bourquin, 52
Brahmins, 8, 12, 18, 38, 121
Brar, Major General Kuldip Singh ('Bulbul'), 201, 206–07
British annexation of the Punjab, 199
   Anglo-Sikh War, First, 72
   Treaty of Lahore, 72–75
   Anglo-Sikh War, Second, 75–77

Punjabi literature after, 177–78
British army in Punjab, 70, 95
   Sikhs in, 105, 229
British Columbia
   Legislature, 132
   Sikhs/Indians in, 131–32, 139
   Supreme Court of, 130–31
British Commonwealth of Nations, 130
British Indian Army, 81, 215
British rule in India, 121
Broadfoot, Major, 69
Buddhism, 6
   theory of nirvana or salvation, 7
Budha Dal (old army), 44
Bulhey Shah (1680–1758), 17
   Kafis, 177
Burma, 123, 220
Burton, Richard, 229
Bush, George, 233

Canada, 131
   anti-Indian riots, 125
   British Columbia, Dominion Election Act of 1920, 125
   Dera Sacha Sauda ashrams, 226
   emigration laws, 129
   Ghadrites, 135, 153
   Immigration Act, 1906, 125, 129
   race legislation, 126

Sikh/Indian emigrants, 124, 126, 128, 129
Canadian Pacific Railway, 124
Canal Colonies, 122, 123, 162, 163
caste, 8, 19, 82, 267
    distinctions, 34, 87, 90
    Hindu system, 33, 194, 195, 197
    taboos in Sikhism, 37–38, 91, 217
    society and, 32
Caveeshar, Sardul Singh, 152
Central Legislative Assembly, 157
Chaitanya, 9
Chamkaur, 21
Chand Kaur, 66, 67
Chandigarh, 207, 213, 217
Chatrik, Dhani Ram, 182
Chief Khalsa Diwan, 101, 102, 141, 142, 143–45, 147
Chillianwala, 77
Chima, Karam Singh, 127
China, 122, 123, 128
Christianity, 6, 222
Churchill, Winston, 107
cis-Sutlej states, 55
civil disobedience movement, 106, 119, 149
'coalition dharma' and the 'compulsions of coalition politics', 234
colour prejudice, 127
communal consciousness, 14, 105

communal riots
    Gujarat, 2002, 210
    during Partition, 158, 164, 184,
Communist Party of India, 153–55
Communist Party of Punjab, 140, 153
Communists, 153–55, 127, 140, 141, 142, 148, 152
Congress Party (post-Independence), 201, 203, 204, 232
    Syndicate, 203
    victory in General Elections, 2004, 234
    victory in General Elections, 2009, 232. *See also* Indian National Congress
Congress Socialist Party, 152
conspiracy cases, 105, 137
Cotton, Henry, *Indian and Home Memoirs*, 96
Court, French General, 57
cow slaughter agitation, 93
Cowan, L., 95
Currie, John, 72, 79

Dalhousie, Lord, 79–82
Dalip Singh, Maharaja, 68, 70, 73, 77, 78
Dalit Sikhs, 223, 225, 227
Dane, Louis, 114
Dard, Hira Singh, 118, 182

Dardanelles, Treaty of, 55
Dasam Granth, the tenth scripture
    of the tenth Guru, Gobind
    Singh, 30
Dedi, Sahib Singh, 100
Defence of India Act, 136
Dera Sacha Sauda, 226
Dharde, Santokh Singh, 128
Dhawan, R.K., 207
Dhillon, Gurbaksh Singh, 152
Dina Nath, Raja, 57
Direct Action Day, 158
Diwan Chand, 57
Dogra, Dhian Singh, 66, 67
Dogra, Hira Singh, 68
Dogra, Suchet Singh, 66
Dogras and Gurkhas, 51–52, 61
Dost Mohammed, 59, 69
Dravidians, 4
Duggal, Kartar Singh, 183
Dutt, Barkha, 223
Dutt, Nirupama, 224
Dyal Das (1783–1855), 87
Dyal Sar, Rawalpindi, 89, 90
Dyal, Lieutenant General Ranjit
    Singh, 207
Dyer, General, 107

East India Company, 64
Edwards, H., 73
Elgin, Lord, 125
Ellenborough, Lord, 69, 70, 71
Emergency, 203
English, and the kingdom of the
    Sikhs, 53–56

English, Shah Shuja and Ranjit
    Singh, tripartite treaty, 60

Farid, Shaikh Ibrahim (1450–
    1535), 10
Faridkot, princely state, 54, 142,
    194
Faridkot, Raja of, 143
Farukhsiyar, 42, 43
Fateh, 147
Fatehgarh, United Provinces, 21,
    78
Ferozepur, 21, 56, 70–72, 81, 101,
    122, 161, 196; occupied by
    British, 1835, 56
First War of Indian Independence
    (Mutiny, 1857), 80, 82, 89, 91,
    215, 220
Five Ks, 18–20
Ford Foundation, 212
Forsyth, commissioner of Ambala
    Division, 95
Forward Bloc, 152

Gandhi, Indira, 201, 203–04, 207,
    209, 210, 213, 231
    assassination and its aftermath
        201, 210
    Operation Bluestar and its
        aftermath, 201, 203, 207,
        211
Gandhi, M.K., 106, 108, 110, 153,
    233
Gandhi, Maneka, 203
Gandhi, Rahul, 232

Gandhi, Rajiv, 209, 222, 223, 231
Gandhi, Sanjay, 203–04
Gandhi, Sonia, 232
Ganga Ram, 114
Gardner, Colonel, 57
General Elections, 2004, 201, 202, 233, 235; 2009, 209, 232, 233, 235
General Sales Tax (GST), 233
Germany, 127, 138, 222
    and Great Britain, war, 126, 127, 138
Ghadr ('Mutiny'), 128, 138
Ghadr Party 105, 120, 127, 135, 137–40, 153
Ghadrites, 128, 135–39, 144
Ghallu-ghara or the 'great massacre', 46
Ghazni, 58
Gill, Colonel Niranjan Singh, 152
Gill, K.P.S., 211
Gobind Singh (1675–1708), tenth Guru, 16, 20–25, 28, 29, 30, 32–33, 35, 36–37, 38, 40–42, 46, 88, 99, 104, 176, 177, 179, 193, 194, 224
    Khalsa of, 17–22
    Jup Sahib, 177
    Zafarnama, 22, 176
Gough, General, 71, 77, 79
Govindgarh, 55
Greeks, 4
Green Revolution, 202, 212, 213, 215
Grey, Edward, 125

Grierson, 169
Gulab Singh, Dogra Maharaja of Jammu and Kashmir, 66, 67, 73, 74
Gurdas (1559–1637), 15, 30, 32–33, 42, 176
Gurdaspur, 42
Gurdwara Act, 1925, 115, 146, 228
    and the Akali split, 115
Gurkhas, 50, 53, 57, 65, 70, 81, 107
    Dogras and, 51–52, 61
Gurleen Kaur, 228
Gurmeet Ram Rahim, 202, 226–27
Gurmukhi script, 15, 171
Guru ka Bagh, 112–13, 117
gurumata, 32
Gurus, symbolic representation, 21, 30
Guruship, concept of, 20
guruship, institution of, 40

Haidar, Ali (1690–1785), 174
Hailey, Malcolm, 119
Hall, C.W., 129, 130
Hardayal, 127, 128, 136
Hardinge, Lord, 70–73, 75–76, 128
Hargobind, sixth Guru (1606–1645), 16
Harmandir (Golden Temple), Amritsar, 79, 93, 99, 107, 108, 110, 116, 186, 201, 204, 205, 207

Haryana, carved out of erstwhile Punjab, 212

Hashim Shah (1753–1823), 174

Hassan, Chaudhri Mohammed, 164

Hastings, Warren, 53

Hazara, 59, 73, 159

Hazare, Anna, 234

Himachal Pradesh, creation of, 212

Hindi Association. *See* Ghadr Party

Hindu
Bhaktas, 8–10, 13
caste system, 33, 191
concepts of God, 9
converts, 7–8
encroachments on the Sikh way of life, 88 nationalism, 14
schools of thought, 5
Sindhis in Pakistan, 229
theory of retributive justice – karma and life hereafter, 9

Hinduism, 5, 87, 122, 157
and Islam, conflict, 5–6
renaissance, 5, 157
and Sikhism, relations, 37–39, 191, 197, 198

Hindu–Muslim riots, Amritsar, 114

Hindus
anti-Muslim prejudice, 173
conversion to Sikhism, 198

forcible conversions to Islam, 5

and Sikhs, relations, 74, 82, 211, 212, 226

Hira Singh, Maharaja of Nabha, 66

Holkar, Jaswant Rao, 52–53

Honduras: Sikh emigrants, 125–26

Hopkinson, 139

Hukum Nania, 89

human comprehension, 25

Huns, 4

Hunter, Justice, 131

Hussain, Madhu Lal (1539–1593), 116

Hussain, Mian Fazli, 116

immigration to Canada and the United States, 123, 125, 129, 131, 133

Indian National Army (INA), 152, 154, 164

Indian National Congress, 86, 106, 107, 108, 112, 115, 118, 145, 146
and the Communists, 141, 142

Indo-Pak Wars (1965 and 1971), 214

Indo-US nuclear deal, 233

Indus Valley, 4

Ingress Ordinance, 134, 135, 138

Inter State Intelligence (ISI), 217

intercaste marriage, 37

international communism, 85
Ionians, 4
Iqbal, Muhammed, 156
Islam, 14, 173
    forcible conversions, 5
    and Hinduism, conflict, 5
    and Sikhism, relationship, 6,
        14, 37–39
Islamic
    brotherhood, 6
    invaders, 6
    Sufism, 6–8
    theology, 176
Iyengar, Srinivas, 112

Jagat Ram, Pandit, 137
Jagiasi Abhiasi Ashram, 90
Jaito, 115
Jallianwala Bagh massacre, 107
Jamrud, 59
Janam Sakhis, 177
Janata Party, 203
Jang-i-Azad, 155, 183
Jats, 38, 43, 62, 97, 192, 194, 195,
    196, 197
    and non-Jats, 195
Jawahar Mal, Bhagat (*d*. 1862), 90,
    91
Jehangir, 16
Jenkins, Evans, 160
Jhabal, Amar Singh, 118
Jind, 52, 54, 142, 194
Jindan, Rani, 71, 74, 75, 76
Jinnah, M.A., 156

Josh, Sohan Singh, 155, 183
Judaism, 6
Jup Sahib, 174, 177

Kabir (*d*. 1398), 9, 30
Kabul, 58
Kairon, Pratap Singh, 152, 213–14
Kalyug, 11
Kamram, 59
Kanheya *misl*, 47, 48, 49, 50
Kanimozhi, 234
    (founder of Bahujan Samaj
        Party), 262
Kanshi Ram, Pandit, 128, 137,
    224
Kapur Singh, Nawab, 44, 48, 152,
    186
Kartarpur Gurdwara, 202
Karunanidhi, M., 233
Kashmir, 48, 58, 59, 65, 66, 73, 74,
    90, 170, 172, 210
Kasur, 51, 173
Keay, F.E., 169
Keshgarh, 21
Khalistan movement, 202, 204,
    206, 211, 222
Khalsa Advocate, 108
Khalsa College, Amritsar, 100, 101,
    145, 149
Khalsa Nationalist Party, 145
Khalsa of Gobind Singh, 17–22
Khalsa Samachar, 100, 102, 179
Khalsa schools, 100
Khalsa Sewak Punjab, 108

Khalsa Tract Society, 100, 102, 179
Khan, Hakim Ajmal, 112
Khan, Mohamed Azam, 165
Khan, Rana Nasrullah, 165
Khan, Rana Zafrullah, 165
Khan, Sikander Hayat, 149, 156
Khan, Syed Ahmed, 156
Khan, Wazir, governor of Sirhind, 22, 41
Khan, Yahya, 43
Khan, Zakarya, 42, 43, 44–45
Kharak Singh, Prince, 66, 67
Khosla, Gurdial Singh, 185
King, Mackenzie, 125, 126
Kirti Kisan (Communist) Movement, 183
Koer, Ram, 177
Koh-i-noor diamond, 78
Komagata Maru incident, 129
Koran, 6, 7, 19
kosher meat (halal), 19
Kythal, 54

Lahore, 56, 57, 58, 59, 65, 68, 69, 70, 72, 75, 77,
   Durbar, 78
   Ranjit Singh's occupation, 46, 49
   Resolution for Pakistan, 156
   Sikh confederacy, 40
   Sikh power, 46, 53, 75
   Singh Sabha movement, 99
   state of affairs, 68
   Treaty of, 72
Lahore Chronicle, 78, 79, 81
Lahore Conspiracy Case, First, 137; Second, 137
Lajpat Rai, Lala, 135
Lake, General, 52
Lambro, Byrons, 73
Lansdowne, Lord, 100
lawlessness in Punjab, 174
Lawrence, George, 79
Lawrence, Henry, 79, 80
Lawrence, John, 80
Le Corbusier, 213
Lodhis, 10
Login, John, 78
Lohgarh, 21
Longowal, Harchand Singh, 206
Lumsden, 73

Macauliffe, M.A., 101
Maclagan, Edward, 110, 113
Macnaughton, William, 69
Mahatma Gandhi National Rural Employment Guarantee Act (MGNREGA), 233
Mahmud, Shah, 58, 59
Mahrattas, 41, 43, 45, 46, 50, 52, 61, 62, 82
Majha Sikhs, 49, 53
Majhail, 149, 150, 151
Majithia, Kirpal Singh, 145
Majithia, Sundar Singh, 101, 130, 144, 145, 148, 149, 150, 187
Majithia, Surjeet Singh, 145, 152

Malaviya, Madan Mohan, 112
Malay States, 122
Malerkotla, 46, 94, 95, 97, 142
Malwa Sikhs, 49
Mamdot, Nawab of, 164, 165
Mandi Gobindgarh, 216
Mandi State Conspiracy Case, 137
Mangatrai, Edward Nirmal, 213
Manji (weekly), 182
*manji*s, 15
Mannu, Mir, 43
Mansel, C.G., 80
Marxism, 121
Maya, 147
Mayawati, 224
Maynard, John, 106, 108, 113
McGregor, 73
Meerut Conspiracy, 155
Mehta, Harshad, 232
Mellor, Andrew, 163
Metcalfe, Charles, 54, 55
Mirabai, 9
*misl*s, 47–49
Modi, Narendra, 210
Mohammed, Prophet (A.D. 623),
    6, 9
Mohenjodaro and Harappa
    civilizations, 4
Mohkam Chand, 57
Mongols, 5
monotheism, 6, 24
Montagu Chelmsford reforms,
    106
Mool Mantra, 24
Morrison, Justice, 131

Mountbatten, Louis, 160
Mughal Empire, 21, 37, 43, 58,
    199
    disintegration, 58
Mughal rule in India, 82
Muktsar, Ferozpur, 21
Mulraj, 75, 76
Murphy, Justice, 130
Musafir, Gurmukh Singh, 152,
    182
musicians (*ragis*), 36
Muslim invasions, 5–7, 37
Muslim League, 150, 154, 155,
    156
Muslim League National Guards,
    160

Nabha, 54, 95, 100, 114, 117, 119,
    142
    dispute, 114
Nadir Shah, invaded India, 43,
    44–45
Nagoke, Udham Singh, 149, 151
Nalwa, Hari Singh, 48, 57, 59, 97,
    197
Namdev, 9
Namdhari or Kooka movement,
    90, 91, 178
    cow slaughter agitation, 93
Nanak, Guru (1469–1539), 9, 11,
    29–30, 172, 173
    Babar Vani, 174
    on caste, 33–34
    founding of faith, 11–14
    on conception of God, 24–28

preached for togetherness of
 Hindus and Muslims, 13
 on prayer, 35
 his successors, 14–17
 teachings, 11–14, 15
 the times, 10–11
Nanda, I.C., 121
Nankana Sahib, 116
 massacre, 113–14
Naonihal Singh, 66, 67, 91
Napier, Charles, 79
Narain Das, Mahant, 109
Narain, Govind, 109
Narang, Labh Singh, 147
Narcotic Drugs and Psychotropic
 Substances Act, 218
nationalism, 14, 85
Nehru, Jawaharlal, 115, 147, 213
 Interim Government, 147
Nehru, Motilal, 118
 Nehru Report, 118
Neo-Platonic Greek philosophy, 6
Nicholson, Captain, 71, 73
nirankar (formless), 23
Nirankaris, 23, 87, 90, 91
non-co-operation movement, 157
North-west Frontier Province
 (NWFP), 90, 156, 159

O'Dwyer, Michael, 114, 128, 136
Ochterlony, David, 55
Operation Bluestar and its
 aftermath, 203, 211
Operation Woodrose, 207
Osman, Jalal, 151

pacifism and use of force, 36–37
Pakistan, 202, 207, 210, 213, 214,
 217, 223, 229, 236
panchayats, 65
Panipat, battle of, 1761, 45
Panth Sewak, 108
pantheism, 6
Paonta, 21
Parma Nand, Bhai, 135, 137
Parthians, 4
Partition, 32, 86, 90, 141, 147, 150,
 151, 153, 154, 156
passive resistance movement, 120
Pathans, 51, 57, 81
Patiala, 44, 54, 55, 95, 104, 118,
 142, 171, 194
Patiala and East Punjab States
 Union (PEPSU), 142, 171
Perkins, Colonel, 95
Perron, 52
Persians, 5, 58, 60
Peshawar, 57, 58, 59, 65, 69, 79,
 82, 87
Petman, Bevan, 137
Pheruman, Darshan Singh, 152
Phillaur, 55
Phoola Singh, Akali, 57
Phoolkias, 49, 50
Phulwari, 182
Pingley, Vishnu, 122, 135
Pipa, 9
Preet Lari, 183
Pritam, 147, 182
professional scripture readers
 (*granthis*), 36

progressive writers in Punjabi
language, 183
Punj Piyaras, the Five Beloved,
18
Punj Darya, 184
Punjab
collapse of local
administration, 43
joblessness in Punjab, 217
the land of five waters, 3
from prosperity to decline,
211
Punjab Agriculture University
(PAU), Ludhiana, 214
Punjab Assembly Elections, 2017,
235
Punjab Irregular Frontier Force,
81
Punjab Legislative Assembly, 147,
149, 154
Punjab Provincial Congress
Committee, 152
Punjab Provincial Muslim League,
164
Punjabi Hindus, 177, 229
Punjabi language, 172
Punjabi literature, 170, 172, 176,
185
Akalis, 170
after annexation, 177
progressive writers, 183
Singh Sabha writers, 178. *See
also* Gurmukhi

Qazilbashes, 59

Quit India movement, 153
Qutubuddin (*d.* 1172) of the
Chisti order, 10

Radcliffe, Cyril, 162
Raghunath, Dr, 132
Rahatnama, 92
Raja, A., 234
Rajputana, 3, 53
Ram Chandra, 138
Ram Das, fourth Guru (1534–
1581), 15, 174
Ram Singh (1815-1885), 92–97
Ramanand, 9
Ramanuja (1017–1037), 8
Ramgarhia, Jassa Singh, 44, 47, 50
Ramgarhias, 49
Rana Surat Singh, 179
Randhawa, Mohinder Singh, 213
Ranjit Singh, Maharaja of Punjab
(1780–1839), 38, 44, 49,
50–51, 60
and the Afghans, 58–60
army, 66–68; reorganization
of, 56–57 character, 60–63,
65
death, 60, 67, 68, 73, 83, 91
and Dogras and Gurkhas,
51–52, 61, 62
end of the Sikh kingdom,
64–66
and the English, 53–56, 57,
58, 60, 61, 66
free of religious prejudices,
65–66

looks, 64–65
the Mahrattas, 52–53, 61, 62
rival factions, 68–69
succession, 68
successors, 69–71, 81
Rao, P.V. Narasimha, 201, 231
Rashtriya Janata Dal (RJD), 233
Rashtriya Swayamsewak Sangh
(RSS), 160
Rattan Chand (1870–1908), 89,
90
Rawalpindi Bomb Case, 137
religious mentor (*pir*), 7
religious reformation, movements,
87
religious tolerance, 173
Ribeiro, Julio, 210
Right to Information Act (RTI),
216, 233
righteousness, 17, 91
Rikab Gunj gurudwara, 105, 108
Ripduman Singh, Maharaja of
Nabha, 108, 114, 119
Rogers, Robert, 130
Round Table Conference, 150
Russians, 60

Sabraon, 72
Sada Kaur, 50
Sadhana, 9
Sahajdharis, 20, 23, 104, 193
Sandhawalia, Ajit Singh, 67, 68
Sandhawalia, Attar Singh, 67
Sandhawalias, 66, 67

Sandhu, Gulzar Singh, 214
Sankara, 9
Sansar Chand, Dogra ruler of
Katoch, 51
Saptah Path, 31
Saraba, Kartar Singh, 127, 137
Sarbat Khalsa, 48, 53
Scindia, Mahadaji, 52
Scythians, 4
separatism, 204. *See also* Khalistan
movement
Seva Ram, 177
Shabeg Singh, Major General, 205
Shah Nawaz, 43
Shah Nawaz, Begum, 165
Shaheed, Charan Singh, 182
Shahidgunj, Lahore, 45
Shakargunj, Sufi Faridudin of Pak
Pattan, 10
Sher Singh, Prince, 66, 70, 78, 79,
81
Sher-Gil, Amrita (1913–1941),
187
Sher-i-Punjab, 147
Shiromani Gurudwara
Parbandhak Committee
(SGPC), 108, 113, 114, 146,
151, 226
Shuja, Shah, 58–59, 60, 69
Sidhu, Navjot Singh, 235
Sikh: attitude towards Pakistan,
158
Sikh Congressmen, 152
Sikh confederacy

anarchy and persecution,
43–44
confederate organization,
46–49
rise of, 40–49
Sikh diaspora, 202, 219
Sikh identity, 39, 82, 202, 224, 228
and the Dera phenomenon,
223
identity crisis, 204
Sikh Kingdom, 52, 60
end of, 64
British preparations to annex
Punjab, 68
Anglo-Sikh War, First, 72
Treaty of Lahore, 72
Anglo-Sikh War, Second, 75
Sikh League, 108
Sikh politics, 86, 119, 141, 150,
159
Sikh Princes, 143, 144
Sikh religion, 23–39
conception of God, 24–28
the Guru or teacher, 29
pilgrimage, 32
prayer, 34
the scripture – Granth Sahib,
30
society and caste, 32
subsects, 23
Sikh reorganization, 44
Sikh terrorism, 210
terrorists' control of
Harimandir (Golden

temple), 206. *See also*
Bhindranwale, Jarnail Singh
Sikhism
background, 5–11
caste system, taboos, 37–38,
91
and its relation to
Hinduism and Islam, 37
transformation into a
militant sect, 16
Sikhs and the government, rift,
106
Guru ka Bagh, 112
and the mahants, friction, 104
Nabha dispute, 114
Nankana massacre, 109
Sikhs from prosperity to decline,
211
Sindh, 3, 7, 56, 58–61, 100, 156,
157, 177
Singh Sabha movement, 99, 102,
143, 144, 178, 181, 199
and social reform, 98
Singh Sabha writers, 178, 182
Singh, Ajit, 135
Singh, Ala, 44
Singh, Amar (*d.* 1949), 147
Singh, Amarinder, 235
Singh, Arjan, 231
Singh, Atar, 104
Singh, Baba Balak, 90
Singh, Baba Jawala, 155
Singh, Baba Midhan, 155
Singh, Baba Nidhan, 173
Singh, Baba Rur, 155

Singh, Baba Wasakha, 127, 137, 140, 155
Singh, Bachittar, 147
Singh, Bakhshish, 137
Singh, Baldev, 147, 149, 163
Singh, Bant, 224, 225
Singh, Bela, 139
Singh, Bhai Vir (*b.* 1872), 145
    Guru Nanak Chamatkar, 179
    Kalgidhar Chamatkar, 179
Singh, Budh, 97
Singh, Chattar, 76, 77
Singh, Cheyt, 67
Singh, Darbara (1855–1870), 89
Singh, Dasaundha, 149
Singh, Ganda, 48
Singh, General J.J., 211
Singh, General Mohan, 152
Singh, Giani Zail (1916–1994), 204
Singh, Gurbaksh, 49
Singh, Gurdit (*d.* 1947), 89
Singh, Gurdit of Sarhali, 131
Singh, Gurmukh, 99, 137, 152
Singh, Guru Hari. *See* Singh, Budh
Singh, Gyan, 177
Singh, Gyani Kartar, 149, 150
Singh, Hara, 89
Singh, Hari, 48
Singh, Harnam, 137, 162
Singh, Jagjit, 97
Singh, Jai, 48

Singh, Jamadar Khushal, 65
Singh, Jawahar, 68
Singh, Jhanda, 48
Singh, Jodh, 116, 145
Singh, Jogendra, 185
Singh, Jowala, 127
Singh, Kahan, 100, 182
Singh, Kesar, 140
Singh, Kishen, 120
Singh, Lal, 71, 71, 74
Singh, Lehna, 67, 68
Singh, Maha, 49, 50
Singh, Mahtab, 108, 111, 116, 118, 146, 148
Singh, Mani, 30, 43, 45
Singh, Manmohan, 201, 211, 230
Singh, Master Tara (*b.* 1885), 108, 111, 118, 146, 160, 182, 197
Singh, Mewa, 139
Singh, Mohan, 152, 184
Singh, Mota, 152
Singh, Nanak (1922–2001), 183, 184
Singh, Nand, 120
Singh, Pratap, 67, 97
Singh, Prem, 183
Singh, Puran, 182
Singh, S.G. Thakur, 187
Singh, Sangat, 100
Singh, Santa, 120
Singh, Santokh, 177
Singh, Sarabjeet (*b.* 1923), 188
Singh, Sobha, 187

Index

Singh, Sohan of Bhakna, 127, 128, 135, 137, 155
Singh, Sundar, 101, 130
Singh, Tej, 71, 72, 74
Singh, Trilochan, 145
Singh, Ujjal, 145, 150
Sirhind, 21, 41
Sistani, Harbans Singh, 147
Sivaji, Mahratta hero, 121
society and caste, 32
Spaniards, revolt against France, 55
Stevens, H.H., 133
Sudhar Committees, 120
Sufis, Sufism in India, 6–8, 9–10, 13, 173, 182, 225
Suhrawardy, Hasan Shaheed, 158
Sukerchakia *misl*, 47, 48, 49, 50
Sukerchakia, Charat Singh, 44
Sultan Bahu, Shah Sharaf (1639–1691), 174
Sundarji, Lieutenant General Krishnaswamy, 207
Sunder Das, Mahant, 112
Sundri, 42, 43
Swaminathan, M.S., 212
Swatantra, Teja Singh, 155

Tagore, Abanendra Nath, 186
Takhts (Amritsar, Anandpur, Patna and Nander in Hyderabad, Deccan), 104
Taruna Dal (young army), 44, 47
Tegh Bahadur, ninth Guru, 16, 17, 30, 32, 174

Thanesar, 54
Thapa, Amar Singh, 51
theological intellectuals, 6
theological systems, 29
Thomas, George, 50, 52
Tilak, Bal Gangadhar, 121
Tilsit, treaty of, 54
timelessness, 24–25
Timur invaded India, 10
Tiwana, Malik Khizr Hayat, 157
Treaty of Lahore, 72
Trilochan, 9
Trump, Donald, 219
Tukaram, 9
Tulsidas, 9
Turkey, 54
Turks, 5, 59
Turun Tarun gurudwara, 15, 32, 108, 116
2G spectrum, 234

Udasi subsect, 99, 104
Unionist Party, 158
United Progressive Alliance (UPA), 233
United States
    economic crisis, 1906–1907, 124
    Ghadr Party, 138, 139
    race legislations, 126
Sikh emigrants, 122, 126–28
untouchability, 33
Urara, Channan Singh, 151
Uzbeks, 59

Vaidya, General Arunkumar
    Shridhar, 207
Vaishnav, P.H., 211
Vaishnavites, 8–9
vegetarianism and austerity in
    food, 35
Ventura, French General, 57, 65,
    67, 70
Vivekananda, 121
Vohra, N.N., 210

Wahabis, 59

Warris Shah (1735–1798), *Heera
    Ranjah*, 177
World War I, 85, 105, 144, 221
World War II, 140, 141, 144, 152, 157
Wurley, Lord, 125

Yadav, Lalu Prasad, 233
Yusufzais, 59

Zafarnama, 22, 176
Zaman, Shah, 51
    invaded India, 1798, 51
Zoroastrianism, 6